FOOTBALL FEUDS

The Greatest College Football Rivalries

KEN RAPPOPORT & BARRY WILNER

The Lyons Press
Guilford, Connecticut
An imprint of The Globe Pequot Press

The Lyons Press is an imprint of The Globe Pequot Press.

10 9 8 7 6 5 4 3 2 1

Printed in the United States of America

Designed by Kim Burdick

ISBN 978-1-59921-014-8

Library of Congress Cataloging-in-Publication Data is available on file.

The great thing about strong family support is that it eliminates all rivalries. I want to thank all my family members for their help and encouragement — BW

For Bernice, the one perfection in an imperfect world — KR

Contents

Acknowledgments

The authors wish to thank the following for their help with this book: Greg Beacham, Terry Donahue, Josh Dubow, Clem Gryska, Brent Harris, David Housel, Gary Migdol, Larry Lage, Bill Miller, Rusty Miller, Paul Newberry, Bill Newton, Bob Rose, Bob Wagner, John Zenor, Loran Smith, Dan Magill, Rollie Stichweh, Roger Staubach, Ben Kotwica, Bob Kinney, Dick Farley, Dick Quinn, Renzie Lamb, Brian Dowling, Steve Conn, Jim Finnen, Brian Klingerman, Ann Kline, Frank Downing, Nick Martucci, Shelly Poe, EJ Borghetti, Beano Cook, John Heisler, Tim Tessalone, Tom Duddleston, Matthew Russell, Scott Miller, Brad Nadeua, Haywood Harris, Dave Meyer, Kenneth Mossman, Ryan McGinty, Leland Barrow, Brent Kallestad, Elliott Finebloom, and Richard Korch.

Introduction

Which is the best college football rivalry in America?

Ask that question to any number of sports fans around the country and you'll get any number of answers.

Here is what we've gathered after a combined sixty-plus years of sportswriting at The Associated Press covering every major sport out of New York, and writing more than seventy-five sports books between us.

We've rated the rivalries and have come up with our own Top-25 all-time list.

So how do you rate the best? On Rivalry Weekend, every college football fan has someone he or she especially wants to beat—whether it's Michigan versus Minnesota for the Little Brown Jug, or Idaho-Montana for the Little Brown Stein.

Here, then, is our criteria for the best:

—Historical impact. (See Harvard-Yale, two schools that basically invented football, and Southern Cal-Notre Dame, which raised football to a new level with high-profile intersectional play.)

—Traditions. (The march to the stadium by 6,000 Middies and Cadets at the Army-Navy game. Or the players' walk down Spring Street in Williamstown, Massachusetts, to St. Pierre's barbershop following a home victory by Williams over Amherst.)

—Pageantry. (Can you beat the spectacular "Battle of the Bands" between Grambling and Southern at the Bayou Classic? Or the marching bands of Ohio State—which is often called "The Best Damn Band in the Land"—and Michigan when these two teams meet?)

—Continuity, yes, but also competitiveness. (With the teams just two games apart after 107 meetings, the Army-Navy game certainly qualifies. So does Wabash-DePauw, only two games apart after 113 clashes.)

—Intensity of spirit; some call it "hate." (Consider the "Backyard Brawl" between West Virginia and Pitt, fostered by played-upon class distinctions between the schools. Same thing goes for Texas-Texas A&M. Or the "Duel in the Desert" between Arizona and Arizona State, which became political in the 1950s when one school tried to deny the other university status.)

—Familiarity. (Southern Cal and UCLA share a city and for many years shared a stadium. Also see Lehigh-Lafayette and North Carolina-Duke, two other backyard rivalries just a few miles apart.)

—Classic coaching matchups. (Hard to top the ferocious "Ten-Year War" between Ohio State's Woody Hayes and Michigan's Bo Schembechler. Or the classic battles between Florida's Steve Spurrier and Florida State's Bobby Bowden, and Oklahoma's Barry Switzer and Texas's Darrell Royal).

So here's our Top-25 list numbered in order of importance, in our opinion the very best rivalries that college football has to offer. What do you think?

1. Army-Navy
2. Southern Cal-Notre Dame
3. Ohio State-Michigan
4. Harvard-Yale
5. Texas-Oklahoma
6. Alabama-Auburn
7. Cal-Stanford
8. Miami-Florida State
9. Southern Cal-UCLA
10. Texas-Texas A&M
11. Florida-Georgia
12. Lehigh-Lafayette
13. Florida-Florida State
14. Grambling-Southern
15. West Virginia-Pitt
16. Williams-Amherst
17. Wabash-DePauw
18. Arizona-Arizona State
19. Mississippi-Mississippi State
20. Alabama-Tennessee
21. Kansas-Missouri
22. Washington-Washington State
23. Georgia-Georgia Tech
24. Oregon-Oregon State
25. Toledo-Bowling Green

Chapter 1

A Rivalry Like No Other: Army-Navy

For two memorable, magnificent Army-Navy games, Roger Staubach and Rollie Stichweh were on opposite sides of the field. Now they were in the same backfield.

The occasion was the 1964 North-South Shrine Game in Miami. Staubach, Navy's Heisman Trophy winner, was at his usual quarterback position in the all-star game and Stichweh, normally a quarterback for Army, was playing halfback.

"Toward the end of the game," Stichweh remembers, "we were in the huddle and Roger said to me, 'I've got to get you a touchdown here.' So he called a play where he, a Navy man, handed the ball off to an Army man for a touchdown. It was the first time Navy ever handed Army a touchdown on purpose."

Indeed. Since it began in 1890 on the windswept plain at West Point, the Army-Navy rivalry has been as contentious, competitive, and colorful as any in college football.

And extremely close to say the least. After 107 games through 2006 played in fifteen different stadiums, with games mostly in Philadelphia, Navy led the series by the slim margin of two games: 51-49-7.

The significance of the series was made clear to Staubach not long after he dropped his luggage in his room as a freshman at the Naval Academy.

"The day you walk into the Academy, they give you a haircut and they say, 'Beat Army,'" Staubach said.

For Stichweh, it happened even earlier than that.

"When I was visiting West Point in the spring of my senior year of high school, I would say the indoctrination process started right then. We were going

1

to be playing Army football and, believe me, you got that message quickly what the mission was."

The mission, of course: Beat Navy!

Staubach and Stichweh were involved in two of the most entertaining and thrilling Army-Navy games. These served as a backdrop for a lifelong friendship.

"We felt that that was not a one-act play, but a two-act play," Stichweh said of the 1963 and 1964 clashes.

Act One: In 1963, time literally ran out on Army with the ball on the Middies' 2-yard line and Navy barely survived, 21–15.

Act Two: Stichweh and Co. gained revenge with an 11–8 victory in another heart-thumping thriller.

"It was so disappointing to come so close but not be able to get the job done," Stichweh recalled of the 1963 game. "But those same two teams had a head-to-head rematch the following year and we won that one. Believe me, it took a lot of the pain away from '63."

In 1946, it was Navy feeling the pain. In a remarkable similarity to the 1963 game, the Middies were driving for the winning touchdown in the final seconds against a great Army team featuring Doc Blanchard and Glenn Davis. But the Middies fell short, 21–18, when they ran out of time at the Army goal line. Talk about déjà vu.

Such close shaves have been ridiculously common in this highly competitive rivalry, Navy's lopsided domination from 2002 to 2006 notwithstanding.

Prime examples of six recent games, all decided by four points or less:

In 1989, Frank Schenk kicked a 32-yard field goal with 11 seconds left to give Navy a comeback 19–17 victory.

In 1992, Patmon Malcolm's 49-yard field goal with 12 seconds remaining led Army to a 25–24 victory after the Cadets had fallen behind by 17 points in the third quarter. It capped the greatest comeback in Army-Navy history at that point.

In 1993, Navy came back from a 16-point deficit in the rain to pull within two. But Army held on to win 16–14 when Navy kicker Ryan Bucchianeri missed an 18-yard field goal at the end.

In 1994, Kurt Heiss kicked the longest field goal in Army-Navy history with a 52-yarder late in the fourth quarter to give the Cadets a 22–20 victory.

In 1995, John Conroy scored a touchdown with 1:03 remaining to cap a remarkable 19-play, 99-yard drive and lift Army over Navy 14–13.

In 1996, the Cadets rewrote their own record books by coming back from an 18-point deficit to beat Navy 28–24.

Ben Kotwica played in four of those games for Army, from 1993 to 1996.

"Those were all great games," said Kotwica, co-captain of the 1996 Army team, "but I'd have to say the last one was the best. There was a little bit more on the line. Not only was the Commander-in-Chief's Trophy on the line, but we also presumed that the winner of that game would end up going to a bowl game, which neither of us had done for some time."

Although Army trailed 21–3 in the second quarter, Kotwica said there was no panic on the Cadets' sideline.

"We had games that year where we had been behind, so there was a quiet confidence. Bob Sutton was our head coach and he did a really good job of having a quiet confidence about him, and we were able to follow that."

Early in the third quarter, running back Bobby Williams took a pitchout from quarterback Ronnie McAda and raced 81 yards down the left sideline for a TD—second longest in Army history. It trimmed Navy's lead to 21–19.

"I think that run was a defining moment just to get us back into the game," Kotwica said.

The Cadets went ahead to stay, 25–21, on a touchdown plunge by fullback Demetrius Perry. After trading field goals, two late drives by Navy deep into Army territory were repelled by the Cadets, the last when Garland Gay intercepted a Navy pass at the goal line with 10 seconds to go.

"We had a very tight group that year," Kotwica said. "Our theme in that ballgame was that we were playing for some *one*. We weren't playing for some *thing*. We weren't playing for a trophy or to go to a bowl game, we were playing for each other. That camaraderie and that unity helped pull us through when we were down 21–3."

The win extended Army's success to four straight victories over Navy—Army's senior class didn't lose to the Middies—and marked its first 10-victory season, which sent the Cadets to the Independence Bowl.

"Defensively, we were able to shut them down at the end," Kotwica said. "That was a huge, huge win for us. My class that year had never lost to Navy. I didn't know what that was like. We went four years in a row there and had a good run."

As good as the games can be, sometimes the spectacle surrounding the Army-Navy game is even more compelling.

About three hours before the game starts, the entire corps of Middies and Cadets—6,000 to 7,000—march to the stadium in lockstep and form columns from end zone to end zone. Thousands of fans arrive early to watch the breathtaking spectacle.

Just before the game, fighter jets roar overhead followed by Apache helicopter gunships and colorful parachutists that make a direct landing on the field.

Once the game begins, the Middies and Cadets lose all sense of decorum. They sing, shout, and sway, hurling insults and sometimes water balloons at each other. And they stand through the entire game.

"One year some of our spies at the Naval Academy told us that the Navy was going to come prepared with mortar tubes that shoot tennis balls across the field," longtime Army sports information director Bob Kinney remembered. "So we gave our cadets tennis rackets, and as the Navy fired the balls across the field, we hit them back."

After every score and every quarter, a cannon goes off. Freshmen make a mad rush to the end zone to do push-ups, the number decided by their team's points.

At the end of the game, the players from both teams stand at attention together while the alma mater of each school is played by the respective bands.

Part of this spectacle, of course, are the Navy goat and Army mule, two of the most famous mascots in sports.

And all's fair in love and war when it comes to pranks involving these mascots.

At the 1971 Army-Navy game, a limousine drove into JFK Stadium with the presidential flags flapping and guards jogging alongside. Excitement rippled through the stadium. It was rumored that President Nixon would be at the game and thousands in the stands strained their necks to catch a glimpse of America's No. 1 fan. As the limo drove by the Army stands, the Cadets stood stiffly and saluted. The car proceeded to the Navy side, where it stopped in front of the Middies. The door opened, and the Middies started laughing as out stepped the Navy goat, to the Middies' delight and the Cadets' chagrin.

For a good part of the rivalry, before the practice was outlawed, kidnapping each other's mascot was a high priority for both academies.

In one memorable episode, a group of Midshipmen disguised as Army cadets sneaked into West Point and made off with four Army mules after tying up the handlers. After the successful mission, the mules were a featured attraction at Navy's pre-game pep rally before the Army game.

Another time the Cadets kidnapped the highly prized Navy goat, Billy XIV, before the 1953 Army-Navy clash. Professing "deep regret," West Point sent the animal back to Annapolis with a military escort commanded by a colonel, who issued this statement upon arrival:

"They say in the Army there are four general classes of officers: aides, aviators, asses, or adjutants. I am an adjutant at West Point, have been playing aide to a goat all day, and feel like a bit of an ass."

As for the action on the field, the rivalry has produced so many riveting and stunning games that it's hard to pick a top five, or even ten, all-time.

Start with the 1926 clash. It's generally considered the all-time classic of the service series. Like a Super Bowl, it was as much an event as a game. Everyone wanted to be there, from the man on the street to the man in the White House. And almost everyone was.

The site was sparkling Soldier Field in Chicago, one of the sports world's newest wonders. There was plenty of fanfare for this Army-Navy game, the first time it was played out of the East. And Soldier Field was beyond packed with 110,000 fans, the largest crowd ever to see a football game in America. The crowd included Vice President Charles Dawes and Mayor Jimmy Walker of New York.

Before sending his players out onto the Soldier Field turf, Navy coach Bill Ingram gave them a bit of advice: "In going out for your warm-ups, I want you to stop at the end of the runway and look as long as you want at the largest crowd ever to witness a football game, 110,000 people, and then to forget the crowd."

With an unbeaten record, Navy was gunning for the national title. Army had lost only once, and also had championship aspirations.

Chicago had been hit by a blizzard the day before. The temperatures were freezing and the wind biting. On game day, the field and football were wet, but that didn't stop the teams from keeping fans frozen to their seats. Or at least on the edges of those seats.

Navy took an early 14–0 lead as Howard Caldwell and J. B. Shuber scored on short touchdown blasts. In the second period, "Lighthorse" Harry Wilson scored on a 17-yard dash and Norris Harbold crossed the goal line after recovering a Navy fumble to pull Army into a 14–14 tie.

Chris Cagle then scored on a 43-yard run in the third quarter to give Army a 21–14 lead.

In the fourth quarter, Navy's Alan Shapley made a huge interception on the slippery turf to stop an Army drive at the Middies' 35 with four minutes to play.

With time running out, Navy captain Frank Wickhorst gathered his teammates around him on the sideline. He pointed at the goal line 65 yards away: "We are going across that goal line without losing the ball," he said. "Let's go!"

And so the Middies did. Shapley, who had made the key interception, scored on a slick double-reverse from 8 yards out.

Then with darkness fast descending, Navy backfield star Tom Hamilton drop-kicked the tying point "in a field almost as silent as a tomb," according to one observer.

Final: Navy 21, Army 21.

Navy claimed the national championship. No one would dispute it, with the exception of Army, of course.

And no one could dispute the passions evoked by this clash of titans. Across the Pacific, emotions were just as high among military men who had gathered in an Army-Navy club in Manila to hear the game on Navy radio. These high-spirited loyalists partied through the wee hours of the morning, Manila time, as the game went on. After the final touchdown and Hamilton's tying kick, a fight broke out among the revelers.

That kind of competitive spirit has been going on ever since Navy challenged Army to a football game on November 29, 1890.

The game was played at West Point on a cold, gloomy day. Even so, a good-sized crowd showed up—a foreshadowing of the next one-hundred-plus years.

The new game thrilled the spectators, who had never seen the awesome V-Wedge formation in person. Apparently neither had the Army team. With Charles ("Red") Emerich running behind a vicious V-shaped formation in the backfield, the Middies gobbled up big chunks of ground play after play.

To say the Cadets were somewhat unprepared and overmatched was an understatement. The Middies had been playing football since 1879 and continuously since 1882. The Cadets were making their first appearance in a football game against another school. They seemed a bit confused.

On one play, an Army tackle grabbed a Navy back and spun him around. When the spectators cheered, the Army tackle thought they were voicing their disapproval. So he let the Navy runner go—and the Middie ran right over the Army goal line.

The Cadets didn't have a chance, and the Middies marched off with a 24–0 victory. When news of the resounding win reached Annapolis, a contemporary account reported that the Middies fired twenty-four guns on campus to reflect the score and then paraded through the streets of the town blowing horns.

The following year, Army returned the favor with a 32–16 licking of Navy behind Elmer Clark. The Army victory was then cause for celebration at West Point. The Cadets marched around the post, fired eleven guns for each member of the team, and started bonfires.

The rivalry was off and running.

But not so fast.

The 1893 game, won 6–4 by Navy, was marked by some disturbing violent play. And the ferocity wasn't limited to the field. In the stands, an admiral and a brigadier general challenged each other to a duel. It's not known if the duel came off, but President Grover Cleveland ordered a halt to the series, and it wasn't played again until 1899.

That five-year break was the longest in the rivalry, but not the only one. The 1909 game was canceled because of a player's death. The 1917 and 1918 games were canceled because of the First World War. And games were canceled in 1928 and 1929 because of a dispute over player eligibility.

There was no stopping any Army-Navy games after that, not even during the Second World War. In fact, the war was put on hold momentarily by General Douglas MacArthur to send a congratulatory telegram to Army coach Earl Blaik following the Cadets' victory over Navy in 1944.

Blaik received this message on December 2, 1944 from MacArthur's headquarters in the South Pacific: "The greatest of all Army teams-STOP-We have stopped the war to celebrate your magnificent success. MacArthur."

Those were the nonpareil days of Army's Blanchard and Davis, whom Blaik called "the best one-two punch that college football ever saw."

Hard to argue with that. From 1943 to 1946, Felix "Doc" Blanchard and Glenn Davis combined to score 97 touchdowns and 585 points, still NCAA standards for a backfield pair.

Blanchard, "Mr. Inside," was Army's first Heisman Trophy winner in 1945 when he scored 19 touchdowns. Davis, "Mr. Outside," won the Heisman in 1946 and was Army's touchdown leader for three straight seasons. His 59 TDs are still a school record and his 11.5 yards a carry in 1945 and 8.26 yards per carry for his career remain NCAA 1-A standards.

During the early part of the forties, Navy dominated Army, winning five straight from 1939 to 1943. Then Blanchard came to West Point from South Carolina and Davis from California to help turn the series around with wins in 1944, 1945, and 1946.

During that era, Navy produced some strong teams of its own, with the help of transfers due to the war. But if Navy was good, Army was just that much better with three straight unbeaten seasons from 1944 to 1946 behind its fabulous "Touchdown Twins."

But even in such high times for Army, Navy could still be a dangerous opponent—as witnessed by the memorable 1946 game that typifies the impassioned series.

During the 1940s, Blaik was at the height of his glory with those stunning Cadets teams.

Blaik was considered the savior of Army football, the greatest coach in the Academy's history. In eighteen seasons from 1941 to 1958 at Army, he won two national championships, seven Lambert Trophies as the best team in the East, and 121 of the 164 games he coached.

Against Navy's Eddie Erdelatz, however, he was merely human. Blaik had a losing record of 3-5-1 against his fiercest coaching rival. In eighteen games overall versus Navy, Blaik was 8-8-2, stunningly mediocre for such a great coach.

Like Blaik at Army, Erdelatz had been brought to Navy to resurrect a floundering program, and of course, to beat Army. In his first year at the Naval Academy in 1950, the Middies only won three of nine games. However, one of them was a victory over the Cadets that is generally considered the greatest upset in the series.

The Cadets were 8-0 that season before the Navy game, extending an unbeaten streak to 28. They were ranked No. 2 in the country.

The Middies were 2-6 during Erdelatz's first season at Navy, but played their greatest defensive game of the season against Army and prevailed, 14–2. Erdelatz called it "the greatest team effort I've ever seen."

Blaik couldn't agree more. "They outcharged us," he said. "They overwhelmed us."

Adding to that bitter defeat for Blaik were his feelings toward Erdelatz. The coaches were not exactly buddies, according to some observers, further fueling the rivalry between their teams.

"Eddie Erdelatz and Earl Blaik wouldn't give each other the time of day," said Steve Belichick, a scout for Navy for three decades and father of New England coach Bill Belichick.

They certainly wouldn't give each other game films of their teams, a common practice among coaches. "The schools started trading films in 1959 for the first time," Steve Belichick said. "Prior to that, they didn't trade anything. Wayne Hardin [of Navy] and Dale Hall [of Army] started the direct exchange, and every coach has done that since."

Blaik actually had to resurrect the Army football program twice, the second time after an academic cheating scandal involving thirty-seven of his players in 1951 left the football squad decimated.

One of those players was none other than Blaik's own son, Robert, a quarterback on the Army team in 1949 and 1950. Young Blaik himself did not cheat on tests, but was deemed equally guilty for failing to report his teammates to authorities.

A total of ninety Cadets were dismissed, leaving Blaik heartbroken. He considered resigning, but was urged to stay on and rebuild the Cadets by one of the few people who could influence him: General MacArthur.

In 1955, Blaik hoped to get back in the victory column against Navy after losing four of the five previous games. Navy appeared to have a big edge over Army at quarterback with George Welsh, who later became a highly successful coach at Annapolis. The Cadets had an out-of-position quarterback the media had dubbed "Blaik's Folly." That was Don Holleder, an All-American end who had switched to the quarterback position because Blaik had no one else available.

But Holleder performed magnificently against Navy, outplaying Welsh even though he was unable to complete a single pass, leading the Middies to a shocking 14–6 victory.

The innovative Blaik was always full of surprises. He wasn't afraid to take chances or introduce new wrinkles. His most dramatic: the "Lonesome End" in the person of Bill Carpenter.

When the Cadets lined up, there was the lonely figure of Carpenter way out on the fringe, standing 15 yards from the rest of the team. Nor did he return for huddles. Blaik wanted him to conserve energy. Carpenter received the plays through a series of hand signals from quarterback Joe Caldwell.

The idea was to spread the field and improve the Cadets' passing game. Furthermore, with Carpenter already in position, the Cadets could get off plays faster.

The strategy worked, leading to a stronger passing game and opening the field for running star Pete Dawkins, who went on to win the Heisman Trophy. Blaik's idea also opened a new path for football: the beginnings of the split end and wide receiver.

Both Blaik and Erdelatz left the academies after the 1958 season. Blaik's Cadets went 8-0-1 in his final year, including a 22–6 victory over Navy. That completed his sixth unbeaten season in eighteen years at West Point and remained the last unbeaten Army team through the 2006 season.

Following Army's 1958 win over Navy, the stage was set for a turnaround in the Middies' football fortunes—and two Heisman trophies. Joe Bellino and Roger Staubach won Heismans within a four-year period, the only two in Navy history.

Bellino, a gifted all-purpose running back from New England, won the Heisman in 1960. Staubach, a scrambling quarterback from Cincinnati nicknamed "Roger the Dodger," won in 1963.

At 5-foot-8 and 181 pounds, Bellino was not the biggest player on the field—except for his oversize calves. They were so big that his football pants had to be slit down the back so he could fit into them. That's where much of his running power came from. And run he did.

"I figure I've got at least one 50-yard run in me in every game," he told reporters.

Very often he was right, and Bellino was never better than when he played against Army.

One touchdown dash against Army exemplified why Bellino was such a creative runner. The play called for Bellino to go off right tackle and cut to the middle. But he found a big hole on the right side, swung over to the sideline, and raced 15 yards untouched into the end zone.

"I was supposed to cut to the middle," Bellino explained, "but it's easier to go outside—especially when there's no one there."

Bellino hailed from Winchester, Massachusetts, a small residential town of some 15,000 and about eight miles west of Boston. There was a big Navy flavor to Boston, with shipyards, a Naval hospital, and several Navy juniors whose fathers were stationed in the area.

"We had quite a few of them that went to our high school," Bellino recalled. "And there were at least six retired Navy admirals in my town."

When Bellino started to make his athletic mark in high school, one of those retired Navy officers "put a bug in my ear" to become a Middie. So did the family doctor.

"They sort of pushed me toward the Naval Academy," Bellino said.

Not that he didn't receive interest from other schools—many others, including Army, favorably looked at him. Bellino was only a sophomore when one day he was called out of class. His football coach wanted him to meet somebody.

That "somebody" turned out to be none other than Doc Blanchard. Bellino was thrilled, to say the least.

"At the time he was stationed at West Point and doing some recruiting for them," Bellino said. "So that was my first taste of speaking to a college recruiter."

Many more recruiters would be banging on his door, particularly after he scored three touchdowns against a big rival in his first game as a high school senior. Bellino opened some eyes by scoring in almost every way possible: on a long run, interception, and punt return.

Now the letters were really flying in, and so were the visitors. Bellino realized he had to start narrowing his choices. His short list came down to Army, Navy, and Notre Dame.

Then it was Army or Navy.

"After I interviewed with Notre Dame, I felt they thought I was a little too small to play in their program," Bellino said.

Bellino felt he needed a year in prep school before joining one of the academies.

"I played three sports in high school—football, basketball, and baseball—and my foundation just wasn't there," Bellino said. "I wanted a year of gearing up. I didn't want to take any chances of not doing well in college."

Army was only willing to send Bellino to a six-week school. Navy obliged Bellino with a full year, if that's what he wanted. Basically, that was how he decided on Navy, his natural leanings toward the Naval Academy notwithstanding. That, and, to a smaller extent, an experience he had visiting both campuses.

"I visited West Point in February of my senior year in high school," he said. "It was a rainy, icy day. Overlooking the Hudson River, the water was white-capped. With the gray uniforms and the gray buildings in that February cold, I said to myself, 'This is like going to prison.'

"Conversely, when I went to the Naval Academy, it was in the springtime. The sailboats were out, the Midshipmen were wearing white uniforms, the flowers were blooming . . . and there were pretty girls all over the campus. I said to myself, 'This is a place I want to go to.' So I decided on Navy."

Bellino made his first appearance in an Army-Navy game as a sophomore in 1958.

"As a sophomore, it was almost like being a rookie at the game," Bellino said. "If you've never walked into a stadium and looked in the stands to see 105,000 people, it is an awesome sight. A lot of guys who play their first [Army-Navy] game, they'll say, 'I don't remember what happened in that game.'"

Bellino, though, wouldn't forget it. He scored a touchdown out of Eddie Erdelatz's newly designed formation called a "double wing-T offense."

"He came up with one of these split offensive formations where the center and the quarterback were pretty much alone," Bellino recalled. "There was no one in the backfield. The left part of the line was way over on the left side and the right half of the line was on the right side of the field. And the backs were spread out, too. So we were scattered, and I caught a pass and ran it in for a quick score."

Bellino was Navy's whole offense that day in a losing cause. That's something he would not have to experience in his final two games against Army, each with its own unique element.

In the 1959 game, a 43–12 Navy rout, Bellino scored three touchdowns and could have had more except he actually rejected a coach's orders to go for it.

"I had scored three touchdowns and late in the game, we were going in for another touchdown," Bellino remembered. "We were on the 1-yard line and a play came into the huddle for me to take the ball in. I refused to take it: 'I already have three touchdowns, give it to Ronnie Brandquist.'"

Brandquist was a senior and had played a great game, and the unselfish Bellino felt his teammate deserved to have the chance to score.

The Navy quarterback called timeout and went over to speak to coach Wayne Hardin on the sideline.

"Gee, coach, Joe won't take the ball."

Hardin didn't know what to do, except to give the ball to Brandquist.

"So Ron scored the touchdown and the coach was mad at me," Bellino said.

"As I tell the story, at the time four touchdowns would have broken the Army-Navy record.

"Had I known then," Bellino continued with a chuckle, "I would have taken the ball in."

It was a major triumph in a so-so season for the Middies (5-4-1), who had been struggling with a number of injuries. Bellino, for one, was limping quite badly a good part of the year with an injured calf muscle. But the bye week before the Army-Navy game gave the Middies extra time to heal.

"We played hurt all year," Bellino said. "But we all came back healthy at the same time for the Army game."

The 1960 game capped a Heisman-winning season for Bellino. To say that Bellino was all over the place against Army would not be an exaggeration. He rushed for 85 yards, caught two passes for 16, and returned two kickoffs for a total of 46 yards. But it was an interception he made at the end that was the biggest story of the game.

The Middies built a 17–0 lead at halftime. But the Cadets came back with two quick scores. It was 17–12 Navy late in the game when Bellino fumbled, handing the ball over to Army.

"Actually, it was a good defensive play," Bellino remembered. "The defensive end knocked the ball out of my hand as I was going through the line. Army recovered, and it looked like they were going in for the go-ahead touchdown. Fortunately, I had the chance on defense, because I also played defense, to redeem myself."

Bellino intercepted an Army pass in the end zone and ran it out to the 50-yard line as time expired.

After the game, an excited Navy publicist told Bellino, "That interception won you the Heisman Trophy!"

"Are you kidding?" Bellino responded. "It saved me from being the goat. I fumbled the ball."

Not long after that, Bellino was sitting in electrical engineering class one day when he was called out to go to the superintendent's office.

"I thought I was in trouble academically," Bellino said. "I couldn't imagine why I'd be called out of my electrical engineering class. So the midshipman officer of the watch escorted me out of the classroom and across the campus to the superintendent's office. It's not always a good feeling to be called to the sup's office."

When Bellino arrived at the office, there were a number of people there—among them the football coach, the sports publicity officer, and a couple of gentlemen in civilian clothes.

The superintendent stood up to read a telegram from the Downtown Athletic Club. It advised Bellino that he had won the Heisman Trophy.

"And that's how I was notified," Bellino said. "To be truthful with you, my first reaction was, 'Whew, thank God! I thought I was in trouble academically.'"

Three years later, Staubach became the second Navy player to win the Heisman and the third from the service academies in a six-year period. A product of Cincinnati's strong Catholic Youth Organization, he was nicknamed "Roger the Dodger" for his ability to slip away from the opposing team's defenders. It was a taste of things to come in the pros, where he starred for many years with the Dallas Cowboys after serving in Vietnam.

From 1962 to 1964 at Navy, Staubach thrived under Hardin's coaching.

"Wayne was a very smart coach," Staubach said. "He was a very good X's and O's coach, very creative. We had a wide-open offense and he recognized my ability to run. He really understood how an offense works against a defense and how to exploit your opponent's weaknesses. I learned a lot from Wayne."

In 1963, Staubach's junior year at Annapolis, he led the Middies to the No. 2 ranking in the country and a berth in the Cotton Bowl. Then he proceeded to set Cotton Bowl records for pass completions and yards passing.

More memorable to Staubach were two victories over Army, including the 21–15 decision in 1963. Although Staubach won two Super Bowls with the Cowboys, he still considers those games against Army the most significant of his career.

The buildup for Army-Navy started for him when he was a freshman, long before he played in the game.

"First you hear, 'Beat Army,' as a plebe. Then you go to the game and sit in the stands. Oh, my, the pressure of playing in this game. I'm watching as a plebe and then next year, I'm starting the game. I was really nervous the night before. It was probably the only time I couldn't sleep the night before a game."

Nerves didn't seem to bother Staubach on the field. He threw two touchdown passes and scored twice in the 1962 game to lead Navy to a 34–14 rout of Army. Staubach was now in the national consciousness.

He was only getting started. In 1963, Staubach won the Heisman while quarterbacking a strong Navy team, some say the best in Navy history. Staubach was the highest-profile figure as the Middies rose to No. 2 in the country. Along the way, Navy beat such teams as Michigan and Notre Dame and was the only team to beat Pittsburgh that year.

And, of course, the 21–15 victory over Army in one of the most controversial games of the series was Navy's highlight of the season.

"You felt a little guilty because of the way it ended," Staubach said, "but everyone has to realize the big thing was that we won the game. If we lost, it would have totally ruined our season."

The game was played in the wake of an American tragedy, the assassination of President Kennedy.

The Middies were at practice a week before the game when they heard the news. Hardin abruptly stopped practice. Staubach remembers Hardin saying in effect, "You guys take the afternoon off. I don't know what's going to happen." Neither did the players for a while.

"We got word that the game probably would be canceled," Staubach said, "and then the word came back that the Kennedy family wanted the game to be played." And so it was—one week later than the scheduled date.

Staubach remembered the pall cast over the pre-game activities because of the assassination.

"There weren't a lot of pep rallies, the usual stuff. There was a somber atmosphere."

But once the game got underway before a sellout crowd of 102,000, Municipal Stadium in Philadelphia was electric. The Middies came running out of the locker room with DRIVE FOR FIVE stitched on the back of their gold uniforms, signifying their bid for a fifth straight win over the Cadets.

"From an entertainment standpoint, many feel that was one of the most exciting games ever, not just Army-Navy games, but one of the more exciting games, period," said Stichweh, Staubach's opposite number at Army.

It was historic as well, for another reason. Instant replay, which would become a TV staple—does anyone remember watching televised games without it?—made its debut in the '63 Army-Navy game. It was the brainchild of Tony Verna, a former Cadet who was working in television with CBS.

"The Army-Navy game was a good place to introduce it," Stichweh said. "And Roger, of course, was the obvious candidate to display the new technology, having won the Heisman Trophy. So they had the camera on him, with the intent of capturing him with this first technology."

Stichweh crossed them up by scoring first, however, on a 1-yard run in the first quarter.

When the replay was shown, announcer Lindsey Nelson quickly told his audience of millions, "This is not live. Ladies and gentlemen, Army did not score again."

Army's 7–0 lead only held until the second quarter when Navy halfback Pat Donnelly scored a touchdown. Then he scored another one in the third to give Navy the lead. And yet another in the fourth, as Navy sprinted ahead, 21–7.

Army was an 11-point underdog at the start of the game. With a little more than ten minutes left, Army was down by 14. Few gave the Cadets much chance of winning.

"We moved the ball pretty well," said Staubach, who directed touchdown drives, mostly on the ground, of 47, 80, and 91 yards. A penalty in the first half cost Navy another touchdown.

Then it was Army's turn in the fourth quarter. Stichweh, a converted half-back who was a running threat as well as a passer, took the Cadets downfield on a 52-yard drive.

"Rollie was an option-type quarterback," Staubach said. "He was just a great athlete."

Stichweh dashed the final yard of the drive, then scored the 2-point conversion himself to cut Navy's lead to 21–15 with 6:19 remaining. Was he finished? No.

Stichweh, who also played defense, then recovered an onside kick to get the ball back for Army at the Navy 49-yard line.

With Stichweh at the controls, Army inexorably moved downfield again. On the Navy sideline, Hardin pulled Staubach aside and started plotting strategy in the event Army scored and went ahead.

"I'm watching the clock and they're moving the ball," Staubach recalled. "I said, 'Hey, coach, we're not going to get the ball back.'"

The Cadets seemed to have everything going for them—except the clock. They were out of timeouts.

"Touchdown! Touchdown!" the Army rooters yelled.

"Stop them! Stop them!" answered the Navy stands.

By this time, the clamor was building to ear-splitting intensity at Municipal Stadium.

"The noise level was not unlike a New York subway . . . maybe ten times a New York subway," recalled Stichweh, who was born in Brooklyn and grew up on Long Island.

That noise level would play a big part in the outcome.

"I've never been in a situation where the noise was so loud," recalled Army SID Kinney, who had left the press box and come down to the sidelines with about four minutes to go.

He wasn't the only one. As the final minutes ticked away, thousands of fans had begun spilling onto the field and encroaching the very end zone toward which Army was advancing.

With 1:38 left, Army had the ball on the Navy 7-yard line. Don Parcells gained 2 yards, Ken Waldrop gained another yard, and then 2 more.

It was fourth down and Army had the ball on the Navy 2-yard-line. Sixteen seconds to go.

"People were screaming," Stichweh said. "The place was pandemonium."

Kinney, standing right on the goal line, recalled that someone at his elbow was yelling at him. "I couldn't hear him."

Nor could the Army players hear Stichweh's signals. "Our captain, Dick Nowak, was one of our guards, and he was up out of his stance on the line," Stichweh said. "He was turning to me with his hands out. 'Can't hear you! Can't hear you!' "

Stichweh tried to call signals again. The place was bedlam. He turned to referee Barney Finn, asking him to call a timeout to quiet the crowd, just as he had done a little while earlier.

"I was saying, 'Can't hear ourselves. Can't hear ourselves,' " Stichweh remembered. "For reasons that were never really explained, he decided just to let the clock tick off."

Game over! Time had simply run out on Army.

"The game should have been decided by the players rather than have it end on that basis," Stichweh said, recalling the event more than forty years later.

Almost forgotten in the chaotic finish was Navy's great goal-line stand for at least the first three downs of that final Army drive. And Stichweh's extraordinary performance in the face of adversity.

"On those drives, he was tired as can be," Staubach pointed out. "He was playing some defense, too. He was almost exhausted."

For Staubach and the rest of the Middies, the victory was more a feeling of relief than triumph.

"When the gun went off, Tom Lynch, our captain, grabbed that football and just ran off the field as fast as he could," Staubach recalled. "It wasn't a done deal that they were going to score, but we sure didn't want to give them another chance to score."

In the Army locker room, shock.

"Everybody was kind of stunned," Stichweh remembered. "There was a fair amount of anger and emotion . . . you know, where's the justice? And there was sadness and disappointment at having come so close to knocking off one of the top teams."

Wait till next year? The Cadets couldn't wait.

"The preparation for the '64 game began literally in the hours following the '63 game," Stichweh recalled. "For the seniors on our club, the 1963 game was the last game. We dedicated the next game in 1964 to the seniors of 1963, and it provided a lot of motivation."

Another close battle in '64, but a different finish. This time, Army held on for an 11–8 win.

"We moved the ball," Staubach remembered, "but Army kept making plays. Rollie had another good game."

Stichweh threw a touchdown pass and Barry Nickerson kicked a 20-yard field goal in the fourth quarter for Army's winning points. For Stichweh, the victory erased some, but not all, of the pain from the 1963 loss. "Anyway, we went out on a positive note."

Something else positive happened in the wake of those games: a close friendship developed between Staubach and Stichweh. Between Navy QB and Army QB.

"We didn't know each other until that '63 game," Staubach said. "That's when I really got to know what a great athlete Rollie was. We formed respect for each other from that game."

While visiting each other's campuses on Exchange Weekend, the two forged a strong bond. They had a mutual friend in Skip Orr, who had known Rollie since his high school days and was Staubach's roommate at Navy. Staubach recalled that he and Stichweh actually switched uniforms in a moment of lighthearted fun at West Point.

"We were walking around to see if anybody recognized us."

After serving in Vietnam, Stichweh was on the Army coaching staff before starting a successful career with a consulting firm. Back from war duty, Staubach went into pro football with a purpose. In eleven years, Staubach took the Cowboys to four Super Bowls, winning in the 1971 and 1977 seasons. Like Stichweh, he later went into private business as a consultant and has his own real estate company in Dallas.

The two kept in contact over the years. They have stayed at each other's homes, but haven't lost their competitive spirit. Each year, they have an annual bet of one dollar on the Army-Navy game.

The best of friends, the worst of enemies. The Army-Navy rivalry has been called that. But there is also a mutual respect because of their unusual circumstances as members of the Armed Forces. In the case of Staubach and Stichweh, their relationship exemplifies the finest aspect of this unique rivalry. A rivalry, yes, but also a brotherhood.

"You learn how to say 'Beat Army' so it becomes a real part of your life," Staubach said. "But everybody understands the commitment you make to the military, and so you sure understand what teamwork means after football and after the academies."

Chapter 2

Cross-Country Classic: Notre Dame-Southern Cal

What is it about the Notre Dame-Southern Cal football rivalry that makes it so unique?

Is it the combined twenty-two national championships the schools claim "plus parts of lots of others," suggested by Notre Dame sports information director John Heisler?

The fourteen Heisman Trophy winners and three-hundred-plus All Americans they have between them?

The historical impact that the rivalry has had on college football?

Yes—all that, and more.

Southern Cal-Notre Dame is simply the best intersectional college football rivalry in the country. No one—if there is a second place—even comes close.

Some rivalries are based on geographic proximity or league affiliations; this one is based on pure excellence.

You want impact players? Try these Heisman winners at Southern Cal: Mike Garrett, O. J. Simpson, Charles White, Marcus Allen, Carson Palmer, Matt Leinart, and Reggie Bush. And these at Notre Dame: Paul Hornung, Johnny Lujack, Leon Hart, Angelo Bertelli, John Lattner, John Huarte, and Tim Brown.

Coaching greats? To name a few: Knute Rockne, Frank Leahy, and Ara Parseghian at Notre Dame. Howard Jones, John McKay, and John Robinson at Southern Cal. And Pete Carroll, most recently making his mark with the Trojans.

The USC-Notre Dame rivalry could also very well lead the college football world in exciting and meaningful games. When the two met at their 2006 showdown, Notre Dame and Southern Cal were both ranked in the Top Ten for the eighteenth time in the rivalry.

It turned out to be a Southern Cal blowout. The game that fans will never forget, an instant classic, was the 2005 clash at South Bend.

When the Trojans visited Notre Dame that season, Irish coach Charlie Weis said he received more than three hundred requests for tickets. That was many more than he received while coaching for New England in the Super Bowl.

Tickets were going for $1,500 on the Internet. Hotel rooms in South Bend were going for $499 a night—if you could find one.

On the Friday night before the game, 40,000 people, including former star quarterback Joe Montana, attended a rally on campus.

As has so often happened in this series, the favored team had its hands full. Southern Cal, the two-time defending national champion with twenty-seven straight wins, was a 14-point favorite. That meant nothing to the Irish, who gave the Trojans the battle of their lives.

The game actually had two endings.

With Southern Cal trailing by three points, Leinart kept the Trojans' hopes alive with a last-chance 61-yard pass to Dwayne Jarrett.

But Leinart fumbled at the Notre Dame goal line. The clock showed 0:00. Thousands of the 80,795 fans in feverish Notre Dame Stadium came pouring onto the field to celebrate the Irish's apparent 31–28 victory. On the sidelines, Notre Dame coach Weis raised his arms triumphantly.

But the celebrations were premature. Leinart's fumble had gone out of bounds with seven seconds remaining. After a short conference, officials put the seven seconds back on the clock.

With the ball inside the 1-yard line, Leinart and the Trojans had a second chance.

"I did not want to go into overtime," Carroll said, dismissing a game-tying field goal. "I had already told our guys before the last possession, 'We're going for it the whole way.' "

Leinart lined up under center and turned to tailback Bush, who had already scored three rushing touchdowns.

"Do you think I should go for it?" Leinart asked with a smile, needing reassurance for a quarterback sneak.

"Yeah," Bush said.

So Leinart did, with a little help from Bush. "I used all two-hundred pounds of my body to push Matt in," Bush said. This time, the celebrating was on the other side of the field as Southern Cal escaped with a 34–31 win.

Add another spectacular game to Southern Cal-Notre Dame lore. And add another expression that identifies special moments in the history of this great rivalry: the "Bush Push."

Southern Cal's victory continued a winning streak that would reach five against the Irish in 2006.

In that period, Notre Dame had the misfortune of facing three Southern Cal Heisman Trophy winners in four years from 2002 to 2005: Palmer in 2002, Leinart in 2004, and Bush in 2005.

In 2002, Palmer passed for 425 yards and four touchdowns, the most ever allowed by Notre Dame, in a 44–13 Trojans laugher.

In 2004, Leinart led the Trojans to a 41–10 rout of the Irish en route to the national championship. Losing 10–3, USC scored 38 straight points against the Irish defense.

And, of course, there was that three-TD performance by Bush in the 2005 Bush Push game.

Carroll felt more relieved than triumphant after that one. "We'll be happy to leave South Bend," he said.

Many other coaches have felt much the same emotion following a clash of these college football titans. Even when the teams are going through a down cycle—and there have been long droughts on both sides of the rivalry in recent years—there is still a sense of importance about this game like no other.

At the 2001 matchup, both Notre Dame and Southern Cal had losing records and neither was nationally ranked. No matter.

"This is a seventy-five-year tradition," said Irish offensive tackle Kurt Vollers, who was from the southern California area. "Even if both teams are below .500, this is a feature game all over the nation. That speaks for itself in that we can be under .500 and everyone still wants to watch."

The rivalry has featured great coaching matchups, none better than when Parseghian was at Notre Dame and McKay at Southern Cal in the 1960s and 1970s.

"We had an intense rivalry and virtually every year each team came into the game having an influence on the national championship in one way or another," Parseghian said. "It was incredible."

In Parseghian's eleven years at Notre Dame, nine of the games with Southern Cal had national significance. On five occasions, the winner of the game went on to win the national championship. Four other times, the loser got knocked out of title contention.

In their head-to-head rivalry, McKay had the better of Parseghian 6-3-2, but shared equally in some of the highest—and lowest—moments in their football programs.

As far as a sense of humor was concerned, there was no contest. McKay had it all over Parseghian.

At the 1965 game with Notre Dame, the Trojans' Mike Hunter slipped and sprawled on a rain-slick field after taking the kickoff.

"Oh, my God, they've shot him," McKay quipped.

No one could tell if he was kidding; the USC-Notre Dame rivalry has been *that* intense.

McKay was not only funny, but also a man of superstition to a certain extent. Noted his wife: "For a while he wore what he called his lucky pants, but he hasn't put them on since the day they split down the seat at a Notre Dame game."

The 1964 game typified the heated rivalry. The year before, the Irish had gone 2-7 under Hughie Devore. Parseghian had come from Northwestern to take over the struggling Irish football program. Notre Dame won its first nine games of the 1964 season and held the No. 1 ranking in the country.

Against Southern Cal, the Irish rushed to a 17–0 lead at halftime behind Heisman winning quarterback John Huarte. Parseghian was but thirty minutes away from an undefeated season and a crack at the national title in his very first year at Notre Dame. But the Trojans scored 20 points in the second half and shut down the Irish to pull out a 20–17 victory.

"That was traumatic, after having gone through all those games and leading in that game, 17–0, to have it snatched away from us in the fourth quarter," Parseghian remembered.

Doing the snatching for Southern Cal was Rod Sherman, who caught a TD pass from Craig Fertig with 1:33 remaining.

Fertig ended up on his back after throwing the football and didn't actually see Sherman making the catch. All he saw was the L.A. Coliseum crowd go wild. Then the mad dash to the celebratory locker room.

"We just barely got to the locker room," Fertig recalled. "Coach McKay was really emotional. Notre Dame was his favorite team as a kid, so he made the Notre Dame game really important. He was overcome with emotion. It was the first time a lot of us had ever seen it."

The emotions in the Notre Dame dressing room, meanwhile, were obviously much different.

"It was a blurry tunnel to the dressing room, full of tears, full of sobbing young giants," Notre Dame assistant coach Tom Pagna wrote in his season diary. "Ara allowed no one into the locker room. Ara composed his feelings rapidly. He asked the team to kneel and he led them in prayer. The sobs of the men were apparent as Ara fought for tranquility. 'Dear God,' he said, 'Give us the strength in our moment of despair to understand and accept that which we have undergone.' Each player who participated blamed himself. It was perhaps the most humble moment we would ever know."

Ten years later, Parseghian had to be experiencing some form of distasteful déjà vu. The Irish held a 24–0 lead over Southern Cal shortly before the half. But the Trojans scored a staggering 55 straight points, all in less than seventeen minutes, to rout the Irish 55–24.

Anthony Davis, Notre Dame's greatest tormentor, scored four touchdowns against the Irish, including a rally-inspiring kickoff return for a TD at the start of the second half.

"It was one of those freak things that happens when the momentum shifted in the game on Anthony Davis's kickoff return on the opening play of the second half," Parseghian said in an interview many years later. "The momentum just completely turned around."

With his team trailing 24–6 at the half, McKay made no Rockne-type speeches in the dressing room.

"John did what he always did," said former Trojans quarterback Mike Sanford. "He turned the lights out so you could think about the game. His only comment was, 'Gentlemen, we're behind.'"

For Davis, it was all in a day's work. In a 45–23 rout of Notre Dame in 1972 to complete a perfect season for the Trojans, AD scored a remarkable six TDs. Davis was considered Public Enemy No. 1 by Notre Damers.

"After that '74 game, I was walking out of the locker room," Davis remembered. "There were about twenty Irish fans milling around and one of them, this lady, walked up to me. I don't know if she was serious or not, but she pulled out a small crucifix on a chain and started swinging it in my face. And do you know what she said? 'Nobody's ever done that to Notre Dame, AD. You've got to be the devil.'"

In-between 1964 and 1974, there was some payback for Parseghian against Southern Cal.

There was the so-called "Remember Game" in 1965. To say the environment at South Bend was hostile was a gross understatement.

"Every two feet on the sidewalk on the campus were signs that said KILL MIKE GARRETT," Fertig recalled of the vicious sentiments directed at the Trojans' Heisman Trophy winner.

Larry Conjar turned out to be the star of the day, scoring a modern Irish record of four touchdowns as Notre Dame romped, 28–7.

That was followed by the "Humiliation" game in 1966, when the Irish returned to the scene of Parseghian's greatest disappointment and whacked the Trojans 51–0 at the L.A. Coliseum. It was the worst beating in Southern Cal history.

"Before that game, Ara came into the locker room and wasn't like himself," remembered Jim Seymour, one of Notre Dame's all-time great ends. "Normally, he would leave the players completely alone, except maybe talking to the quarterbacks or receivers. But this time he came into the locker room and after we knelt down in prayer, he went over to the blackboard and wrote down '1964' and circled it and said, 'Let's go!' "

It took a long time for McKay to forgive Parseghian for that merciless beating—and he never forgot.

How sweet it was for the Southern Cal coach to spoil a perfect season for Notre Dame in 1970. Even sweeter in 1972, as the Trojans routed the Irish behind A.D.'s monster day and went on to win McKay's third national championship. McKay would add a fourth in 1974 before giving way to Robinson, who had equally good luck against the Irish with a 6-1 mark.

One of the games Robinson would fondly remember was Southern Cal's 27–25 thriller over the Irish in 1978. The Trojans blew a 24–6 third-quarter lead, then battled back to win on Frank Jordan's 37-yard field goal with two seconds left.

One Robinson would like to forget is the "Green Jersey" game in 1977, his only loss to Notre Dame.

Some background: Dan Devine had replaced Parseghian in 1975 and was finding out how difficult it was to coach at Notre Dame. After his second straight 8-3 season, which would have been fine at most any other school, there were already "Dump Devine" movements on campus.

Now it was 1977. Devine had a secret plan, and it had nothing to do with game strategy. It was all about game jerseys.

Traditionally, Notre Dame players wore blue jerseys with gold numbers at home. But Devine wanted to shake things up in '77. So he ordered green jerseys to be worn in the Southern Cal game. It had been done before at Notre Dame for motivational purposes. Why not against the Irish's biggest rival? When the jerseys came in, Devine allowed his four co-captains to try them on. But he insisted that it must be kept secret.

"It was the only secret ever kept on this campus," Devine said, apparently referring to the movement to fire him and the suspension of one of the Notre Dame players for dorm violations. "The coaches didn't even know."

Against Southern Cal, the Irish players warmed up at Notre Dame Stadium wearing their traditional blue jerseys. Then they headed to the locker room to find the surprise. There, hanging in their individual lockers, were brightly colored shamrock-green jerseys with gold numbers. The players whooped and hollered.

"We went totally crazy," remembered senior defensive back Ted Burgmeier. "It was as emotional as I've seen us. What a super idea it was."

Southern Cal didn't have a chance. The Irish made their fashion statement when they rushed on the field, then made their football statement with a 49–19 rout of the Trojans. It opened the door for another of Notre Dame's national championships.

It was the only time from 1974 to 1982 that Notre Dame brought home the bejeweled Shillelagh, the Gaelic war club that is the coveted prize of the series.

The Notre Dame-USC rivalry was brought together by a casual gentleman's agreement. In 1921, Rockne's Fighting Irish had been upset 10–7 by an Iowa team coached by Jones. It was the only loss on Notre Dame's eleven-game schedule. After the game, Rockne met Jones at midfield, shook hands, and made him promise to play Notre Dame again.

When Jones took the coaching job at Southern Cal, he remembered his promise to Rockne. He set up a home-and-home series with Notre Dame, and one of the country's grandest—not to mention most lucrative—college football rivalries was born.

Pro football wasn't much to speak of in those days. College football was king. And here was a natural rivalry of football giants from different sections of the country. It was the first time a Midwestern team had visited the West Coast for a game other than a bowl game. The rivalry caught on as quickly as, well, a Midwestern prairie fire, and fueled national interest.

It has been an annual event since 1926, with the exception of three years during the Second World War. After seventy-eight games, the Irish led the series, 42-31-5.

The first game, a closely fought 13–12 battle won by Notre Dame, was a sign of things to come. So were the highly publicized trips the Irish took to the West Coast, a publicist's dream.

On those weeklong train trips to California from South Bend, the Irish would make scheduled stops to work out. Of course, Rockne, ever the promotional genius, would stop and talk to reporters. By the time Notre Dame reached the West Coast, all of America was well aware of the game.

Southern Cal's weeklong train trips to South Bend also stirred up plenty of interest.

When the Trojans traveled to Chicago to take on Notre Dame in 1927, a record crowd of 120,000 was on hand to greet the teams at elephantine Soldier Field. That broke the crowd record of 110,000, set just the year before at Soldier Field for the Army-Navy game. The fans saw another close contest, this time won 7–6 by the Irish.

Rockne, known for his "inspirational salesmanship," went to great lengths to motivate his team. He seemed to save his best moments for the games with Southern Cal.

In 1929, the Irish hosted the Trojans at Soldier Field before another monster crowd of 112,912. Everyone was there, it seemed, but Rockne. The Notre Dame players were told he was in a sickbed with leg problems.

At the half, the teams were tied 6–6 and the exhausted Notre Dame players slumped wearily into their locker spaces. Suddenly, the locker-room door creaked open and there was Rockne, in the flesh. Everybody perked up.

He was sitting in a wheelchair, in apparent pain, as two managers pushed him to the center of the room. Rockne proceeded to give his players a fiery pep talk, exhorting them to "play them hard."

"Rock will be watching you," he added in a passionate voice.

That was all he had to say. The Notre Dame players charged out to the field and beat the Trojans, 13–12.

P.S.: Rockne may or may not have been as sick as he looked. But knowing how Rockne operated, it would not have been beyond him to fake the seriousness of an illness merely for inspiration purposes. And it didn't matter whose illness it was.

Before one game against Georgia Tech in 1922, Rockne walked into the locker room with a handful of telegrams. One was from his son Billy, who was supposedly critically ill in a South Bend hospital. Rockne started to read it to the team.

Jim Crowley, one of the famed Four Horsemen, remembered the words that struck home to the players: "I want Daddy's team to win."

"God, we knocked Rockne down, went through a pole on the door, and got on the field about ten minutes before game time," Crowley said. "We took a hell of a beating from this great Georgia Tech team, but we won the game for little Billy, 13–3.

"Well, when we got back to South Bend, there must have been 20,000 people to greet us the next morning. And as we stepped off the train racked in pain, the first face we saw was Rockne's kid. He was in the front line. There was 'poor, sick, little Billy' looking like an ad for Pet Milk, and we were all basket cases."

Rockne knew just what buttons to push to get his Notre Dame team started. The 1930 game with Southern Cal in Los Angeles had Rockne's touch all over it.

The Irish had won their first nine games, but were losing the war of attrition. Several of their top players were sidelined either by injury or ineligibility. Rockne had to do something to get his team sparked up for the USC game.

At one stopover to practice on the trip to California, Rockne thought his players looked apathetic. He decided to use a little reverse psychology. He threatened to desert them and go back to South Bend rather than coach a team that "did not seem interested in the game ahead."

Rockne's players begged him to stay, which of course he did. And then this suddenly revitalized Notre Dame team crushed Southern Cal 27–0 to complete a perfect season.

Notre Dame's performance was truly amazing considering the circumstances. En route to an 8-1 record, the Trojans had outscored opponents 382–39 and posted five shutouts.

It was one of the worst losses handed a Howard Jones team in Los Angeles, and the worst loss to Rockne.

Jones, a coaching giant in his own right, never had the opportunity to pay back Rockne personally for that whipping in 1930. The Notre Dame coach died in a plane crash before the 1931 season.

But Jones would go 5-4-1 in the next ten years against the Irish.

It's hard to believe there was a game more important to Jones than the Trojans' victory over Notre Dame in 1931, regarded as a turning point in the Southern Cal football program.

Hunk Anderson, Rockne's faithful assistant, was the new coach at Notre Dame. But nothing else had changed much at South Bend: The Irish were still considered the greatest team of their generation.

They had not lost a game since the 1928 season. In 1929, they went 9-0 despite playing every game on the road because Notre Dame Stadium, Rockne's dream house, was under construction. The Irish came into the 1931 game against Southern Cal with a twenty-six-game unbeaten streak.

"There is every reason to believe that the team we buck up against Saturday is much stronger than the one which trounced us 27–0 last year," Jones said en route to South Bend on the "Trojan Special."

Not that the Trojans weren't confident. After all, they had won six straight games and usually gave the Irish a terrific battle.

"We are in excellent shape physically, if that means anything, and we are ready to give them the best we have," Jones said while sending his squad through a brisk workout in drizzling rain during a stopover in Hutchinson, Kansas.

Covering the November 19 workout, The Associated Press reported: "Thirty-four squad members spent nearly two hours on a local athletic field today in scrimmage, passing and punting. A crowd of 2,000 met the Californians and escorted them to the gridiron. Quarterback Gaius [Gus] Shaver was a spectator owing to a slight foot infection that is not expected to keep him benched at South Bend Saturday."

Despite all their preparations, the Trojans fell behind 14–0 when Steve Banas and Marchy Schwartz scored touchdowns. Notre Dame held that two-touchdown lead heading into the final quarter.

Sensing victory, Anderson pulled out most of his regulars and handed the ball over to the subs to finish the job. It wasn't such a bad idea—they were fresh and, in the opinion of many observers, as good as any first-team players in the nation.

The move backfired.

Shaver, his infection apparently no longer a problem, scored twice as Southern Cal stormed back to make it a 14–13 game.

If Anderson was thinking about reinserting his regulars, his hands were tied. There was no free substitution in those days. Players who were taken out of a game were not allowed to return in the same quarter.

Anderson could have kicked himself. As it was, the only kick that counted was one by Johnny Baker. Baker, who nearly walked off the team in a spat with Coach Jones and had earlier missed an extra-point try, kicked a 23-yard field goal with one minute left.

Final: Southern Cal 16, Notre Dame 14.

On the way home, there was plenty of merriment on the Trojans' train. Even Jones, the sober "Head Man," got in on the fun. When the train went through the snowbelt, the Southern Cal coach found plenty of the white stuff to dump on people—and it didn't matter if it was the athletic director, his assistant coaches, or the players. Anyone within reach was a victim. Seeing the normally reserved Jones spreading the white stuff around on the train like a snowblower was an amazing sight, but it was nothing like the sight that greeted the players when they stepped off the train in L.A.

Some 300,000 people were on hand to give the Trojans a rousing welcome. The players, outfitted with bowler hats courtesy of a Chicago haberdashery, stepped into cars at City Hall and rode through L.A. like the conquering heroes they were.

As described in the *Los Angeles Examiner*: "A reception never before equaled for athletic stars turned downtown Los Angeles into a half holiday as the triumphant Trojans rode through the city at the head of a three-mile parade beneath a barrage of confetti and flowers . . . men and women poured from every building."

Los Angelinos—and just about everyone else in America—had the opportunity to hear the broadcast of the game on national radio. It was the early version of the Super Bowl and *Monday Night Football* wrapped into one brightly colored package. Then football fans had the chance to see it at the Loews State Theater in L.A. The contest was captured on film and rushed into production at Metro Goldwyn Mayer as a feature-length movie. Sometime between dinner one night and breakfast the next morning, local sportswriter Braven Dyer did the narration at the MGM studios.

At first the game film was shown as part of a double feature at the State Theater. And the crowds kept coming. Soon, management dropped the Hollywood feature in favor of showing just the Notre Dame-Southern Cal game on the silver screen. The film broke all house records at Loews, the top movie theater in L.A.

Launched by the victory over Notre Dame, Southern Cal went on to win its second national championship in four years under Jones. He would win two more before his premature death in the summer of 1941.

By then, Frank Leahy was turning out uncompromising Notre Dame teams that USC found hard to match. One of the few times the Trojans did literally match the Irish, it cost Notre Dame the national championship.

Returning from the World War II to retake the coaching reins, Leahy led the Irish to national championships in 1946 and 1947. He was on his way to another when the Irish pulled into Southern Cal for the 1948 game.

Notre Dame, which routed Southern Cal 38–7 the year before, was unbeaten and ranked No. 1 in the country. But the Trojans put up unexpected resistance to an Irish team that featured four All-Americans, including pass-catching star Leon Hart and running back Emil "Six Yard" Sitko, and a superb quarterback in Frank Tripucka.

The Trojans played one of their best defensive games of the year, knocking Tripucka out of the contest at the end of the first half. The Irish were pushed to their limit and needed a spectacular kickoff return by Billy Gay in the final three minutes to save them from defeat. Notre Dame came out with a 14–14 tie and because of it, dropped in the polls to No. 2.

Leahy made up for that stunning tie with the undermanned Trojans the following season, beating Southern Cal 32–0 to win his third national title in four years.

For most of the rivalry, such lopsided scores haven't been exactly the norm. Until Southern Cal beat Notre Dame by an average of 31 points from 2002 to 2004, thirty-one of seventy-three games were decided by a touchdown or less.

Even when Notre Dame posted a thirteen-game unbeaten streak against the Trojans from 1983 to 1995, there were excruciatingly close contests such as the 1986 classic at the L.A. Coliseum.

The Irish trailed 30–12 in the third quarter before coming back behind quarterback Steve Beuerlein. Beuerlein fired three TD passes and John Carney kicked a 19-yard field goal with no time on the clock as the Irish nipped the Trojans, 38–37.

That was the first encounter Lou Holtz had with Southern Cal as the Irish coach, and one of nine victories over the Trojans in his eleven seasons at South Bend.

That contest was so typical of the rivalry, which is always played at the highest level even when the teams are at their lowest points.

Consider Notre Dame victories that spoiled unbeaten seasons for Southern Cal in 1927, 1947, 1952, and 1973, and ruined a perfect season in 1968. The Trojans returned the favor in 1931, 1938, 1964, 1970, and 1980, not to mention the tie in 1948 that ended Notre Dame's quest for the national title.

"There's no hitting like the hitting in a USC-Notre Dame game," said Nick Pappas, a top Southern Cal running back of the 1930s. "Any Trojan who ever played in a Notre Dame game remembers every tackle, every block, every play called in the huddle."

And every Notre Dame man, too.

"I think the greatest rivalry in the country is Notre Dame and Southern Cal," said Jack Snow, an all-time great receiver at South Bend. "They're always screwing each other up. Seems when you're going for a national championship, one team or the other will gum up the works."

Chapter 3

The Ten-Year War—And Then Some: Ohio State-Michigan

Bo was gone.

On the eve of quite possibly the biggest, most anticipated game in the history of the great Michigan-Ohio State rivalry, Bo Schembechler, the Wolverines' beloved former coach, passed away.

Doctors said his heart just stopped working and even acknowledged that the excitement leading to the 2006 contest could have contributed to the seventy-seven-year-old Schembechler's death.

Just two days earlier, as the Wolverines and Buckeyes prepared for their first meeting ever as the No. 1 and No. 2 teams in the nation, Schembechler spoke to the maize and blue players. Sadly, it was the last time he would address them.

"He told our team, 'You're going to go out and do a lot of great things in your life, but you are never going to have the great experiences you've had at Michigan,'" coach Lloyd Carr said.

"He just said if we want to win, we've got to come out and win the line of scrimmage," Wolverines star running back Mike Hart recalled. "That's Bo—offensive and defensive lines win games."

Hours later, Bo was dead.

Until 2006, nothing more defined the Michigan-Ohio State rivalry than Schembechler's battles with Buckeyes coach Woody Hayes, who died in 1987. The battles were known in Ann Arbor and Columbus as "The Ten-Year War."

In fact, despite all of the great players—nine Heisman Trophy winners, including the only repeat recipient, OSU running back Archie Griffin—and All-America honors, the matchup between these Big Ten powers always will be known for the Bo and Woody Show.

They overpowered the game itself with their strong personalities, coaching styles, and their famous feud. And now, as the schools prepared for the most momentous matchup in more than a century of gridiron face-offs, Bo was gone.

His death certainly tempered enthusiasm among the Wolverines for their trip to Ohio Stadium.

"We have lost a giant at Michigan and in college football," said Carr, who was hired by Schembechler in 1980. "There was never a greater ambassador for the University of Michigan, or college football, than Bo. Personally, I have lost a man I love.

"I'm a little mad at him because he didn't stay around for this game. But it wouldn't be fair to use that in any way, and we don't."

Buckeyes coach Jim Tressel, an Ohio man through and through, also paid tribute to Schembechler, who actually began his coaching career as a graduate assistant for Hayes at Ohio State and was from Barberton, Ohio.

"Bo Schembechler touched the lives of many people and made the game of football better in every way," Tressel said. "He will always be both a Buckeye and a Wolverine and our thoughts are with all who grieve his loss."

And so many grieved, throughout the football world and beyond. President Gerald Ford, a former Michigan player himself, had requested that Schembechler be a pallbearer at his funeral. That was done in memoriam after Ford passed away a month later.

"We've lost two of our greatest icons," former Wolverines running back Jamie Morris said after Ford's death. "It's tough. Michigan football is known by those two. Who is going to carry that flag for the program?"

The current Wolverines would be asked to carry that flag proudly at the Old Horseshoe in Columbus with a spot in the national championship game on the line.

Indeed, there was conjecture that a rematch in January between these two powerful teams was possible, depending on the outcome of the game and the intricacies of the Bowl Championship Series (BCS).

It already had garnered more attention than most matchups in the storied series. In fact, Dr. Kim Eagle, Schembechler's personal physician, reasoned that the hype for the game between a pair of 11-0 teams could have contributed to Schembechler's death.

"I believe that's entirely possible," Eagle said. "It's fair to say Bo wanted to live his life with vigor."

Before Schembechler's passing, Carr described the significance of this particular Michigan-Ohio State encounter in the kind of terms that, well, very much fit when the top two teams in the nation meet in mid-November.

"We've played this game now, Michigan versus Ohio State, for 102 years," Carr said. "To have this be the first time in over a century that both teams are ranked one and two [makes this very special]. It's a dream to not only coach in this rivalry, but to be able to play in a game like this certainly is very, very special."

Tressel, who had won four of his first five Michigan-OSU games, echoed those thoughts.

"It's a tremendous feeling to be a part of something that so many people are excited about and so many people count special," said Tressel. "I got an e-mail from a guy who said he's flying to Las Vegas to watch the game with his son because he couldn't get tickets to the game. He's flying home that night, but he just wants to be with his son. I can relate to that and it's special. You can feel the electricity and the energy."

For only the third time since 1935, the schools both had perfect records.

"It's going to be the biggest game of probably everybody's life on this team," Hart said. "We're undefeated, they're undefeated, we're playing for a Big Ten championship and a chance to go to the national championship, so I don't think there's a bigger game out there."

There almost never is.

But this one—WOW!

The Buckeyes already had won a No. 1 versus No. 2 matchup when they beat defending national champ Texas 24–7 on September 9. In Austin.

Ohio State had gotten even better since, running rampant through much of its schedule, led by eventual Heisman Trophy winner Troy Smith at quarterback; star receiver/kick returner Ted Ginn Jr.; steady receiver Anthony Gonzalez; sturdy running back Antonio Pittman; and a staunch, big-play defense sparked by All-Americans Quinn Pitcock on the line and James Laurinaitis at linebacker.

Michigan began the year ranked 14th, which seemed charitable considering it was 7-5 the previous season, one of Carr's worst years. But the Wolverines were returning Hart, receiver Mario Manningham, and quarterback Chad Henne on offense plus defensive standouts Alan Branch and LeMarr Woodley on the line, Leon Hall in the secondary.

As each team knocked off opponents worthy and bogus throughout the autumn, it became clear that the Big Ten had the nation's two best programs. And that they were headed for one hellacious showdown on November 18 in Columbus.

As the Wolverines and Buckeyes secured their eleventh victories each, the frenzy over their meeting built. Some high schools moved their kickoffs for playoff games to Friday or earlier on Saturday to avoid conflicting with Michigan-OSU.

"We've never had anything of this magnitude that has caused us to make such drastic changes," said Ohio High School Athletic Association assistant commissioner Bob Goldring.

There also was concern about how fans might react after the game. Fresh in government officials' minds was the rioting and couch burning of 2002. Security was ratcheted up throughout Columbus, including a heavier police presence on campus.

"I want you to know that we have a game plan off the field and that game plan will be one where, frankly, there will be no tolerance of any inappropriate behavior," Columbus mayor Michael Coleman said.

Ticket prices on the black market had rocketed all the way to $1,500. "This is probably the biggest game that's ever come to Columbus," said Tony Mollica, general manager of the Varsity Club near Ohio Stadium.

At the Frog Bear & Wild Boar Bar, the establishment separated Buckeyes and Wolverines fans. Each side had decorations for their team and even sound systems through which they could play their own music—particularly their fight songs.

Tim Keil and Heather Rogge were married one week before "The Game," as it's called in both states. Somehow, their marriage would have to survive the upcoming weekend: Keil roots for OSU, Rogge for Michigan. Indeed, Keil wore a scarlet and gray tie and vest at the wedding ceremony. At the reception, Rogge donned a Wolverines jersey.

"We might start out [watching the game] together," Keil said. "We'll tease each other, but we won't get nasty." At least not so soon into the marriage.

"It amazes me how people are really very split," said Dr. Coral Matus of Toledo, Ohio, near the Michigan border. "Everybody gets involved and picks a side even if they really don't care."

The players were especially caught up in the intensity of the rivalry. Both sides had natives of the opposing state suiting up for them, a common occurrence in Big Ten games. Or players had other ties to the opposition.

Ohio State guard T. J. Downing grew up in Canton, home of the Pro Football Hall of Fame and about as staunchly Buckeyes territory as any place in Ohio. But Downing's father, Walt, was an All-American lineman for the Wolverines before playing in the NFL. So T. J. grew up rooting for Michigan.

"Obviously, we always wanted to see the Buckeyes lose," he said. "It was always cool following the Wolverines. They were a huge part of my growing up. I loved the success they had in the nineties."

Yet, when it came time to choose a college, Downing stayed in-state, heading to Columbus. And now he was about to be part of a truly historic Michigan-OSU contest.

"I'm glad that I've been able to bring an end to that success [for Michigan] here in the 2000s," he said with a smile. "This is my team, the Buckeyes. I bleed scarlet and gray now. I would die for these guys in this locker room."

National TV outlets took the hyperbole to even more outrageous extremes—if you can imagine that without wanting to blow out your brains. More media credentials were issued for the game than for any other at the Horseshoe.

Could this ever live up to such grand expectations?

Well, yes.

But first, with both squads standing at attention and the 105,708 fans on their feet, a video tribute was paid to Glenn "Bo" Schembechler:

"Bo was born in Barberton and played for and graduated from Miami of Ohio. He earned his master's degree from the Ohio State University and later served four years as an assistant coach for the Buckeyes on Woody Hayes's staff.

"Bo became the head football coach at the University of Michigan in 1969 and when he retired in 1989, he had led his teams to thirteen Big Ten championships and was the winningest coach in school history.

"Bo was more than a coach. He was a mentor and friend to the hundreds of young men whose lives he touched.

"Michigan has lost a coach and patriarch. The Big Ten has lost a legend and icon. Ohio State has lost an alumnus and friend. The Schembechler family has lost a beloved father, grandfather, and husband.

"Bo made the game of football better in every way. Our thoughts and prayers are with his family and everyone who mourns his passing."

Signs honoring Schembechler adorned the stadium.

BO AND WOODY IN HEAVEN: PLAY NICE read one.

WIN IT FOR BO! read another.

The Wolverines looked as if they would do exactly that early on. They stunned the Buckeyes with an 80-yard, seven-play drive that Hart capped with a 1-yard run. Just two-and-a-half minutes into the Game of the Century, 2006 version, Michigan led 7–0.

How would the Buckeyes respond? They rarely trailed all season, and certainly weren't used to being manhandled on the opposition's opening series.

"We needed to answer them right away," Smith said.

They answered three times: Smith throwing touchdown passes to Roy Hall and Ginn, and Chris Wells, Pittman's backup, breaking a 52-yard run.With 6:11 left in the first half, it was 21–7 and looking like a rout.

But the Wolverines weren't just any opponent. They weren't about to be trampled like so many Northwesterns and Minnesotas.

Hart, who was playing brilliantly, burst free on a 30-yard run, then Henne hit a wide-open Adrian Arrington down the left side for a 37-yard touchdown.

"There was no doubt we were going to come back right at them," Henne said.

But they also came back too quickly, leaving 2:33 on the clock. Smith used all but twenty seconds of that time to guide yet another 80-yard drive—the third of the half; OSU also had a 91-yarder—before hitting Gonzalez for eight yards and a 28–14 halftime lead.

What had happened to the defenses? They were allowing a combined 20 points a game heading into The Game. They'd yielded 42 in thirty minutes, on the way to the second highest-scoring game in the series.

This was not a style that Bo and Woody would have recognized. Three yards and a cloud of dust? How about two quarters and a sky full of footballs? And a scoreboard in overdrive?

"I thought it would be a low-scoring game," said Woodley. "It kind of shocked everybody."

The Wolverines knew they couldn't keep trading big plays and points with the Buckeyes. They needed some stops, some takeaways, some breaks.

Hart capped the first foray of the second half with a 2-yard TD run, and when Garrett Rivas made a 39-yard field goal, the Wolverines were within 28–24.

Throughout the season, the Buckeyes, when challenged, responded with game-defining plays. This situation called for just that, and Pittman delivered with a 56-yard gallop to a 35–24 lead. The score came only two plays after Rivas' field goal.

"That's what great teams do," Smith said. "You make a big play, we'll make a big play, but we'll make more of them."

Perhaps. Michigan was only thinking about how to respond, and who else but Hart would find a way. The tailback scored his third TD of the game early in the fourth quarter as Michigan converted a turnover into seven points.

It was 35–31. Michigan was coming.

"Hart was the best back we faced all year," Pitcock said.

Still, as much as Michigan managed on offense, led by Hart's 142 yards rushing, its defense uncharacteristically struggled. And when it needed to shut down Smith and the Buckeyes, it came up short.

And it came up with an undisciplined move that pretty much ended its chances.

The Wolverines forced OSU into a third-and-15 at the Michigan 38 with just under seven minutes to go. A stop, and Michigan figured to get back the ball with plenty of time and, at worst, a seven-point deficit if Tressel opted for a very long field goal—and it was made.

Smith rolled to his right under pressure, but his pass came nowhere near intended receiver Brian Robiskie. As he let the ball go, though, Smith was slammed helmet to helmet by Michigan's Shawn Crable. The flags flew, Crable was penalized 15 yards for roughing, and Smith connected with Robiskie three plays later for the clinching TD.

"That was a big play in the game because if we don't have a penalty, then they probably are going to punt the ball or it's going to be fourth down and 15," Carr said. "But I'm not complaining about the call. I do have some questions about the situation.

"But when a quarterback is scrambling, when he's running around, I'm not sure I'm clear on exactly what the rule is."

The call surely appeared correct, though, and it's aftermath was clear. Although Michigan struck back once more on Henne's 16-yard pass to Tyler Ecker to complete an 81-yard march—the Wolverines also made the 2-point conversion to close within a field goal—the Buckeyes had a big enough edge to win this epic confrontation, 42–39.

The victory meant each OSU player would get a gold charm replica of football pants with the year etched on. It was a long-standing tradition at Ohio State following a victory over Michigan.

Before the 1934 game with the Wolverines, Ohio State coach Francis Schmidt created one of the great sporting clichés by saying of the Michigan players that they "put their pants on one leg at a time just like everybody else."

The quarterback from that 1934 Ohio State team, Tippy Dye, was the only starting QB to beat the Wolverines three straight years until Smith achieved it with his twenty-fifth win in twenty-seven starts and his 316 yards passing with four TDs in the 2006 game.

"That means the world," Smith said of the charms. "You have to go through situations and games like today to earn those golden pants."

The ninety-one-year-old Dye was on hand to see Smith clinch the Heisman Trophy, as well as that spot in the national championship game—which the Buckeyes would lose to Florida.

But on this day, there were only celebratory thoughts for the OSU players after securing the school's first outright Big Ten crown since 1984.

Offensive lineman Kirk Barton puffed on a cigar and sipped champagne in the locker room. "I bought us a bottle of Dom Perignon; it was like $350," Barton said. "We kept it on ice in the locker room. That took a big chunk out of my scholarship check."

How did it taste for all that money?

"Sweet," he said.

The tight defeat—and the crushing loss of their beloved former coach hours before—led to heartache and tears in the Michigan locker room.

"It was definitely difficult for us," Henne said. "Coach Carr loves him dearly and so do we. . . . It's sad to see him go. We dearly miss him. We tried to fight for him today."

They fought valiantly, a testament to what Schembechler meant to anyone he'd touched at Ann Arbor.

Or elsewhere.

Said former Southern Cal coach John Robinson: "All of you guys can say, 'I'm a Michigan man. I played for Bo.' All you coaches can say, 'I coached for Bo.' All the rest of us can say, 'I loved Bo Schembechler.' "

And from one of Schembechler's successors, Gary Moeller:

"The players know, 'The team, the team, the team,' there's nothing more important. That was Bo's message, always."

Perhaps the most enlightening testament came not from a former Michigan football player, but from a one-time Wolverine hockey player, Aaron Ward, who told The Associated Press:

"I think the most meaningful interaction [with Bo] came after I was a pro. Bo invited me to his golf tournament. . . . We had just won the Stanley Cup, and it wasn't, 'Hey, Aaron congratulations on the Stanley Cup.' He looked at me, plain as day, put his hand out and said, 'When are you going to finish your degree?' There was no congratulations.

"Bo set a standard by which the coaches of every varsity program or the people in the athletic department held themselves to. You do it as a team. Team, team, team. You hold yourself to a certain level, and you do it the right way.

"Once you've left the university, and even though you weren't part of the football program, you're still a member of that university and a member of that athletic department and you have deep ties."

The height of the Wolverines-Buckeyes series was the decade that became known as the Ten-Year War. From 1969 to 1978, the schools staged the kind of games that lift a rivalry to the most elite level.

Hayes and Schembechler were nearly always referred to as Woody and Bo, except by their respectful (and fear-filled) players, who were awe-inspired in their presence. To them, they would always be nothing other than "Coach," then and forever.

That Hayes and Schembechler would become fierce adversaries, as well as close friends, was pure destiny. Their backgrounds, their philosophies on life and sports, their very makeups guaranteed it.

Both were from small towns in Ohio and went to mid-major schools before heading into the military. Both earned master's degrees at Ohio State and, of course, coached there.

While Woody was the master of the conservative "three yards and a cloud of dust" offense, backed by an aggressive defense and solid special teams, Bo was the student who learned well from the master.

"They acted exactly alike," said John Hicks, an All-American tackle during his four years [1970–73] in Columbus. "They both grumbled, complained, and cussed all game. And everybody loved one or hated the other in Ohio and Michigan."

Their passion for their jobs and the stress of the game of football—not to mention "The Game" in November—might also have led each to having heart problems. Schembechler once mentioned he figured that, like Hayes, his heart would simply give out one day.

Just a few days before his death in November 2006, Schembechler reflected on his career—and his relationship with Hayes.

"I escaped from Columbus when I got the head coaching job at Miami," he said, his tongue firmly planted in his cheek, the smile on his face and the twinkle in his eye giving away just how precious these memories of Ohio State were.

"But I had a wonderful experience there because I coached for Woody when Woody was really Woody. He was the most irascible guy that ever lived, and the worst guy in the world to work for. But I wouldn't change that experience for anything in this world because I learned a lot. And we won a few games here and there."

The Buckeyes even won a national championship in 1968.

"I loved Woody Hayes," Bo wrote in his book, *Man in Motion*. "I am not ashamed to say it. In the thirty-seven years I knew him, he coached me, humbled me, employed me, angered me, and taught me more about the game than anyone could. I guess I was about as close to him as anyone, but to the day he died, I never considered myself his equal."

Schembechler recalled attending an alumni dinner in Cleveland in 1961, when the Buckeyes went 8-0-1. The Buckeyes had routed the Wolverines 50–20 and Hayes was expecting to take his team to the Rose Bowl in Pasadena, but the OSU faculty board voted against it.

Hayes left the dinner, with Schembechler in tow.

"Now, this banquet is packed, because we had a great year and beat Michigan and all that. And we started walking through the streets of Cleveland until it was nine o'clock, I guess," Schembechler said. "We talked some and walked in silence some. When we got back to the hotel, Woody went to the podium and gave one of the great speeches you ever heard.

"He said that nobody took into consideration the players and the people that had worked hard to go through an undefeated season, because that's a very difficult thing to do."

What was not difficult for Schembechler was deciding to take the job at Ann Arbor. Although he knew he would be heading to the Buckeyes' staunchest rival, and that Hayes would never publicly give his blessing for the move, Bo also knew that Woody would understand. Who turns down one of the prime coaching positions in America?

So when Schembechler donned maize and blue, Ohio State versus Michigan was elevated to the very highest level of sports rivalries.

The Ten-Year War might not have featured the very best versions of the Buckeyes and Wolverines. There might not have been titles on the line each year, and there might have been better rivalry games in other locations from 1969 to 1978. But nothing could have been more intense—and more personal—than what occurred between Ohio State and Michigan during that decade.

"It was a very personal rivalry," said Earle Bruce, who played and coached for Hayes, then succeeded him as head man at OSU. "And for the first and only time, it was as much about the coaches as it was about the game.

"Bo and Woody were very close because Bo played for Woody at Miami of Ohio, then coached with him at Ohio State. But their friendship was put on hold when Bo took the Michigan job because it was the protégé against mentor."

And it was "that state up north," as Hayes always called Michigan, against the state that many consider the cradle of coaches.

It was simply Hayes's nature to hate Michigan. Whether it's apocryphal or accurate, there's the famous story about Hayes on a recruiting trip to Michigan. On the way home, his car ran out of gas close to the Ohio border. Refusing to spend a cent in Michigan, he pushed the vehicle into Ohio before getting it serviced.

When push came to shove, Schembechler would talk about furniture-kicking and chair-throwing fights the two coaches staged.

Schembechler's first meeting with Hayes as his sideline foe came in the wake of controversy stemming from the 1968 contest. In '68, on its way to that national crown, OSU pummeled Michigan 50-14. Late in the game, Hayes ordered a two-point conversion, which enraged pretty much everybody outside of Ohio.

Why go for two, Woody?

"Because I couldn't go for three."

With such disdain on the Buckeyes' part so deeply ingrained in their psyches, the Wolverines in 1969 prepared to meet their fiercest foe, which happened to be the top-ranked team in the nation. With a twenty-two-game winning streak, a second straight national crown was within Ohio State's reach when it journeyed to the Big House.

What sort of humiliation might Hayes conjure up for Michigan and its "turncoat" new coach?

"Going for two points in '68 may have been the best thing Woody ever did for us and the Schembechler era," said Jim Mandich, a star tight end on the 1968 and '69 Wolverines. "It infuriated us and was a huge spark for Bo's new program."

How much of a spark? Well, the first shot of the Ten-Year War was fired by Bo and his boys, hitting the target directly.

Schembechler had his players practice with a small No. 50 on their jerseys as a reminder of the previous year's score. And the Wolverines stunned the Buckeyes 24–12, earning a trip to the Rose Bowl for themselves and ensuring that Ohio State would not win another national crown; Texas got the nod that year.

Hayes's reaction? If anyone expected a warm handshake for his protégé and what he'd done for the Michigan program—forget it.

Hayes stuck his head out of the slightly ajar door of the locker room and held the briefest of news conferences:

"All good things must come to an end and that's what happened today. We just got outplayed, outpunched, and outcoached. Our offense in the second half was miserable and we made every mistake you could possibly make."

He then slammed the door shut on the media—and on OSU's season.

To this day, Mandich says winning that 1969 game was "the most thrilling experience of my life." And he won three Super Bowls.

"It's not even close," Mandich said. "It was the signature event of my life."

And a great start for Schembechler at Ann Arbor, in front of 103,588 fans, the largest crowd in the rivalry to that point. His defense had intercepted six passes.

The only downer was when Schembechler saw references to him as "Little Woody."

Bo and Woody would meet the next November at the helm of undefeated squads—as if the rivalry hadn't gotten juicy enough.

Hayes was haunted by the '69 loss. It was bad enough to fall to the Wolverines in any year, but against his former assistant with a national championship on the line?

So when a Columbus carpetmaker—obviously not a Buckeyes fan—sent Hayes a rug with the 24–12 score on it, the coach didn't burn it. He placed it at the door leading to OSU's practice field. Every day of the 1970 season, the players would trudge on that rug.

And every Saturday, they would trudge on an opponent.

As would the Wolverines.

With a crowd of 87,331 packing the Horseshoe, it was Michigan that broke first. And early. The visitors fumbled the opening kickoff, leading to an Ohio State field goal. Although Michigan would tie it, the Buckeyes had a confident air and a vociferous fan base on their side. They also broke free from their ultraconservative offense of fullback John Brockington running off left tackle, off right guard, or straight up the middle. Quarterback Rex Kern, a bust in the previous meeting with Michigan, used tricky pitches and sprints and, can you believe this, passes.

Ohio State's defense was at its very best, allowing a meager 37 yards rushing in a 20–9 win. When a Woody or Bo team manages so few yards on the ground, it's going to be, well, ground into defeat.

Hayes had plenty of time to gloat and, in his curmudgeonly way, he did his share of it. But the Buckeyes also had a Rose Bowl date with Stanford, and a victory would likely bring Woody his third national crown; the first came in 1954.

But Stanford—Stanford?—would upend OSU in Pasadena, handing the championship to Nebraska.

At least Hayes had gotten even with his former player and assistant.

And in their third meeting, Hayes would break out in the kind of tantrum that, no matter how hard his protégé might have tried, he could never have matched.

Heck, Woody's hero, Gen. George S. Patton, probably never had such a meltdown, and certainly not such a public one.

Hayes's team was not on the level of Schembechler's group in '71, but he had OSU primed for The Game. And the Buckeyes were down 10–7 in the fourth quarter to the third-ranked Wolverines when they began silencing the Big House with a big drive.

When Michigan intercepted a pass to clinch matters, though, Hayes went berserk. Claiming the Wolverines committed pass interference on the play, he rushed onto the field to scream at the referee and other game officials. The coach was flagged for not one, but two 15-yard unsportsmanlike conduct penalties.

That further enraged Hayes, who had to be pushed off the field by his assistant coaches and several players. But a couple of plays later, Hayes took a yard-marker and bent it over his knee, then ripped up a flag on the down-marker.

Normally, Hayes's tirades would be ignored by the local media. Not this one. *Cleveland Plain Dealer* sports editor Hal Lebovitz wrote that the coach needed "to apologize for his immature behavior . . . first ludicrous, then revolting. It's one thing to be a fierce competitor, quite another to be a horse's rear end, which he was at Ann Arbor."

Was Hayes contrite?

"I'd have been ashamed if I didn't go out on the field," Hayes insisted. "It was one of the worst-called plays in the history of college football."

Two years later, it would be Schembechler's turn to flip.

But first, the schools shared the Big Ten crown in 1972, though OSU won their matchup 14–11. A pair of stunning goal-line stands and the running of freshman

Archie Griffin, who scored the winning TD, and fullback Champ Henson, who scored a school record twentieth touchdown of the season, were the difference.

"Woody told us before the game that this would be the most important thing we'd ever do in our lives." Henson said. "I agreed."

In 1973, both teams were 10-0 heading to Ann Arbor. Fourth-ranked Michigan had outscored opponents 235–48. But No. 1 Ohio State was even more imposing, with a 297–27 edge in points.

Under Bo, Michigan had beaten Ohio State every year when the game was at Ann Arbor, so in '73, with yet another Rose Bowl invitation at stake, it figured that he would emerge from the Big House smiling.

Griffin made sure that didn't happen—not that the Buckeyes were grinning widely, either, after a 10–10 tie in which the Ohio State halfback rushed for 163 yards.

Schembechler, who'd had a bald assistant paint a No. 1 on the top of his polished head to emphasize to his players where the Wolverines would be if they vanquished Ohio State, was enraged when a conference committee voted to send OSU to the Rose Bowl. He verbally blasted everyone he could think of in some of the most colorful language ever to emanate from Ann Arbor.

"It was a low point," he later would say. "That decision was not based on fact or logic."

In football, that's often the case. Especially in such rivalries.

Somehow, the Buckeyes, despite routing USC in the Rose Bowl, finished behind Notre Dame for the national title.

Woody would run his unbeaten string against Bo to four (3-0-1) with two more tight victories. While Griffin individually was dominating college football, he couldn't break free for many big gainers against the Wolverines during both of his Heisman seasons. He didn't get into the end zone in 1974, although the Buckeyes prevailed 12–10 on four field goals, and Griffin was held to 46 yards rushing in Ohio State's 21–14 win in 1975.

By 1976, Schembechler was desperate to beat Ohio State. As Bruce would later say, echoing the way Bo was feeling back then: "If you don't win the Michigan-Ohio State game, that's a problem. You're not going to be recognized for too much success."

So Bo and the Wolverines needed success over Woody and the Buckeyes in '76.

"We've never played badly and they've never dominated us," Schembechler said of the four seasons without a win in the series. "The score is the only thing that really has gone against us.

"I'm not going to sit back and say they've beaten the heck out of us; they haven't. We've been playing well enough to win, so now we have to play well and win, as well."

What he would get would pretty much put an end to the Ten-Year War.

Michigan not only stopped its slide against Ohio State in '76, it also did so with a 22–0 shutout that was so stunning in its one-sidedness that Hayes himself declared Michigan the best team in the country.

The Wolverines would win 14–6 at Columbus and 14–3 back home the next two years, meaning in the final three meetings between mentor and student, Bo the pupil would guide his squad past Woody the headmaster by a combined 50–9.

It is one of the sad footnotes of the sport that Hayes's career would end so ignominiously soon after that third straight setback to Michigan.

OSU went to the Gator Bowl, where it lost to Clemson. Tigers linebacker Charlie Bauman intercepted a pass and was run out-of-bounds near Hayes, clinching the win. Hayes grabbed Bauman and, before a national TV audience, threw a punch before he was restrained.

Hayes's legendary coaching career was ended by his equally legendary temper. Ohio State president Harold Enarson and athletic director Hugh Hindman told Hayes he could either resign or be fired. On the team's flight back to Columbus later that day, Hayes announced on the airplane's public-address system that he was through.

Hayes's demise deeply disturbed other coaches, including Bruce, who would succeed Woody at Ohio State, and Schembechler.

"You can't lose three in a row to Michigan and keep your job at Ohio State," Bruce said. "In my opinion, Woody Hayes would not have been fired even after slugging that kid from Clemson if he did better against Michigan at the end."

Some time later, Hayes paid a visit to two old coaching compatriots— Schembechler and Doyt Perry, a coach at Bowling Green. One of Schembechler's prize possessions was a photo of himself, Hayes, and Perry. The meeting took place at Perry's house.

"That was the first time Woody left his house after he got fired," Schembechler said. "I had an agenda. I knew we had to get Woody to apologize for what he did to that Clemson kid.

"Woody said, 'Should I apologize for all the good things I've done?'

"Later, he went back to Columbus to make a speech. Cameras were there because it was the first time he was in the public eye. He said, 'Bo thinks I ought to apologize, but Bo doesn't know everything.'

"That was the extent of his apology!"

That story always made Schembechler laugh.

"Woody was the best," he'd say.

And for a decade, their rivalry was the same.

The roots of Michigan-Ohio State are truly Midwestern, even if both didn't start out as Big Ten members. They were laid by the likes of Fielding Yost, Bennie Oosterbaan, Schmidt, and Chic Harley.

They were carried on by so many great players and coaches—Les Horvath, Howard "Hopalong" Cassady, Tom Harmon, Fritz Crisler, and Paul Brown—all the way up to Troy Smith and Mike Hart, to Jim Tressel and Lloyd Carr.

Staunch defense, strong running games, good special teams. Just about every great squad from Columbus or Ann Arbor had those. And excellent coaching.

OSU joined the Big Ten in 1912. Oddly, Michigan, a charter member, dropped out in 1908, and then resumed membership in 1917, when the schools met for the first time as conference members.

In 1926, guess what! The Big Ten title was on the line—and not for the last time, of course—as more than 90,000 fans gathered in Columbus to see if the locals could hold off Bennie Friedman, Oosterbaan, and the rest of formidable Michigan.

The Buckeyes grabbed a 10–0 lead in the first quarter. Then Michigan got going.

Friedman hit Oosterbaan for a TD, and with thirty seconds remaining in the half, Friedman kicked a 43-yard field goal.

"I think the way we came back showed something about our team," Oosterbaan said.

It showed Ohio State that this would be a difficult, tight game that probably would turn on a break. And it was Michigan that got the break.

The Buckeyes fumbled deep in their territory. Their defense bunkered in, paying extra attention to Oosterbaan. They held for three plays.

But the clever Friedman, well aware that Ohio State would be shadowing every move made by his top receiver, instead lobbed a pass to Leo Hoffman for the go-ahead TD. Michigan added the extra point for a 17–10 lead.

Ohio State would not go quietly, especially at home. The Buckeyes marched downfield as the frenzied crowd anxiously awaited a big play. The fans got it on fullback Marty Karow's short touchdown run.

What they got next—a botched extra point by Myers Clark—was crushing. Michigan won 17–16.

And the Big Ten's top series—indeed, one of the great rivalries in college sports—was off and running. Not passing, at least not too often. But certainly running, blocking, tackling, and kicking.

The Wolverines needed to get past Ohio State in their national championship seasons of 1932 and '33, and did so in style: a pair of shutouts. Then along came the aforementioned Schmidt, whose colorful sobriquet "Close the Gates of Mercy" fit perfectly for his coaching style.

Under Schmidt, the Buckeyes were an offensive juggernaut described by one reporter as "Buckeyes who scored in buckets." They won three Big Ten crowns and, mostly behind Dye at quarterback, they beat Michigan four straight years—by a combined 114–0.

Schmidt used a militaristic approach, which made sense because he was a bayonet instructor during World War I. And his teams didn't let up, often pouring on the points even when games were decided. He had such a command of offense that his clubs could use a variety of formations and still be productive.

And very entertaining, with halfback passes, laterals, and gimmicks galore. "He was a genius," Dye told The Associated Press. "It was not the kind of football people in the Big Ten were used to seeing, but they sure liked it when we were winning all those games."

The wins with Dye at quarterback hardly were the earliest OSU victories in the series. Back in 1919, the Buckeyes won for the first time against Michigan, 13–3. The Wolverines were 13-0-2 in the series up to that point and had outscored Ohio State 369–21.

But Harley, a three-time All-American and the first true star for the Buckeyes, almost single-handedly carried his school to the win. He got the only TD on a 42-yard run, picked off four passes in an era when throwing the ball wasn't common, and averaged 40 yards punting.

Those 13 points were the first the Buckeyes managed off the Wolverines in four years. Maybe the fact Harley was serving in the military in 1918 had something to do with that.

When Ohio Stadium was constructed, in great part because of the dynamic play of the football team, it often was called "The House That Harley Built."

The Schmidt era in Columbus was followed by an equally significant one at Ann Arbor. Crisler, hired in 1938, would turn around the Wolverines' fortunes both on a national scale and in the rivalry with the Buckeyes. Of course, he had the great fortune of having Harmon on his teams for three seasons. The versatile halfback won the Heisman Trophy in 1940—four years before Horvath would earn it for Ohio State.

Crisler was a disciple of the master, Yost, who'd built the Michigan program as a coach and athletic director. He was leery about leaving Princeton and taking the coaching position at Ann Arbor because of Yost's dominating presence.

But Crisler insisted he must be his own man and the school agreed there would be no interference from above. So the crafty coach headed to Michigan and turned the Wolverines into an offensive force the way the Buckeyes were under Schmidt.

Harmon, famed for wearing No. 98, was the key to that offense in Crisler's early days at Michigan.

"Tom Harmon could run inside, outside, throw, catch, quick kick, or be a decoy," Crisler once said of his first star player at Michigan. "He had the power and the speed, he had the agility and the intelligence, and he made the correct decisions. Players like Tom Harmon make coaches' jobs easier."

Especially in 1940, when the Wolverines ripped apart the Buckeyes 40–0. Harmon passed for two touchdowns and scored three times himself in that game. He finished his three seasons at Michigan with thirty-three touchdowns. In comparison, Red Grange, considered the best college football player up to that point, scored thirty in his career at Illinois.

That one-sided romp signaled the end for Schmidt, who resigned rather than be fired by Ohio State. Schmidt died three years later.

Paul Brown, who'd won six high school championships at Massillon in Eastern Ohio, was hired by OSU and it took him all of two seasons to win a national title. He clinched it with a 21–7 win over Michigan.

But Brown's destiny (the Hall of Fame) lay in the pros as founder of the Cleveland Browns and later the Cincinnati Bengals.

As if the rivalry wasn't heated enough, two post–World War II games added to the fire and the lore of Ohio State-Michigan. In 1946, the Wolverines pummeled the Buckeyes 58–6, including Jim Brieske's 12-yard field goal in the dying minutes. Perhaps Woody had that in mind when he went for the two-point conversion twenty-two years later.

And in '49, with Michigan on top 7–0, OSU scored a late touchdown after an 80-yard drive, only to miss the extra point. But the Wolverines were penalized on the play, and Jim Hague made his second try for a 7–7 tie.

The pre-Woody years ended in 1950 with, well, a whiteout. And a stunning 9–3 loss to Michigan.

A snowstorm blanketed the Columbus area, and throughout Ohio snowdrifts and heavy winds made transportation dangerous, even impossible at times. Coupled with low temperatures that froze everything, getting to—or even near—Ohio Stadium became a daunting task.

Indeed, the stands would not be full for one of the few times in the series because, as one reporter wrote: "Columbus is a sealed city."

Stunningly, the Wolverines had gotten to Columbus to face All-American halfback Vic Janowicz (headed for the Heisman) and the vaunted Buckeyes. Actually, the Michigan team boarded a special train, got to Toledo on Friday, then, despite the horrid conditions, made it to Ohio's capital city the next morning.

The players didn't get dropped off at the stadium, though. They had to trek through the miserable weather for about a half-mile. But they did get there.

When they did, the Wolverines were told that OSU coach Wes Fesler wanted to postpone the game. But he was overruled by the athletic departments of both schools, who didn't want to be the first conference teams to back out on a game. They also figured that with both teams on hand, why not play?

After a delay of a couple hours to remove the snow—and the frozen tarp between the snow and the field—the teams kicked off.

And kicked and kicked. There were forty-five punts in the game, with both sides electing to punt on first down several times to avoid turnovers deep in their territory. Every player wore gloves in the windchill that nobody bothered to measure. Michigan didn't manage a first down or complete a pass.

The biggest play was made by Michigan's Tony Momsen, who happened to have a brother, Bob, on the Ohio State team. Tony Momsen blocked one of Janowicz's punts and fell on the ball in the end zone for the only touchdown in the "Snow Bowl."

Fesler was fired after that season, and OSU turned to Miami for its next coach: Woody Hayes.

It took Hayes all of three seasons to have the Buckeyes back on top, riding Howard "Hopalong" Cassady to the national championship in 1954. Cassady, nicknamed after the star of Western films, was a game-breaking runner who operated behind Jim Parker, perhaps the best blocker in history (for the Buckeyes or anyone else). If Cassady got the ball in the open field, he was gone. But he could also pound it if necessary, and with Hayes as coach, that often was necessary.

But it was the defense that carried the day against Michigan in the 21–7 victory.

The Wolverines took the ball to the OSU 1-yard line and quarterback Lou Baldacci was certain they would score on the next play. But what to call?

He opted for a fullback dive rather than a quarterback sneak, reasoning that the power of fullback Fred Baer would be enough to gain the foot or so needed for the TD.

"But as I called the play in the huddle," he said, "I saw that Fred, who had been shaken up a few plays earlier, had been replaced by Dave Hill."

Hill got the call anyway, but he slipped taking the handoff and his fourth-down dive came up short.

Or did it?

In these days of instant replays and slow-motion analysis—not to mention video reviews by officials—the correct call almost certainly would have been arrived at. Back in 1954, without such luxuries, the call on the field would stand.

And the call was no touchdown.

Had Michigan held and forced a punt from deep in Ohio State territory, it could have seized back the momentum. Instead, the Buckeyes covered 99 yards for the go-ahead score on Cassady's 60-yard gallop.

The 21–7 victory carried Hayes and his players to the national crown. He would win another in 1968, leading into the Ten-Year War.

But even in that decade of the Bo and Woody Show, there was nothing like the 2006 matchup of No. 1 vs. No. 2. It's hard to imagine there ever will be another meeting in "The Game" like that one.

Well, actually, it's not hard to imagine at all.

Chapter 4

The Game: Harvard-Yale

As a central figure in the most famous Harvard-Yale game, Yale's Brian Dowling appreciates its historical significance, if not the final score.

"If we would have won the way we could have, no one would have remembered us, or that game," Dowling said. "They would have said it was just another undefeated Yale team. But because of what happened, it was a mixed blessing for us. The notoriety lasted, and it added to the lore of the rivalry."

The year: 1968.

The place: Harvard Stadium.

The stakes: the Ivy League championship.

And a storyline that even Hollywood script writers would find hard to believe: In a battle of unbeatens, Harvard scored 16 points in the final forty-two seconds for a stupefying 29–29 tie.

Since the rivalry began in 1875, the 1968 game is still considered the most exciting of them all. That's saying something, considering that 123 games had been played through the 2006 season between Harvard and Yale.

Like Harvard-Yale, many rivalries call themselves "The Game." Few match the tradition and trappings of these two Ivy League schools who boast the third most-played rivalry behind Lafayette-Lehigh and Princeton-Yale.

"Harvard and Yale are like two families that are very close, that have a lot of respect for each other," Harvard coach Joe Restic once noted.

And the importance of the game is evident to each school. Speaking at a weekly press luncheon, Yale coach Jack Siedlecki pointed out: "At the beginning of each season, there are two goals:

—"First, win the league title.

—"Second, beat Harvard.

"I don't think you're happy if you don't get them both."

Many say the second goal is more important than the first.

"The season is just a moment, but The Game is a lifetime," Restic said.

The blue bloodline of this rivalry traces to the very beginnings of college football. It started in 1875, just six years after Rutgers played Princeton in the first officially recognized football game in America.

Harvard and Yale had been playing different versions of football when they first met in New Haven's Hamilton Park on November 13, 1875. The "concessionary rules" agreed upon favored Harvard's rugby style over Yale's soccer-like game. The Yale players wore yellow caps, blue shirts, and dark trousers. Harvard's players wore knee britches, crimson shirts, and stockings.

Indicating the tone of that era, rules specified that the player carrying the ball "may be tackled or shouldered, but not hacked, throttled, or pummeled." Harvard did better in the tackling department to upend Yale, 4–0.

There were no reports of any throttlings or pummelings.

Yale won the second game 1–0—obviously, scoring rules were different back then—and continued to hold the upper hand over Harvard with a 13-1-1 record over the next fifteen years. Their games were brutal testimony to the violence of the times.

In the 1894 Harvard-Yale game, won 12–4 by Yale, a newspaper reported that seven players had been carried off the field "in dying condition." Played at a popular neutral site in Springfield, Massachusetts, the game was renowned as "The Springfield Massacre."

The first game played in Springfield, in 1889, was also known for something else: the initial appearance of the Yale bulldog, Handsome Dan.

Between them, Harvard and Yale helped to move the game from the dark ages into an age of football enlightenment. Among their developments: the forward pass, downs, yards to gain, the line of scrimmage, tackling above the waist, and carrying the ball instead of kicking it rugby style.

Yale and Harvard not only dominated the early, violent days of American football, they created the sport. Their players and coaches, their formations and their games led football out of the era of the Rugger scrum and rubber nose guard and into something approximating the complex, fast-moving game of modern times.

At the center of all this was Walter Camp, who played for Yale in the 1870s and coached there from 1888 to 1892. Often called the "Father of American Football," Camp helped invent and standardize the basic football rules and, in later years, took personal charge of the All-America teams. For decades, Camp's All-America teams were considered the primary source for the honor.

Camp was a half-pint halfback when he made his debut for Yale in 1876. The Harvard captain cracked to the Yale captain, "You don't mean to let that child play, do you?"

"Look to your business," the Yale captain replied testily. "He may be small, but he is all spirit and a whipcord."

Camp was that, indeed, as he helped Yale beat Harvard 1–0 in a game featuring rugby-style football. That started a string of eleven straight Yale victories that finally ended in 1890.

The East, and particularly the Ivy League, ruled the college football world in those days. Harvard and Yale were usually at the top of the pile. From 1874 through 1927, Yale won eighteen national championships. Harvard won seven between 1890 and 1920.

Though they stopped winning national titles after 1927, Harvard and Yale didn't stop competing at a high level. Yale produced two Heisman Trophy winners in end Larry Kelley and tailback Clint Frank in the 1930s, and both teams could boast of a stream of All-Americas.

Not until the organization of the Ivy League and a de-emphasis of football in the 1950s did the Harvard-Yale game become generally less significant in the national rankings. The schools were still significant to themselves, however, and their own magical place they had created in American football history.

They built lasting monuments to football glory that reflect the long-standing tradition of the rivalry: Harvard Stadium and the Yale Bowl. Harvard Stadium, the oldest sports venue in America still in use, has long passed its 100th birthday. The Yale Bowl opened in 1914, an occasion marked by Harvard's 36–0 rout of the Bulldogs, and is still going strong.

Overall, Yale has the upper hand over Harvard. The Bulldogs held a 65-50-8 edge through 2006, thanks to a fast start in the series.

After Harvard won the opening game in 1875, Yale lost only four games to the Crimson over the next thirty-one years (22-4-5). It was in large part thanks to Camp's leadership and the presence of such brilliant talents as Pudge Heffelfinger, Amos Alonzo Stagg, Pa Corbin, Bum McClung (later treasurer of the United States), Tom Shevlin, Ted Coy, and Frank Hinkey, a four-year All-American.

Harvard had its own luminaries in the early days with Percy Haughton, Marshall Newell, Bernie Trafford, Ben Dibblee, and Charles Daley. But even when Harvard was good, Yale was always a little better.

On ten occasions between 1876 and 1906, Yale spoiled perfect seasons for Harvard.

Heffelfinger was one of the more remarkable players of his day, renowned for his superhuman toughness.

Returning to campus in 1916 some twenty-five years after his final game, the legendary guard asked Yale coach Tad Jones if he could work out with the team. He was forty-eight at the time.

"I had to show the men I was still tough, or they wouldn't have paid any attention to me," Heffelfinger said.

Jones said yes, but it was against his better judgment. He instructed his players to take it easy on the onetime star.

It wasn't Heffelfinger that Jones had to worry about. On the opening snap, Heffelfinger knocked over two players. Then he broke the ribs of Yale's starting tackle.

"A few more plays and four more men were stretched out cold," Jones recalled later. "I finally had to call Heffelfinger off the field and request him to confine his efforts to vocal instead of physical instruction."

Heffelfinger played in the era of the Flying Wedge, featuring the ball carrier running behind a wedge of seven or eight blockers placed in the backfield with him. This was ultimately outlawed when rules were changed following the turn of the twentieth century to lessen the savagery in football.

The 1890s were the days of such mass momentum in football, resulting in a large toll of injuries and deaths. The 1894 Harvard-Yale game was a bloodbath, sparking so much public indignation that the series was called off until 1897. When they resumed, the teams played to a mighty 0–0 tie highlighted by Haughton's incredible 86-yard punt through the rain. The Harvard players were so disappointed in their performance against Yale that they refused to accept varsity letters that year.

Jones, by the way, was an impassioned speaker with a feel for the dramatic. He uttered his most famous quote once before the Harvard game: "Gentlemen, you are about to play Harvard in football. Never again in your whole life will you do anything so important."

The rivalry is replete with legendary stories, some of them hard to believe but all of them fascinating. Before the Yale-Harvard game in the early part of the twentieth century, a Harvard coach supposedly choked a bulldog to death and threw the carcass at the feet of his players to motivate them.

Apocryphal or not, the message is clear: Harvard-Yale brings out strong emotions on both sides. Things haven't changed much since John Reed, Harvard Class of 1910, wrote a song proposing to "twist the bulldog's tail" and "call up the hearse for dear old Yale."

It was 1908 that Harvard's fortunes against Yale started to change, thanks to the hiring of Haughton as coach. In Haughton's first year, the Crimson completed an undefeated season with a 4–0 victory over Yale. Following a loss in

1909, Harvard started an unprecedented run over its chief rival and continued it even after Haughton had left.

From 1910 through 1922, a period of eleven games, Harvard lost only once to Yale. Few victories were sweeter for Haughton than in 1914, when his Crimson routed Yale and spoiled the opening of the Elis' Yale Bowl, one of the world's newest sports wonders. The Bowl was filled to capacity with nearly 70,000 fans and one magazine called it "the greatest athletic field in the country."

Haughton not only produced good teams, but also introduced a number of unique ideas to college football: the unbalanced backfield; spinner plays; shifting defenses; five-man defensive lines; defensive signals; and the mousetrap play. The mousetrap was especially devious, allowing a defensive player to cross the line of scrimmage so he could be blocked from the side. "We'll let 'em through and then cut 'em down," Haughton said of the mousetrap. Haughton's successful teams were built on timing, speed, and the perfect execution of relatively few plays.

Bob Fisher succeeded Haughton as coach and produced four straight victories over Yale and an undefeated team in 1919 that won the Rose Bowl.

When Yale finally broke the Crimson spell with a 13–0 victory in 1922, some eight hundred riotous Elis poured out of the Yale Club in New York City, and marched over to the Harvard Club to lord it over their rivals.

In the late 1920s and early '30s, Yale's Albie Booth and Harvard's Barry Wood were two of the biggest names for their teams. The games usually revolved around the personal rivalry of these two great backs.

Wood led Harvard to three straight victories from 1928 to 1930 before Booth drop-kicked a field goal that pushed Yale ahead to win 3–0 in 1931.

The days are long gone since these teams hotly competed for national glory, but that hasn't cooled the passions for The Game. If anything, the ties are stronger with the thousands of old grads who come pouring back to the campus with flasks in hand, just like homing pigeons, for The Game. The weekend kicks off with parties on Friday night. On game day, the stadium lot is one big tailgate party.

Sounds like college football anywhere, right? Well . . .

"Sure, everyone wants to win," said Larry Brunton, Harvard, '69. "But the experience is more important than the outcome of the game."

Once The Game begins, there are also elaborate pranks. And not necessarily from just the Harvard or Yale side.

In 1982, the teams were playing the ninety-ninth contest of the series when suddenly a buried black balloon sprang from the field at midfield in the second quarter. Attached to a motorized device and operated by remote control, the balloon started to expand to reveal the letters, MIT. It rose about twelve feet before it exploded and spread baby powder all over the field.

The ingenious prank wasn't the only one pulled off that day by a student from the Massachusetts Institute of Technology. Members of the MIT band masqueraded as the Harvard band and managed to play the MIT fight song on the field.

"Although Harvard was declared the numerical winner, 45–7, MIT was considered to have won the moral victory," the *Los Angeles Times* reported.

A clever ruse, yes. But when it comes to pranks on their own turf, Harvard and Yale students take a backseat to no one.

One year, a group of students who called themselves the "Harvard Pep Squad" ran up and down the aisles at Harvard Stadium giving out 1,800 red and white pieces of heavy construction paper. They told the fans if they held up the paper simultaneously, it would spell out, "GO, HARVARD."

But the Harvard Pep Squad members were actually Yale students. And when the fans held up the paper on command for the rest of the stadium to see, the message was quite different.

The message: WE SUCK.

Not exactly. Harvard beat Yale 35–3 that day.

As for the Harvard and Yale bands themselves, they're just as competitive as the teams. One year, Yale stole Harvard's big bass drum. The thieves were picked up in their truck by police thirty miles west of Boston and wound up spending the night in jail.

"The judge was a Harvard man," reflected one observer.

It is traditional in the pregame show for the bands to march on the field and form giant Y and H letters. One year the Harvard band members tried to put one over on Yale. Instead of forming their usual H, they planned a giant X, thus X-ing out the Yale Y.

Somehow, Yale found out about the plot. As Harvard marched on the field the Yale band members quickly shifted into a large H, thus making the Harvard band X-out itself.

Anything goes in this battle of the bands—and very often, they'll go over the top and spare nothing to disgrace the other.

In the early 1960s, several Yale students were suspended for their alliance with a girl named Susan. The Harvard band members didn't miss a trick. As they marched onto the field for the Yale game, they played, "If You Knew Susie Like I Know Susie."

Probably most of the students at Harvard and Yale would be hard-pressed to tell you the name of their quarterback, or who's on the football schedule from week to week. But all that changes and a fever hits campus like a linebacker's blitz in the late days of November when the archrivals meet in the last game of the season.

And it *is* the last, make no mistake. The Ivy League bans postseason play, thus outlawing bowl games or any other Division I-AA playoff game. The best Harvard and Yale can do is to win the Ivy League championship. Better yet, beat each other in the process of winning the title.

It has happened on a number of occasions, the most recent in 2006 when Yale snapped a five-game losing streak to beat Harvard 34–13 and claimed a share of the Ivy League title with Princeton.

Yale has won fourteen Ivy League championships, including ten from 1960 to 1981. Harvard has won eleven. On more than a number of occasions their season-ending games have had an impact on the league title.

Reflecting on the rivalry, Harvard coach Restic said: "It will be remembered forever. You can beat everybody else on your schedule, but if you lose to Yale, you've lost it all. This is the one that makes history."

Very often, the unexpected happens.

Try these:

—In 1937, Yale was unbeaten, but the Crimson upset the Bulldogs 13–6 with an 80-yard drive late in the game behind the running of Frank Foley.

—In 1974 Yale was going for its twelfth straight victory and the undisputed Ivy League championship when it was upset by Harvard, 21–16. Quarterback Mike Holt led Harvard on a 95-yard touchdown drive in the final minutes, scoring with only fifteen seconds left, as Harvard tied Yale for the conference crown.

—In 1979, Yale came into The Game unbeaten and Harvard had a woeful 2-6 record. Undaunted, the Crimson upset the Bulldogs 16–7.

—In 1989, Yale had a chance for the undisputed Ivy League title, but Harvard stunned the Bulldogs, 37–20, at the Yale Bowl. The shocking loss forced the Bulldogs to share the Ivy League championship with Princeton.

The 1999 game featured an inspirational performance by a player with an inspirational story.

Joe Walland was a freshman defensive back in 1996 when Jack Siedlecki arrived as the new Yale coach from Amherst. One day, Walland walked into the coach's office and told him he wanted to play quarterback.

Siedlecki couldn't have been thrilled. He remembered the 5-foot-10 Walland wasn't even a full-time starter in high school. Walland also threw with his left hand, unorthodox for most QBs. And he didn't help himself, either, when he threw poorly on the first day of practice. Still, Siedlecki stuck with Walland because he had no quarterback with varsity experience.

Walland's first season as the Yale quarterback in 1997 was rocky. He threw for a less-than-startling 767 yards in a 1-9 season, including a 17–7 loss to Harvard.

"It was rough on me that year, but it was kind of a building block for the next year," Walland said.

In 1998, Walland improved, and so did Yale with a 6-4 record. One year later, Yale was in the running for the Ivy League championship.

When it came time for the Harvard weekend, Walland wasn't feeling well.

"I felt sick watching the J.V. game Friday afternoon and the doctors thought I should go to the hospital," Walland said.

Walland checked into the Yale infirmary with a sore throat and 105-degree fever. Walland was also nursing a sprained thumb suffered in the previous week's game against Princeton. He surely wasn't at his best. "But there was no way I wasn't going to play," he said.

The following day, he left his hospital bed to suit up for the Harvard game. Actually, he did more than suit up: Walland completed 42 of 67 passes for 437 yards to lead Yale to a 24–21 victory and a share of the Ivy title. Eric Johnson caught Walland's last pass of the day for the winning TD with twenty-nine seconds left, the quarterback's third touchdown toss of the game.

"Quarterback Joe Walland earned a place in the Yale Bowl pantheon today with one of the greatest performances in the annals of Eli football," the *New York Times* reported.

When it comes to quarterbacks at Yale, though, Brian Dowling may be the most beloved. A campus hero, he was immortalized as the helmet-wearing BD in Yale grad Gary Trudeau's *Doonesbury* comic strip.

Dowling, a star at St. Ignatius High School in Cleveland, had more than one hundred scholarship offers. But his father, Emmett, wanted him to go to Yale.

"In Cleveland, the Yale alumni group is pretty strong," Dowling said, "so my father knew a lot of Yalies."

Emmett Dowling took his son on visits to Yale and other Eastern schools, and Brian liked Yale the best.

"The Yale Bowl was pretty impressive," Dowling said, "so I sort of kept that in the running."

There was only one catch: Yale, or any of the other Ivy League schools, wasn't handing out scholarships. No matter. Dowling's father offered to pay for his education.

Brian finally decided to go to Yale. "The fact that a lot of other Parade All-Americans were going to Yale and [basketball star] Bill Bradley was going to Princeton played into my decision."

Dowling joined a talented group of players at Yale, including running back Calvin Hill, who later starred in the NFL.

"Our Yale team could have beaten a lot of schools in the major conferences," said Dowling. "We had a lot of depth."

The '68 team, in Dowling's estimation, was the strongest offensive team he played on at Yale.

"I think we were fifth or sixth in the country in average total offense per game," Dowling said. "So I had a lot of choices [in offensive plays]. At the end of the season, the difference between our running and passing attack was about 100 yards. That's how balanced we were. So it was very easy to call plays."

In his first year with the varsity as a sophomore, Dowling missed most of the season with an injury. He missed three games in his junior year because of a broken bone in his hand. When he finally got into action to stay, he was literally unbeatable.

From the fourth game of his junior year until the end of his senior year fifteen games later, Dowling never lost a game he could finish. His overall record was 15-0-1 and he played in two of the greatest games in Yale history against Harvard, in 1967 and 1968.

"The two games I played against Harvard were pretty special," Dowling said. "One because in my junior year, we had already clinched [the Ivy League championship] and we had a full Yale Bowl, which was 68,000. It was pretty exciting. And in my senior year, both teams went into the game undefeated, which hadn't happened since about 1910."

Dowling recalled that, except for a few plays, he "didn't play particularly well" in the 1967 game.

The game seesawed—Yale went up 17–0, but Harvard came back with 20 straight points. With three minutes, five seconds to go, Harvard led 20–17 and appeared on its way to a fourth straight victory over Yale.

Dowling had been having a miserable afternoon and with time running out, he had one last chance. It wasn't going to be easy. The goal line was 70 yards away.

As he took charge of the huddle, Dowling said he was thinking, "I wanted to end the game with more completions to Yale than to Harvard. I only had three completions. I think I had four interceptions at the time. So I threw one short pass, sort of a gimme."

Then came the big play.

"I was just trying to do the two-minute drill going down the field, but on the third play, I rolled out and Calvin [Hill] was in the slot running down the middle and Del Marting was the split end. Marting just beat his guy by a wide margin, so I just threw it way up and it was one of the easiest touchdowns we ever had."

There was only one problem: The Bulldogs had scored so quickly that Harvard had a chance to drive downfield. The Crimson did, but ended up fumbling deep in Yale territory as time ran out.

Yet another classic game in the series. But the 1968 game topped them all.

"I tried to take each opponent at a time," Dowling said. "But after four weeks, you sort of knew what everybody's record was. We kept an eye on Harvard. They were undefeated. We knew it was going to come down to the last game."

Both teams had 8-0 records in 1968 and The Game was expected to be a classic. At first it was more of a romp as Dowling and Hill, two of the best pro prospects in the Ivy League, led favored Yale to a 22–0 lead.

Harvard's starting quarterback George Lalich was benched late in the second quarter in favor of backup Frank Champi.

"We knew Frank had the arm, but we felt he was a little inexperienced for the job," said Harvard guard Tom Jones, later known as the actor Tommy Lee Jones. "He was a junior and he was sort of nervous all year."

Champi was the coolest customer around, though, when he got into the game. With thirty-nine seconds left in the first half, the balding history major threw a 15-yard touchdown pass. In the second half, he led Harvard to another TD, but Yale still led 22–13 going into the fourth quarter.

Then Dowling carried the ball over the goal line on a 5-yard rollout and Bob Bayless kicked the extra point for a 29–13 Yale lead.

It would take a miracle for Harvard to come back—no less than two touchdowns and a pair of two-point conversions in the final minute.

A miracle, it was.

Champi threw a 15-yard TD pass to Bruce Freeman with forty-two seconds left and Harvard picked up two more points on a conversion to cut Yale's lead to 29–21.

With no other choice, the Crimson tried an onside kick as the seconds ticked away. And recovered it.

Dowling wasn't worried. "After they recovered the onside kick, I looked up at the scoreboard and saw us with an eight-point lead," he said. "I felt there was no way we could lose."

Lose? Probably not. But Champi wasn't giving up. He ran and passed Harvard to another TD. With time running out and darkness descending on Harvard Stadium, he found Harvard captain Vic Gatto in the end zone for an 8-yard TD pass to cut Yale's lead to 29–27. Then Champi completed a bullet pass to Pete Varney for the two-point conversion that tied the game at 29.

A tie in name only.

"HARVARD BEATS YALE 29–29" proclaimed the headline in the *Harvard Crimson* in faultless Ivy League logic.

As far as Dowling was concerned, in some ways it felt like a defeat. He has called it "the first time I lost at Yale." Actually, he hadn't lost since grade school.

"It was a frustrating game and a blemish on my career at Yale because I thought we had a better team," Dowling said.

As for the game's historic impact, he notes, "The circumstances became larger than life the farther away from it you go."

In retrospect, players on both sides of the ball realized they had been part of something special—something bigger than themselves. The fans, too.

"It is a game by which people remember events in their lives," Gatto said. "People have a desire to remember for that reason, like anything historic in the world."

The game personified the rivalry, as far as Gatto was concerned.

"You never play as well as you can until you're threatened, and we always felt that way about Yale," he said. "And I know Yale felt that way about us."

Adds Dowling: "Once you've graduated, the rivalry becomes larger than life. It goes beyond just a game. It transcends football."

Chapter 5

Texas Two-Step: Texas-Texas A&M and Texas-Oklahoma

When the Texas Longhorns look ahead to a football game with their archrival, they have to look twice.

As if one Big Game isn't enough in a season, the Longhorns have two: Oklahoma and Texas A&M.

Each is unique in its own way—except for one thing, of course: the intense nature of competition.

As Darrell Royal, an Oklahoma player and Texas coach, said of the Sooners-Longhorns rivalry: "It is no place for the timid."

Say the same for Texas-Texas A&M, a Texas-size institution in the land of chicken fried steaks and oil wells.

Tradition runs deep and emotions run high in this passionate intrastate rivalry that features a history of hard feelings between the students.

This caustic relationship was fostered by overplayed social distinctions between Texas and Texas A&M. For many years, Texas students looked upon A&M with disdain—seeing themselves as urbane "blue bloods" of society and the Aggies as a "lower-class" cow college.

"UT students view Aggies as simple-minded farm boys [A&M's first female student was admitted in 1963] who were thrilled to wear soldier suits," an observer once said.

Founded in the 1870s as the "Agricultural and Mechanical College of Texas," the school offers an opportunity for students to earn commissions in any of the military branches.

It doesn't matter to Aggies followers that Texas holds a huge lead in the series (74-34-2). Their team has managed to have its moments during the storied history that started in 1894.

The Aggies peaked in 1939 when they won their only national championship. That season they crushed Texas 20–0 and went on to an 11-0 record under Homer Norton.

Another blissful moment for the Aggies: 1956, when they broke a jinx at Texas's Memorial Stadium that had lasted from 1924, a total of sixteen games.

Bear Bryant, who later became a legend at Alabama, was coaching the Aggies then. He remembered the tension late in the game.

"We were about five touchdowns better than Texas, yet I recall we were leading by only one touchdown as late as the fourth quarter."

Texas was driving, but Lloyd Hale intercepted a pass, and the Aggies added an insurance touchdown for a 34–21 win.

"I was impressed by how much the Longhorns played over their heads," Texas sports information director Jones Ramsey said. "A&M was really never in danger of losing, but Aggies who respected the Memorial Stadium tradition lived in fear until the end."

Mostly, it's been Texas in the driver's seat.

The game is for bragging rights, pure and simple. The Longhorns can also brag that they have won more national championships (four) than the Aggies (one). The Longhorns won in 1963, 1969, 1970, and 2006.

Texas also leads in Heisman Trophy winners, 2-1. Earl Campbell won in 1977 and Ricky Williams in 1998 for the Longhorns, while John David Crow did it for the Aggies in 1957. All were running backs.

The Aggies were especially happy to see Williams graduate. Dubbed the "Texas Tornado," he was a 200-pound thorn in their side as the Longhorns won three of four games during his tenure in Austin. Those victories included an upset 26–24 win in 1998 when the Aggies were ranked No. 6 and the Longhorns unranked.

In perhaps the most emotional game of the series, the Aggies beat the Longhorns 20–16 in 1999 after twelve A&M students were killed and dozens more injured when the structure for a pregame bonfire collapsed.

The tradition of "Bonfire" was started in 1909, when Aggies students ignited a pile of junk, mostly just to keep warm. But it exploded into a statewide event, the bonfire symbolic of the Aggies' "burning desire to beat t.u." The "t.u." was presented in lower case in any printed matter as a sign of disdain for the Longhorns.

Students worked round the clock to cut thousands of logs and stack them multitiered around a "Centerpole." At times, it looked like a teepee, other times a wedding cake.

Texas at one time also featured pregame bonfires, and that literally added spark to the rivalry. There was no shortage of pranks involving these bonfires.

In 1949, four Aggies students drove onto the Texas campus in broad daylight and attempted to preignite the Longhorns' woodpile with gasoline. But the sabotage backfired when flames leaped to the car and burned two of the Aggies.

Burned once, that did not stop the Aggies from trying again. The next day, they were successful.

Even more spectacular was the daring prank pulled off by Texas students, who piloted a two-seater private plane over the A&M campus and dropped incendiary bombs into the Aggies' woodpile.

By 1969, Bonfire literally reached its peak on the Aggies' campus with a 109-foot structure made up entirely of logs—too big, the university thought. The school soon capped the height at fifty-five feet.

In the early-morning hours of November 18, 1999, as the students hurried to finish their work on Bonfire, the huge structure collapsed and buried dozens of them "beneath a snarl of logs the size of telephone poles," said the *New York Times*.

Rescuers, afraid of causing any more of the logs to collapse, were forced to work slowly and remove each log by hand. Rescue operations took several days.

The worst accident in Texas A&M history caused the university, faced with litigation from grief-stricken parents and outrage from the community, to suspend the event. But that did not stop A&M students from taking Bonfire off campus in later years, continuing the tradition in a more modest manner.

The Aggies' victory in the 1999 game came in the midst of their most dominant period in the series. Under Jackie Sherrill and R. C. Slocum from 1984 to 1999, the Aggies were 12-4 against the Longhorns.

Most of the time, it's been the Aggies who have eaten the Texas dust. Some of the great matchups in this series:

In 1920, the Aggies hadn't been scored on in two years, but took a stinging 7–3 loss to Texas in a battle of unbeaten teams.

In 1940, the Aggies were on their way to an unbeaten season and the Rose Bowl. They wound up with neither after a 7–0 loss to Texas stopped their nineteen-game winning streak.

In 1963, the down-on-their-luck Aggies had an upset in their grasp before Tommy Wade came off the bench to help Texas stave off A&M.

In 1990, the Longhorns nipped the Aggies 28–27 in a scintillating battle of two bowl-bound teams. The victory earned Texas a berth in the Cotton Bowl, while the Aggies settled for the Holiday Bowl.

The schools are located only about one hundred miles apart, the Longhorns in Austin and the Aggies in College Station. In the mammoth state of Texas, that's like being in your opponent's backyard.

So familiarity has bred contempt—and disrespect—between these two schools. The series was once canceled because of fighting between the players. They weren't alone. Fighting among the students was also a part of the history.

One of the most memorable stories of the rivalry had nothing to do with fights. This was instead a sneak attack on the Texas campus by a group of Aggies one day in 1915. The devilish A&M students branded the Texas mascot, a longhorn steer, with the score of their 13–0 victory that season.

Some intellectuals from the University of Texas, however, reportedly used a running iron to turn the numbers into the name "BEVO," which has since been the name of the Texas mascot.

The series has been so high-profile in Texas that coaches have staked their jobs and reputations on the outcome of these games.

Despite a glittering 22-3-1 record over three years at Texas, Berry Whitaker was fired shortly after a 14–7 loss to A&M in 1922. And one year both coaches got fired because the game ended in a tie.

Both the Longhorns and Aggies played in the Southwest Conference for most of the twentieth century. Many of the SWC teams hadn't even been born when the Aggies and Longhorns hooked up in their first game on October 9, 1894.

One UT writer praised the Aggies for their "gentlemanly" behavior while visiting Austin. As for comparative football skills, that was another story.

The "Varsity Boys," as the Longhorns were called then, humbled Texas A&M 38–0 in a day when touchdowns counted four points. After the game, A&M publicity director T. B. Ketterson wrote, "A crowd estimated at five hundred piled into buggies and drove back to town."

By 1908, Texas continued to extend its mastery in the rivalry, but things suddenly went from "gentlemanly" to ugly with a brawl among students. One of two games between the schools was played in Houston as part of a carnival called No-Tsu-Oh (Houston spelled backward). With their team leading 14–0 at the half, some 1,200 Texas students paraded onto the field with broomsticks on their shoulders to mock A&M's military-style school.

Aggies cadets, inflamed by the Texas students, hopped the fence and a battle royal that was to become typical of this carnival was underway.

Texas A&M started to make a U-turn in the rivalry with the arrival of Charley Moran, the school's tenth football coach. He was hired in 1909, partly to see what he could do about Texas's domination in the series. Since the rivalry started in 1894, the Aggies had lost the first seven games by shutouts and only had one victory to show for the initial seventeen games.

Moran's teams proceeded to whip Texas three straight times, including twice in one year. He was the only Texas A&M coach to do so.

Moran won three of four meetings with Texas. Maybe his success had something to do with his use of illegal players, which forced a suspension of the series after the 1911 game. By the time the series resumed in 1915, the first year of the Southwest Conference, Moran was gone.

The 1915 game was the scene of one of the greatest punting performances in SWC history. The Austin American reported that the Aggies' Harry Warren "Rip" Collins punted the ball twenty-three times for an amazing 1,026 yards, an average of 45 yards a punt. Other reports inflate the figure to 55 yards a punt. Whatever, the Aggies clearly would not have won without him.

"It was better than they say," said Ricky Key, a classmate of Collins. "A&M didn't have much of a team and Texas had an awfully good one, but A&M won it largely because the Texas safety man couldn't handle his punts."

Collins capped his brilliant day with a touchdown run in the Aggies' 13–0 win. One thing was for sure: Collins was motivated. When he was trying to make a decision about a college, Texas coach Dave Allerdice made it for him with a slur about Collins's competitive nature. Collins decided on A&M and lived for the day when he could show Texas his best.

There have been notable crossovers between schools. The most significant: Dana X. Bible, a defensive wizard who coached at A&M from 1917 to 1928 (minus a year away for World War I), then at Texas for ten seasons from 1937 to 1946.

Dare any football coach to match Bible's unfathomable start at Texas A&M: twenty-five straight shutouts before the Texas game on the last day of the 1920 season.

While fashioning a 24-0-1 record in that time, the Aggies outscored their opposition by a grand total of 771–0!

The great Aggies teams of those days featured Jack Mahan, Roswell "Little Hig" Higginbotham, Tom Griesenbeck, Scotty Alexander, and Kyle Blum, who later became a turncoat by joining the Longhorns.

The 1920 game versus Texas started out pretty much as expected as the Aggies took a 3–0 lead at the half on a 22-yard field goal by Bugs Morris.

Ho hum. Another game for A&M, another shutout. And another SWC title.

Then the unexpected happened, after Texas had been repelled just inches from the goal line on an earlier series.

It was the fourth quarter when the Longhorns marched to the Aggies' 11-yard line. The stubborn Aggies defense held for three downs, leaving Texas with a fourth-and-7.

Instead of going for a field goal that would have tied the game, the Longhorns decided to shoot the works. They made a first down by inches, then scored on the next play to pull out a 7–3 victory and clinch the SWC title.

"You can understand why it was such a bitter defeat," Bible said in later years, "and it was compounded by the loss coming late in the game. That loss was the hardest to take of my coaching career."

It was one of only nineteen defeats in one hundred games at A&M for Bible. He had less success at Texas, but still turned out some formidable teams in his ten years at Austin. His major impact: seven straight victories over his former team from 1940 to 1946.

In the 1950s, Royal brought unprecedented success to Texas. In a twenty-year coaching career from 1957 to 1976, Royal won eleven SWC titles and three national championships while his Longhorns played in sixteen bowl games.

The former Oklahoma player also gained attention with his intricate offensive formations, including the Wishbone. At one point, the Longhorns won thirty straight games and six straight SWC championships with that formation.

His overall record at Texas: 167-47-5. That included a 17-3 mark against Texas A&M, which Royal was equally proud of.

"It has been an institution in the lives of many Texans," columnist Clark Nealon once wrote in the *Houston Post* about the Longhorns-Aggies series. "This is a traditional event by which so many measure births, marriages, wars and other events to call to mind."

It's as big as, well, Texas.

Like Texas-Texas A&M, the Texas-Oklahoma rivalry is also tough on head coaches.

"To put the Oklahoma coaching job in its proper perspective as a coach," Bud Wilkinson once said, "you have to beat Texas to have a good year."

And so he did while building a power in the forties and fifties at Oklahoma, at one point winning nine of ten games over the Longhorns. Royal, who once played for Wilkinson at Oklahoma, turned the tables for Texas in the late fifties and sixties.

Add Oklahoma's Barry Switzer in later years to the list of successful coaches in the "Red River Shootout," or "Battle of Big D," as it has been called. Those are just two of the nicknames of this traditionally famous border battle of proud neighboring states separated by the Red River and steeped in rich football history.

Forget the nicknames. Mostly, it has been a battle of huge hearts, with a succession of impressive games that have impacted the national rankings time and again.

Talk about a high-quality rivalry:

—Since 1945, at least one of the teams, and usually both, has been ranked in the Top 25 in all but a handful of games.

—The schools have combined for eleven national championships: seven for Oklahoma (1950, 1955, 1956, 1974, 1975, 1985, and 2000) and four for Texas (1963, 1969, 1970, and 2006).

—And both are ranked in the Top Ten in all-time victories.

Texas leads the series by a solid margin, 57-39-5, despite a recent surge of five straight Oklahoma victories from 2000 to 2004.

The game, played in the Cotton Bowl in Dallas since 1912, takes on a festive atmosphere as the centerpiece for the Texas State Fair. Dallas becomes a modern-day "Dodge City," with crowds, cars, and celebrative visitors creating a choke hold in the downtown area.

A big party: "The city comes under siege of drunks, wanderers, rooters, shouters, music-makers, and pranksters," said a *Sports Illustrated* writer covering the 1969 game. "They jam side streets, thoroughfares, hotel lobbies, restaurants, and bars and try to see if they can break the NCAA record for arrests."

In addition, celebrities usually show up for the events surrounding the game. In 1969, it was comedian Bob Hope.

The Fair donates a handsome trophy called the "Cowboy Hat," a gold hat mounted on a block of wood, to the winning team. Along with bragging rights, the winner gets to "own" the Red River on the Texas-Oklahoma border until the teams play again the following year.

The intensity of the rivalry has deepened from the numerous high school players who have crossed over to play in the other state—particularly from Texas to Oklahoma.

But the most famous turncoat in the series happened to be a coach. Royal grew up in Oklahoma and played his high school and college ball in the Sooner State before events led him to the Texas coaching job. That was tough for Oklahomans to swallow, tougher still when Royal began beating the Sooners on a fairly regular basis and winning national championships.

Naturally Sooners football fans had a comeback, claiming that the Longhorns had to hire an Oklahoman to lead them to higher ground.

In earlier days of the series, it didn't seem to matter who was coaching for Texas. The Longhorns won the first game in 1900 by a 28–2 score, and through 1946 held a 28-11-2 edge in the rivalry with a combination of twenty-one coaches. The three that made the most impact for Texas: Dana X. Bible, Clyde Littlefield, and Jack Chevigny.

Because of the early Longhorns domination of the rivalry, the 1908 game—won 50–0 by Oklahoma—stood out that much more. Until Oklahoma beat Texas 65–13 in 2003, the 1908 game stood as the largest margin of victory in the rivalry.

The game was played on Friday the Thirteenth, the coldest day that Norman, Oklahoma, had experienced in ten years.

Oklahoma rooters were so thrilled with their team's success that they didn't mind the cold. Delirious with joy, they started celebrating when the Sooners took a 17–0 lead into the halftime dressing room. Some three hundred Sooners rooters, led by Professor D. W. O'Hern of the geology department, did a snake dance on the field and threw their hats over the goal posts at old Boyd Field.

The Oklahoma offense featured a strong ground attack keyed by two of the best tackles in the college game, Ralph Campbell and Willard Douglas. But the highlight of the 1908 contest was a 90-yard runback of a punt by Charlie Wantland—a school record that stood until Royal returned a punt 95 yards in 1948 against Kansas State.

Sitting in the stands for the 1908 game was Wantland's father, an old cowman. He was shocked by the violence of this hard-hitting rivalry. "This is the roughest thing I ever saw. They ought to make them cut this out instead of steer roping," he said, making reference to recent legislation that outlawed steer roping at rodeos.

Coach of that Oklahoma team was Bennie Owen, the only one to have any real success against Texas before Wilkinson arrived in the 1940s.

Wilkinson had starred at Minnesota as a guard and quarterback and then coached at Syracuse and Minnesota and with the Iowa Pre-Flight football team in the U.S. Navy during World War II.

Coming back from the war in 1946, he joined the Oklahoma team as an assistant to Jim Tatum. When Tatum left the next year for Maryland, Wilkinson took over the head coaching job and also the position of athletic director.

The change in coaching personalities was obvious right away to the Oklahoma players.

"Tatum was a lot more outgoing," recalled Wade Walker, captain on two of Wilkinson's teams in the 1940s. "He would bring himself down to the players' level a lot easier than Coach Wilkinson would. Coach Wilkinson was a person that you didn't feel like you could sit down and talk to. I could, but I was captain for two years. He put a lot of pressure on the captains to help."

Wilkinson, a dashing thirty-year-old who could have been confused for one of his players, was brought in to fire up a football program that hadn't had much success. In the first eleven years of the wire service poll, Oklahoma had been ranked only once.

By the time Wilkinson left Oklahoma seventeen years later, he put the Sooners on the football map with three national championships and a record forty-seven-game winning streak. The high point of the Wilkinson dynasty was the fifties, when the Sooners grabbed the college football world by the throat.

Oklahoma's backfield of the early 1950s was one of the most effective in the school's history: quarterback Eddie Crowder, halfbacks Billy Vessels and Buddy Leake, and fullback Buck McPhail.

They were at their best in the 1952 Texas game, combining for four touchdowns in the first quarter en route to a 49–20 rout of the Longhorns.

Each time the Sooners scored, a group of rabid Oklahoma rooters called the "Roughnecks" fired blanks from double-barreled shotguns right behind the Texas bench. The noise was unnerving to Harley Sewell, a Texas guard who had recently returned from service in the Korean War. Sewell was resting on the Texas bench when the Roughnecks fired a volley to salute a Sooners score.

Just then, Longhorns coach Ed Price called out, "Harley, are you rested? Want to go back in?"

"Yeah, Coach," Sewell responded with a pained look, "but this is worse than Korea."

A good part of Wilkinson's success was built on recruiting players from Texas. Some of his best: center Jerry Tubbs and tackle Ed Gray, co-captains of the great 1956 Oklahoma team that walloped Texas 45–0; tackle Jim Weatherall, an All-America in both 1950 and 1951; and J. D. Roberts, an All-America guard in 1953.

This was only the start of high school all-star defections from Texas. In later years such fine players as Joe Washington, Greg Pruitt, Billy Sims, and Brian Bosworth also made the crossover from Texas to Oklahoma.

Wilkinson's impressive collection of Texans led to outrageous claims by Longhorns backers that he had a hidden airfield, on constant alert, ready to send planes out to pick up top high school prospects across the border. The reputed red-colored planes (modeled after Germany's "Red Baron," flying ace of World War I) were even equipped with machine guns, it was said.

Not that Wilkinson needed any kind of strong-arm stuff to lure players to the brilliant Oklahoma football program. Wilkinson also built his dynasty with players from the talent-rich Oklahoma high schools.

His football philosophy was influenced by Tennessee's defensive master Robert Neyland, his teams featuring a solid defense and a strong kicking game.

"Superior execution of the basic fundamentals will usually ensure victory," Wilkinson said. "The main emphasis of the coaching staff should be on the proper development of blocking, tackling, and running."

This sound ball-control philosophy added up to an extraordinary 145-29-4 record for Wilkinson at Oklahoma. But while Wilkinson was generally a world-beater, beating Royal was another matter. In head-to-head clashes, Royal won six of seven games against the man he reverently continued to call "Coach."

The 1958 game was one of Royal's personal favorites and one of Wilkinson's most excruciating losses. Facing an Oklahoma squad that was ranked No. 2 in the country, the Longhorns trailed 14–8 late in the contest.

Time for a Texas rally. And time for Vince Matthews.

Cool and confident, the Longhorns' backup quarterback drove his team deep into Oklahoma territory with time running out. Royal then replaced Matthews with first-stringer Bobby Lackey. Lackey fired a 16-yard TD pass to Bob Bryant. Then he kicked the winning extra point for a 15–14 upset of the Sooners, who had won nine of the previous ten games in the series.

The '63 game was equally painful for Wilkinson. Both teams were unbeaten going into the contest at the Cotton Bowl, which was filled to capacity with more than 75,000 fans. Everyone was looking forward to the game of the season. No one expected the ease with which Texas won.

Led by quarterback Duke Carlisle on offense and tackle Scott Appleton on defense, the Longhorns simply dismantled the Sooners 28–7 on their way to the national championship.

"The Longhorns beat Oklahoma with the simplest offense Darrell Royal could dream up: the hoary split-T option that had been Oklahoma's bread and butter for a decade," said *Sports Illustrated*.

It was the farewell game for Wilkinson and sixth straight loss to his former pupil. He finished with an overall 9-8 record against Texas. Royal would run his winning streak against Oklahoma to eight before finally losing an 18–9 decision in 1966.

The series took a dramatic turn with Royal's arrival.

From 1958 to 1970, the Longhorns beat Oklahoma twelve times in thirteen meetings. In that time, Royal won three national titles to match his mentor.

Royal was an All-American quarterback under Wilkinson in 1949, leading Oklahoma to two victories over Texas in his career with the Sooners. He would make up for that (as far as Texas fans were concerned) in later years as Longhorns coach. In twenty years of guiding Texas football teams, Royal had a 12-7-1 record against Oklahoma.

As a player, Royal was remembered by one writer as "a fine passer, runner, and kicker . . . and he was possibly even stronger on defense."

More impressive was Royal's football intelligence and attention to detail.

"He was a student of the game. He was usually the last to leave the locker room after practice. He would sit there mulling over the day's practice, analyzing the reasons for everything."

Royal had brief head-coaching stints with Edmonton in the Canadian Football League and at Mississippi State and Washington before joining the Longhorns for the 1957 season.

Royal's football philosophy was expressed when he first moved into his office on the Texas campus. He hung up a discarded, dusty picture of a scrawny longhorn steer. "I'm fond of that painting," he said. "I don't want any fenced-in, fat longhorns around here. Just look at him. He doesn't know where his next meal is coming from, and he's not afraid to kick up a little dust. That's the way I want my football team."

If anything, Royal learned his lessons well from Wilkinson, a great organization man with extremely well-prepared teams.

Like Wilkinson, Royal was also a perfectionist. Royal, who introduced the Wishbone offense at Texas and other innovations, had a simple approach to preparing his players for a game:

"You whip the guys across the line of scrimmage and a lot of things will follow."

He also had a folksy, colorful way of making his point. Like Wilkinson, Royal's teams were built on speed. When his running backs failed to move the ball according to his desires, Royal might drawl:

"They sure run like their corns were hurtin' real bad."

That was only one of the "Royalisms" that helped to make Royal the most colorful and popular coach in Longhorns history.

Some others from the witty Texas coach:

—"He's so rich he could burn a wet elephant."

—"We're not exactly a rolling ball of butcher knives."

—And, rating a close game as even: "It's a hoss and a hoss."

His players certainly appreciated one remark that Royal made at the halftime of the 1967 Oklahoma game.

The Longhorns were losing 7–0 and appeared depressed while sitting in the dressing room. Royal looked around the room and noted with a smile: "There's a heck of a fight going on out there in the Cotton Bowl. Why don't you get in on it?" Texas played a better second half and beat Oklahoma that day, 9–7.

In the 1969 game against Oklahoma, Royal faced another challenge. This time, he was coaching against Chuck Fairbanks, who had the Sooners in high gear. The contest featured two evenly matched powerhouses going for a national championship.

"These are the two best Texas and Oklahoma teams since about 1963," Royal said, referring to the year the Longhorns won the national championship. "If we are what we're supposed to be—a contender for that No. 1 thing—then we have to win this one."

But the Longhorns got off to a bad start. Oklahoma zipped to a 14–0 lead in the game's initial eleven minutes.

Royal, whose ground-gobbling Wishbone offense gained national attention in 1968 and was a prime weapon in previous victories over Oklahoma, now went to the air. Big time.

"Get ready to start catchin' the ball," Longhorns quarterback James Street told receiver Cotton Speyrer.

Filling the air with footballs, Street became a high-speed highway for the Longhorns. They came back to win, 27–17, and went on to their second national championship in seven years.

"We played our hearts out," Fairbanks said. "We have nothing to be ashamed of. Our defense played better than it has ever played for me from end to end. . . . Texas just has one fine football team."

In 1971, Oklahoma started to do some dominating of its own, beginning a six-game unbeaten streak against Texas with a 48–27 victory in a battle of Wishbone offenses.

The teams started out scoring so quickly that Royal commented on the sideline, "Everybody looks like they're running downhill out there."

Texas was supposed to have one of its best defenses in years. But Royal said that didn't matter much "when the other side has one of those Corvettes and a guy who knows how to pitch it."

The "Corvette" in this case was running back Greg Pruitt and the guy pitching the ball to him was quarterback Jack Mildren.

Going 0-5-1 against Oklahoma from 1971 to 1976 was bad enough for Royal. But the rivalry really took on a nasty tone when Barry Switzer replaced Fairbanks as the Oklahoma coach and continued to aggressively pursue Texas high school talent.

No doubt frustrated that Texas was losing prime state-grown players to Oklahoma, the Longhorns coach went on the offense. He intimated that Switzer was using illegal, or at least unethical, means to lure these players to Oklahoma. In an obvious move aimed at the Sooners' coach, Royal helped to push through NCAA legislation for new rules that limited the number of visits to a prospect's home.

Was Switzer ticked off? You bet.

Speaking to a Sooners alumni group that summer, the Oklahoma coach was highly critical of the binding visitation rule. Of course he got a dig in at Royal, talking about coaches who "would rather sit at home and listen to guitar-pickers."

Royal did more than listen. He was a huge country music fan who liked to sit in on guitar sessions with friends for relaxation.

Switzer was simmering. He responded by putting himself and his staff through a lie-detector test in 1975 to prove that there was "no sinning." Royal and his staff did the same.

That by no means assuaged the bitter feelings between the coaches. Switzer never lost an opportunity to take verbal shots at Royal. The Texas coach usually answered in kind, but not always so kindly.

The cleaner version of one of Royal's unprintable remarks described Switzer and his staff as "sorry" folks who were, uh, born without married parents. Royal lived to regret this casual off-the-record remark that made headlines and further stirred up the dust of this passionate, explosive rivalry.

Then there was another lie-detector episode in a continuing bizarre turn of events.

Royal accused Switzer of "spying" on his secret practices. The Texas coach reportedly offered Switzer and his assistant, Larry Lacewell, $10,000 each if they would pass a lie-detector test proving they weren't spies. There was no evidence that the test came off, but Royal had clearly made no secret of his dislike for Switzer and his Oklahoma staff.

He disliked them even more after a 24–17 loss to Oklahoma in 1975, the year of Switzer's guitar-picking remark. In a game so typical of this closely fought series, the Sooners twice took 10-point leads, only to have the Longhorns fight back and finally tie the score at 17. With time running out, quarterback Steve Davis steadily led the Sooners downfield. Then from the Texas 33, Horace Ivory scampered off left tackle and shot down the sideline for Oklahoma's winning touchdown with five-and-a-half minutes left.

In 1976, President Gerald Ford must have felt a chill in the air when he walked out with the two coaches for the ceremonial coin toss before the game. The coaches' feelings were dramatically evident for all to see when they refused to shake hands at midfield.

Following Royal's retirement as coach after the 1976 game, a 6–6 tie, the coaching rivalries were not nearly as bitter.

The players did their best to make up for it, often expressing "hate" for the other side.

That didn't change as the new century dawned and the rivalry was marked by the most lopsided margins in the series—first a 63–14 Oklahoma win in 2000, and then 65–13 in 2003.

When the Longhorns finally stopped a five-game losing streak to the Sooners with a decisive 45–12 victory in 2005, Texans all over rejoiced.

A quote by Brad Shearer, a Texas tackle who played in the seventies, pretty much reflected the strong emotions on both sides:

"I just hate Okies, to put it bluntly. They hate me just as bad and that's what makes it a great game."

Chapter 6

The Iron Bowl: Auburn-Alabama

How odd, how IRONic, that the Iron Bowl once united a state in its love for football. Through the years, though, the Auburn-Alabama—or, if you prefer, as a Crimson Tide fan, the Alabama-Auburn—rivalry has become the state's most divisive issue.

It's torn apart friendships and families. It's caused divorces, feuds, and barroom brawls. It's helped decide political races.

Do you bleed Auburn blue or Alabama crimson? Is it Roar Tiger or Roll Tide? Neutrality is not an option.

Alabamans don't band together in support of a pro sports team, because, well, they don't have any. The closest they come are those bastions of higher education—and gridiron glory—in Auburn and Tuscaloosa.

"We do, of course, have college football," said Alabama Sports Hall of Fame marketing director Bill Miller. "And we talk about it 365 days a year, seven days a week. I mean, not having the NFL isn't anything that really bothers us, I'd say."

Adds former Auburn athletic director David Housel:

"It's so tough because Alabama is a small state, there is not a whole lot for Alabama people to brag about and get excited about in sports. That has been true during most of the history of the rivalry.

"With NASCAR becoming so popular and Talladega Superspeedway and golf, that has changed a bit and I don't think it is as torrid and heated as it once was. People have diversified in Alabama. Still, people down here think about the rivalry every day."

The Iron Bowl is about as tame as that fierce animal on the Auburn logo. Or as peaceful as the scowl Bear Bryant would wear when things turned sour, which wasn't often.

Separated by 160 miles, the universities should have plenty in common. When it comes to this sport, though, it might as well be, as one television commentator said, "the Middle East of college football."

Auburn, which also has the distinction of owning more nicknames than just about any other university—War Eagles, Plainsmen, Tigers—won the first meeting 32–22 in 1892 before roughly 450 fans at Lakeview Baseball Park in Birmingham. Neither school had much football experience, and it was a ragged game.

But it was a start. And it didn't last long.

The teams played in Montgomery the next two years, then in 1895 Alabama romped 48–0 under its new head coach, one John Heisman. The game barely drew any newspaper coverage in the state. It would not be a shining beacon in Heisman's illustrious career.

As the site of the game switched between Montgomery and Birmingham, Auburn generally was the better team and won seven of the first eleven meetings. Before the Iron Bowl—so named because Birmingham was built around nearby iron ore deposits—ever took root, however, it disappeared.

And not because of any football tactics. Even a century ago, money was at the base of the dispute that interrupted the series for a mere four decades.

The only true football issue in the disagreement between Auburn and Alabama was over who would officiate the game. More problematic, it turned out, were expense payments to players, which in the days before the NCAA were common and expected. The difference between Auburn's proposal and Alabama's suggestion was all of fifty cents per man, about $34—less than the cost of a good game ticket today.

Not much of a discrepancy? Only big enough to destroy the annual series.

Despite efforts to renew acquaintances, two world wars and a depression would occur between gridiron get-togethers for the Tigers and the Tide.

It appeared no such gap would happen when both schools agreed they should play in 1908, but the accord didn't come until late September. By then, no date for the game could be worked out, in part because Auburn stood by its policy not to play after Thanksgiving.

Only sporadic attempts were made through the next few decades to revive the game. Even the perception of such a rivalry had turned negative, with Auburn president Dr. Spright Dowell saying a renewal would render "other games, contests, and events subservient to the one supreme event of the year."

Well, yeah. And what's wrong with that?

The very foundation of college football, unlike most other sports, is built on such rivalries. Now, well more than a half-century after the resumption of

Alabama-Auburn (OK, Auburn-Alabama for you War Eagles), it is unimaginable that these schools ignored each other for so long.

Well, maybe ignored is not quite correct, because, as former Auburn quarterback Travis Tidwell once told the *Birmingham News*:

"Through the years when the two teams weren't playing, rednecks on both sides didn't want to play each other. We weren't real good in those days when the two teams weren't playing. Alabama was a national power.

"I think the Alabama folks thought playing us might actually somehow help us. Of course, a lot of Auburn folks didn't want to play Alabama, either."

Never did the cause of revitalizing the rivalry seem more lost than in 1944. Auburn suggested reopening the series, but the Board of Trustees at Alabama declined.

The reasoning was absurd. Alabama's Board of Trustees claimed a resumption would create a harmful emphasis on football—in a state where football is king, emperor, and czar. The board also reasoned that coaches wouldn't be interested in working at either school because of the damage done by losing to the Tigers or the Tide in an annual encounter.

So the Iron Bowl stagnated, rusted. As World War II ended and Americans began to prosper as never before, Alabamans felt a sports void as wide as the Alabama River.

The cause appeared hopeless until 1948. With the state legislature supporting the rebirth of the series—but not ordering it, despite some tall tales of the day—Alabama president John Gallalee and Auburn president Ralph Draughon met for exactly that purpose. Their handshake agreement rekindled the series. And the fires that burned crimson or blue.

On December 4, 1948 at Legion Field in Birmingham, the Crimson Tide rolled over the Tigers 55–0. It was the most lopsided outcome in the series, embarrassing Auburn supporters. But at least the Iron Bowl was back.

"What I remember most," Gillis Cammack, Auburn's student body president in '48, told the *Birmingham News*, "is that Bull Connor was Birmingham's police commissioner and he called me and two other Auburn students and three Alabama students to his office. He warned us that there wasn't going to be any fighting, rioting, or other shenanigans in his town. He was a pretty stern fellow."

That game would be memorable only because it marked the return of the series. What would follow, right up until today, was the development of perhaps the greatest intrastate rivalry in all sports.

Tidwell was one of the great characters in the rivalry, and while the '48 game was worth forgetting for him—he finished it not on the field or the bench but in a hospital with a fractured vertebrae—the 1949 contest really got the rivalry revved up. Auburn, which had one victory entering the Iron Bowl, won 14–13.

"What I remember the most about that game was that Alabama scored and Ed Salem lined up to kick the extra point to tie the game," Tidwell said. "I played safety on defense and we made eye contact. I had my hand straight out in front of me, twitching my fingers kind of voodoo-like. He saw that and had a strange look on his face.

"He missed the extra point. I've always said that I put my voodoo on him."

Voodoo and all other high jinks would be cited on both sides as the rivalry grew in intensity. Every traditional sports series includes passion and, well, fanaticism. That's part of the attraction and the charm of a rivalry.

Earl Brown and Red Drew were the coaches who helped renew the series, and the 14–13 win was considered the peak of Brown's tenure in Auburn. But soon, two of the greatest coaches in SEC history—indeed, in college football annals—would take command of their teams and the Iron Bowl.

In 1950, Auburn went 0-10 and lost to Alabama 34–0. That ended Brown's career, and Shug Jordan took over.

"Coach Jordan was a class guy," said Clem Gryska, who played and coached for Bryant at Alabama and now works at the Bryant Museum in Tuscaloosa. "If he lost he had no excuses, if he won he was very humble about it. He was quite a coach, a very successful coach."

Jordan set about straightening out Auburn's fortunes—most notably against Alabama. But he lost his first three tries against the Tide, and Alabama folk began circulating this explanation: AUBURN stood for Alabama Usually Beats Us 'Round November.

But Jordan was a fine recruiter, tactician, and motivator, and the Tigers enjoyed their greatest string of successes in the Iron Bowl under him. They won five in a row from 1954 to 1958, outscoring the Tide 142–15, with three shutout victories. In 1957, Auburn won its only national championship, punctuating it with a 40–0 rout of 'Bama.

Tough times for the Tide.

"You had to win that game or you were second in the state for the rest of the year. The fans would not let you forget it at all," Gryska said. "The game just stood out. You'd have a real good 365 days if you won and the other team and their fans had to hide. If they beat us, they would tell us every day. And if we beat them, we'd tell them every day, 365 days till the next one."

That next one couldn't come soon enough for the Tide during Jordan's five-game winning streak. And the end of the next one couldn't come fast enough, either, as Auburn dominated.

Alabama's answer: Bear Bryant, the man in the houndstooth hat. Bryant was brought in as much to win the Iron Bowl as to get Alabama back in national title contention. Maybe more.

Oddly, though, for Bryant, the Auburn game wasn't always the one he set his focus on each year. Friends of the Bear insist he was more adamant about beating Tennessee, a school he couldn't handle when he coached Kentucky.

And while the Volunteers-Tide rivalry also is among the best in the land, Bryant's bosses at Alabama, not to mention the Tide's legion of vociferous fans, demanded success against the in-state rival, first and foremost.

While Bryant failed initially in a 14–8 loss, the Tide won the next four games by shutouts. They lost a total of three games in those four years. Most importantly, none of the losses came against the Tigers.

If not for a 10–8 win in 1963, Auburn would have fallen ten straight times to Bryant's bunch. Alabama's 34–0 romp in 1961 solidified its national championship.

Auburn's teams weren't exactly slouches in those days, having just one losing season in the 1960s. But Alabama was far ahead in the recruiting race, going outside the state for much of its talent. Auburn relied more on homegrown players, and they weren't able to keep up.

Plus, Bryant simply was the best coach around, as his 323 victories and five national titles attest.

Some longtime participants in the series believe it was the early 1960s when the Iron Bowl forged a lasting reputation.

"In 1964, Auburn was 6-3 going into the game," said Housel, the former athletic director at Auburn, "and Coach Jordan was talking to the team after the Georgia game and about the postseason bowls. One player just said: 'The only bowl we are worried about, Coach, is the Iron Bowl.' So Coach Jordan started calling it that regularly on his TV show. It kind of stuck with Auburn.

"The 'Bama people picked it up over the years."

It wasn't difficult to catch the bug.

"There was a real fever before the game," Gryska recalled. "It used to be, when it was last game of the season, it was a statewide celebration for a week. We had parades, music, all the pageantry. If we'd play it at 1:30 or 2:00 [in the afternoon], Legion Field was filled up by 10:00 [in the morning]. One side was all blue, the other all red."

Most of the time, the red wave would flow.

But Jordan would get one more taste of satisfaction before retiring at Auburn—in merely the most outrageous finish in Iron Bowl history: the "Punt, 'Bama, Punt" game.

Alabama was undefeated and seemingly headed for another shot at the national crown. Auburn was nearly as strong, with only a loss to LSU blemishing its record. The Tide was ranked second in the country and the Tigers were No. 9, but also were a 14-point underdog.

Alabama led 16–0 in the fourth quarter when, finally, the War Eagles got something going, leading to a long field goal—and plenty of boos from the Auburn faithful who felt Jordan was being too conservative.

With about five minutes remaining, 'Bama had to punt. In those days, the Tigers' defensive players made up a majority of the kick teams. Two defensive starters, linebacker Bill Newton—on his way to a phenomenal 21 tackles—and defensive back David Langner were among the special teamers.

Newton had a good feel for the punting game and had blocked one against LSU earlier in the season.

"We had on a similar type punt rush," Newton recalled. "I was rushing from the right side when I blocked the ball, I saw it bounce behind [punter Greg] Gantt. David had broken through, but was pushed to the outside on the right. The ball took a couple of bounces and it bounced up in his arms like a good bounce on the field in baseball.

"Thank goodness Langner was there; a lineman would have fallen on it and we still would never have scored.

"But he went into the end zone."

That made it 16–10. The clock, however, was on 'Bama's side.

The Tide had embraced the wishbone offense by then, and quarterback Terry Davis was a master at it, with the great lineman John Hannah blocking for him. All they really needed was a first down, perhaps two, to cement another Iron Bowl win.

"The feeling when we went back on the field was we had to go back to work," Newton recalls, the pitch in his voice rising slightly as he described the action. "We knew if could stop them, maybe we could have a chance to score. All we wanted to do was turn the ball back over to our offense."

When Auburn's Mike Neel made a one-on-one tackle on third down, Alabama had to punt again. Surely there would be no problems this time, and the Tide would pin down the Tigers deep in Auburn territory and seal the win.

"There was a lot of excitement now, but we all kept our cool. We didn't have a lot of energy to do jumping up and down," Newton said.

They did have plenty of energy to mount another strong rush on Gantt. Incredibly, Alabama's blocking scheme was almost identical to the previous punt. Just as incredibly, Newton broke through again.

"I did not ever feel I would have an opportunity to do it again," he said. "I figured to do my job and maybe somebody else could block it. This was not a Bill Newton pass rush."

But that's the way it turned out. Auburn's one true chance to steal the game was at hand—Newton's outstretched hands, which connected with Gantt's kick.

And guess where the ricochet wound up? Right by Langner, who picked it up and raced into the end zone. The extra point gave Auburn an unfathomable 17–16 lead.

"Jubilation started on the sideline. I know Coach Jordan jumped two-to-three feet off the ground," Newton said with a laugh.

Not so for the Alabama fans.

"I looked over to the side that had the continuous 'Roll Tide Roll' cheer for three-and-a-half quarters, and they were totally silent. That was what was so great about the rivalry then—you could pick out who was rooting for which team in the stands."

Newton was so exhausted he didn't even bother to take credit for Block No. 2. The coaching staff was yelling, "Who got it? Who got it?" and someone else said he had blocked it.

"I thought, 'Maybe you did.' I was so tired I wasn't going to argue."

The Wishbone hardly was an offense for late-game comebacks, and the Tide couldn't mount one. Auburn had the most improbable victory in the series.

"That's the one that stayed with us," Gryska said. "They didn't even get beyond the 50 the whole game. We were so much better, but broke down on that one side and they beat us on two instances. That was enough to win it."

A loss like that can never be erased, but Alabama made some very nice amends the next two years. It won the Iron Bowl both times and also captured the 1973 coaches' poll national title.

By then, the rivalry had taken on mythic proportions in the state. Tales of parents skipping their own daughter's wedding because Auburn was playing Alabama that Saturday might be apocryphal. Then again, they might not.

A preacher performing his duties with a TV set at his side to keep track of Iron Bowl developments? A funeral parlor where even a wake is no excuse to not have the game on? Couples insisting on watching the game in a hospital room while the woman is in labor?

Alabamans swear by these stories. Rivalries certainly can inspire such behavior, especially one that some compared to "in-laws fighting."

A few years ago, Colin "Big C" MacGuire of Greenville, Alabama, was chosen by *The Montgomery Advertiser* as the area's biggest college football fan after readers submitted nominations. Big C, who had seen nearly two hundred Alabama games at the time, was such an overwhelming choice that even Auburn fans voted for him.

"Anyone knows that he is the biggest fan," Greenville resident Kathy Crenshaw, a Tigers fan, told the *Advertiser*.

"I don't know about that, but I'm flattered," Big C added.

MacGuire came by his Tide obsession as an equipment manager in 1978 and 1979, both national title years.

"I got sick before Christmas in 1978, and he wrote me a real nice card," MacGuire said of Bryant. "The thing I remember most about it, though, is that the return address on the outside of the envelope only had his name on it. No address, no city, just his name. It didn't need any more than that."

Like Bryant's name, this rivalry had reached such epic proportions that not even the retirement of Jordan in 1975 lessened it. By then, Alabama was in the midst of a nine-game winning streak as Bryant outcoached and outrecruited just about everyone in the nation, let alone in the state. Every year, the Crimson Tide rode near the top of the national rankings, and even if Auburn was good, 'Bama was better.

In 1978 and '79, Alabama won a version of the national championship. And it kept sending the War Eagles back to the Plains with more disappointment.

"Nine straight? Pure living hell," said Housel, who has BEAT BAMA engraved in his wedding ring. "Some people at Auburn were scarred forever because of that nine-year streak. Those people who were Auburn fans before 1981 and you mention the Alabama game, they would get tight, antsy and nervous."

For good reason. The greatest coach in college football was having no trouble with what many Tide fans commonly called the "Cow College."

In 1981, Auburn hired Pat Dye—a former assistant to the Bear—in an attempt to turn around the program. And, more significantly, to beat 'Bama.

His first try not only ended in the Tide's ninth consecutive Iron Bowl triumph, but Bryant got his 315th career victory, moving past Amos Alonzo Stagg as college football's winningest coach. After the 28–17 comeback win, Bryant received congratulatory phone calls from Presidents Reagan and Carter.

The 1970s had been so good to Bryant and Alabama that the Bear's quote "I'd rather beat Auburn once then beat Ohio State five times" seemed almost superfluous. Beating everyone, including Auburn, had become almost natural for the Tide. So much so that anyone who might have had neutral leanings during those years began siding with Alabama.

At least that is how Bill Porter, a Birmingham businessman and past president of the Auburn Alumni Association, saw it.

"So many people who did not attend school at either place automatically latch on to Alabama," said Porter, who graduated from Auburn in 1957. "They've had tremendous success, and of course they had Bear Bryant. A lot of the allegiance is to Bear Bryant, not so much Alabama. We've had a great heritage, too, but it's been overshadowed."

Particularly during nearly a decade of having the Iron Bowl hammer fall on them.

But the Bryant era was coming to an end. Just as important for Auburn, the Dye era was beginning on the Plains.

Auburn broke its freefall in 1982 in Bryant's final Iron Bowl. Freshman Bo Jackson, who in 1985 would win the Heisman Trophy, soared over Alabama's goal-line defense for a 1-yard touchdown, and the extra point lifted Auburn to a 23–22 victory—and lifted a decade of disappointment for Auburn.

Bryant coached Alabama past Illinois in the Liberty Bowl, then retired. A month later, he was dead. As one longtime associate of Bryant's said, "It was as if he had nothing left in his life after he stopped coaching. And he stopped living."

Bryant's immediate successor, Ray Perkins, had some success in the Iron Bowl, but he also made a pronouncement that Tigers fans bring up to this day. The former star receiver under Bryant at 'Bama stated the Tide would never play at Auburn, and that the Iron Bowl would always be a Legion Field fixture.

One of those Legion Field fixtures is considered by many the greatest win of the series for 'Bama. Van Tiffin kicked a 52-yard field goal into the wind as time ran out for a 25–23 victory in 1985. The lead changed hands four times in the final quarter.

Alabama led 16–10 at halftime against the Tigers, who were led by Heisman Trophy winner Jackson. The previous year, Jackson had missed a block on a running play that thwarted Auburn's comeback and the Tigers fell 17–15.

But in 1985, Bo took over early in the fourth quarter, scoring on a 1-yard dive for his second TD of the game and a 17–16 lead. 'Bama's star freshman, Gene Jelks—who later would be at the center of a scandal that tore apart the program and led to severe NCAA sanctions—answered with a 74-yard touchdown run. Alabama failed on a two-point conversion, as did Auburn after Reggie Ware's 1-yard TD with under a minute remaining.

So the Tigers were up 23–22 and Alabama had one last-ditch opportunity.

"I just felt if we could move the ball a bit, we could get what we needed," Perkins said.

Indeed.

Quarterback Mike Shula led a desperate drive and Tiffin rushed onto the field to make his fourth field goal of the game, setting off unfettered celebrations on the red side of the stadium.

"One of our team managers was in the stands and caught the ball," Gryska recalled of "The Kick."

"We have had a dozen people come by and say they own the ball that Van kicked. I don't know how twelve footballs were kicked up there."

Auburn was still smarting over the loss—and Perkins's pronouncement years earlier—that, perhaps to punish the 'Bama coach, Dye's Tigers pulled off a wild win in 1986, Perkins's final season in Tuscaloosa.

In the final minute, from the Tide 7-yard line with Auburn down 17–14, Dye called for a double reverse. He'd used the play earlier in the game and Scott Bolton gained 21 yards. It was the only play Dye had called all afternoon.

There was one problem this time: Lawyer Tillman was on the field instead of Bolton.

"I couldn't think of his name," a chuckling Dye said of Bolton. "I kept saying, 'I want my wide receiver. I want my wide receiver.' You'd be surprised how hard it is to think of their names out there sometimes."

Sophomore Tillman, who had never carried the ball from scrimmage, realized "I wasn't supposed to be in there," but Auburn ran the play anyway. Tillman, behind a block by quarterback Jeff Burger, dived into the end zone with thirty-two seconds to go for a 21–17 win.

It was the fifth consecutive time the Iron Bowl was decided by four points or less.

"The flavor of this game said it comes out in the last five minutes," Burger said. "It's a great feeling to be on top. It's a terrible feeling to be where Alabama is right now."

Even more terrible when Perkins left for the Tampa Bay Buccaneers and Bill Curry took over—and lost the next two Auburn games, as well.

Auburn now was the school on a roll, and Dye was being lauded for winning five of the last seven meetings when 1989 arrived. Housel calls it "our emancipation," because the Iron Bowl was coming to the Plains for the first time. Clearly, Perkins's prediction was way off.

Curry was a non-Alabama man and he struggled replacing Perkins, a disciple of Bryant. But his team was 10-0 when it headed to Auburn, and a national championship wasn't out of the question.

For five years, or since Auburn expanded Jordan-Hare Stadium to 87,000 seats, it publicly said the '89 contest would be a true home game. It took an agreement with Birmingham to play the 1991 game at Legion Field to get clearance for 'Bama's first visit to the Plains in '89.

"It was the most emotional day in Auburn history," Dye once told Housel. "And it lived up to our expectations."

For all of those years at Legion Field, even though the ticket split was supposedly down the middle, the game usually had a crimson flair. This time, the stands were filled with blue, with only a sprinkle of red anywhere.

"There was nothing wrong with Legion Field," Housel said. "What hacked off people was when they put in the artificial turf, they never talked to Auburn. We read about it in the paper."

'Bama fans who didn't make the two-and-a-half-hour trip fully expected to be reading about win No. 11 the next day. The Tide was ranked second in the nation; Auburn was 11th.

But the SEC title was on the line, too. And there was that fevered pitch of being at home in the Iron Bowl for the first time working for the Tigers.

Final: Auburn 30, Alabama 20.

"Our boys couldn't have been more ready to play," Dye said, "and it surely showed out on the field."

Auburn took a share of the SEC championship and some more satisfaction: Curry, who from 1987 to 1989 went 26-10 and won an SEC crown, never beat Auburn. He left in 1990 for Kentucky.

The succeeding years brought big-time coaches such as Gene Stallings at Alabama—he won the national title in 1992—and Terry Bowden at Auburn. They brought winning streaks for both sides. They brought a ludicrous two-year ban of the "Rammer Jammer, Yellow Hammer" cheer favored by 'Bama fans because of the NCAA's insistence it was taunting.

And, unfortunately, scandals that saw the Tide and the Tigers fall into NCAA limbo.

Stallings's 1992 team was something of a throwback to the great Bear Bryant squads: terrific defense, a workmanlike offense sparked by a superior running back, Derrick Lassic. The Tide was not highly regarded entering the season, but inexorably marched through its schedule until meeting stubborn Auburn.

After a scoreless first half, Antonio Langham intercepted a pass and returned it 61 yards for a touchdown. The Tide's defense never backed off in a 17–0 victory that catapulted Alabama into the SEC championship game, where it beat Florida. Alabama then took out Miami in the Sugar Bowl for its most recent national crown.

The Tigers' insistence on playing at home every other year paid off in a string of victories in the Iron Bowl under Terry Bowden, who left as coach in 1998.

Before he left, Bowden enjoyed another sweet victory at Jordan-Hare Stadium in 1997 against Alabama. For Alabama coach Mike Dubose, who grew up in the state, it was, conversely, extremely bitter.

Alabama's Ed Scissum fumbled a reception when hit by Martavius Houston and Jaret Holmes kicked a 39-yard field goal with fifteen seconds remaining for a heart-stopping 18–17 Auburn win.

After his fourth field goal of the game, Holmes pumped his fist and dropped to both knees. To Tigers fans, this was as important as Tiffin's kick in 1985—the last time an Iron Bowl had been decided by a last-second field goal.

"It can't get any better than this," said Holmes. "Coach Bowden wondered if I could do this, but I wasn't scared at all. It was the biggest kick of my life."

And a final kick at Alabama, which finished 4-7 that season, its worst record in forty years.

When the Tide showed up at Auburn in 1999, it was sick of being 0h-forever on the Plains. Alabama was bowl-bound and Auburn was struggling. Maybe this time, the Tide would find a way to leave the Plains with a victory.

Alabama trailed 14–6 in the second half, but a safety sparked a rally, and the rest was left to superb running back Shaun Alexander. He scored three touchdowns in a 28–17 triumph.

"In the second half, we stepped up and took charge of the line of scrimmage," guard Griff Redmill said. "The last thing we were going to do was leave here with another loss."

The 'Bama fans wouldn't let them leave without a curtain call. About 12,000 of them, chanting "SEC, SEC" as the Tide won the conference's West Division, stayed until the players returned to the field almost twenty minutes later.

Getting vengeance didn't take long for the War Eagles, however. The first Iron Bowl played at Bryant-Denny Stadium in Tuscaloosa was the next year, and the new millennium brought very little offense, all of it belonging to Auburn in a 9–0 win. Damon Duval's three field goals provided all the scoring.

It was a bad omen for 'Bama, who also lost home Iron Bowls in 2002 and 2004. While everyone in red was certain the tide would turn, the agony of such losses doesn't really fade.

"If the players play hard and lose, they can at least walk off the field and live with themselves," Terry Bowden once said. "But that's not the way it is with the fans. In this state, it's the difference between being the brunt of the jokes at the office all year and being the guy who tells them."

Bowden certainly understood the nature of the Iron Bowl rivalry.

"It's a game where pride and state bragging rights override any other factor that might be playing into this game," he said. "Plus, nobody ever really blows the other guy out. Nobody comes into this thinking the other team is going to be so lousy that they're not even going to show up."

Once the game is over, it becomes a continous topic of conversation for many fans.

"Sometimes for our fans, the game's not over," Dubose said. "[They] just keep replaying the game over and over until the game is played again on the field."

Chapter 7

The Big Game: Cal-Stanford

What could be better than two esteemed universities sharing perhaps the most picturesque place in America?

How about merely the greatest ending to a college football game? Not just in their intense series, but in the history of the sport?

Yes, the Big Game between California and Stanford also owns the Big Finish.

Or, as play-by-play announcer Joe Starkey called it in 1982 from the press box at Memorial Stadium: "The most amazing, sensational, dramatic, heartrending, exciting, thrilling finish in the history of college football!"

Exactly.

But the rivalry between Stanford, founded in 1891, and Cal, established in 1868, is graced by much more than the multilateral madness of '82—a game we will discuss in detail quite soon.

Five meetings in the last thirty years were decided on the final play, including the 2000 game. Stanford fullback Casey Moore, a senior that season, caught a 25-yard touchdown pass for the winning score in the only overtime edition of the Big Game.

"This is one of the greatest rivalries out there because of the way everybody in the Bay Area gets excited about it," said Moore. "There's a lot of people in the Bay Area who don't really care about college football until the Big Game, and then they've got their red or gold on."

While neither school is located in San Francisco—you'll find Cal to the east in Berkeley, Stanford to the south in Palo Alto—they both have, at times, owned the city by the bay. And the entire area.

"It is the only time in the Bay Area where the media that week make a big deal out of these schools," said Bob Rose, who was the sports information director at both schools. "There are a lot of colleges in the Bay Area who get some coverage, but this is the only time college sports are treated as a big pro game would be on the same level.

"This is the mix of a big game—'The Big Game'—and you have a major conference represented (Pac-10). There regularly are Nobel Prize winners sitting in the stands, guys who have been awarded millions to figure out an alternative fuel source for the country. So it has a different feel: an intense rivalry that's a little kinder and gentler than, say, the Iron Bowl [Auburn versus Alabama]. But it is very passionate, still."

That passion began in 1892, soon after Stanford opened. A student named John Whittemore, a transfer from back East, organized a football squad that the established players at Cal considered somewhat ragtag. So the Cal players issued a challenge for a game in San Francisco.

Legend has it that nearly 20,000 fans turned out for the second meeting, such a strong showing that the Stanford student manager, one Herbert Hoover—yes, that Herbert Hoover—collected $30,000 in gate receipts, an unheard-of total for the times.

No one, though, showed up at the Haight Street Grounds with a football, and it took nearly an hour to locate one; the owner of a sporting goods store headed to his shop for a ball.

An ignominious start for two such dignified institutions.

The game wasn't so clumsy, with the *Oakland Tribune* dubbing it The Big Game, and Stanford stunned the favored Golden Bears 14–10.

It was the first of seven successive wins or ties for Stanford, with Cal finally tasting victory in 1898 with a 22–0 shutout.

The next year, Billy Erb, a yell leader for Stanford, wanted to enhance his Axe Yell at a baseball game with Cal. So, as some stories go, he bought a 15-inch blade that would become the emblematic prize of The Big Game.

Except several other reports have different versions of the origin of the Axe. Indeed, one claims it was found during excavating work on the school's campus, then was stolen from the foreman's shop.

Regardless of where the Axe came from, it has played a role in the rivalry for more than a century.

Erb supposedly used it to decapitate a blue-and-gold-clad stuffed bear during the baseball game. When Cal won, its fans grabbed the Axe, had the long handle cut off, and kept possession of the talisman for three decades.

The Axe would appear at Cal football and baseball rallies until 1930, when Stanford finally got it back while posing as Berkeley students on a photo shoot.

Still, the Axe was no more official than the name the Big Game—there are, after all, other Big Games in a variety of sports—until 1933, when both schools agreed to make the Axe the annual matchup's trophy.

That also was the year Stanford came up with a mascot and nickname: Indians. Considering that Stanford isn't exactly Wild West territory, nor does it bear any particular Native American connection, that choice might seem, well, strange.

But local cartoonists had depicted an American Indian wielding an axe—you know, hunt down the Cal Bear, trap it, and skin it. So Indian it was.

The Bears, of course, came by their sobriquet impressively. They brought a live bear to the 1895 Big Game.

Into the 1970s, Stanford kept its Indians nickname, and even had a live representative, a local Yurok named Timm Williams. He appeared at games decked out in full Native American garb from the frontier days, calling himself Prince Lightfoot.

Stanford switched to Cardinal (as in the color, not the bird) after school president Richard Lymon recommended dropping any reference to Indians, which many considered offensive to Native Americans, in 1972. With many alumni, it was not a popular decision, and it wasn't until 1981 that Cardinal became the official nickname.

But at least Stanford had another mascot by then: the Tree.

While the Tree is depicted on the city of Palo Alto's official seal, it only comes to life to dance, cheer, and incite when the Cardinal faithful are involved.

The Tree wasn't exactly planted by someone in the botany department at the school. Rather, it's depicted by a member of the Stanford marching band and became so popular among students and faculty that it was adopted as Stanford's rep.

Of course, an Axe can cut down a tree, so whenever Cal wins the Big Game . . .

Stanford won it in 1902 when Bill Trager kicked the first college field goal. But the schools didn't even face off in football from 1906 to 1914.

In those nine years, the sport of choice was rugby, in great part because President Theodore Roosevelt had demanded that football be made less violent throughout the nation.

And for four years, Cal and Stanford didn't meet in either sport because of a dispute over freshman eligibility.

Among the enviable traits of the Big Game today are the off-campus activities of the Big Week. How many other rivalries can brag of cable car rallies or The Big Sail? How about a sing-off between the two schools? Or The Big Splash water polo match? Or the Big Freeze hockey game?

There used to be traditional bonfires on both sides. Cal has continued its pep rally and bonfire at the Hearst Greek Theatre on the eve of the Big Game, and it even includes a Maori war dance performed by a Cal alum. The bonfire draws as many as 10,000 people, and current coach Jeff Tedford helps stir the emotions even more with fiery speeches.

Stanford, however, outlawed its bonfire in 1992 after several breaks in the tradition.

Often, though, the Stanford band's antics supply enough heat to burn up the Bay Area—and tick off Cal fans everywhere. As irreverent as college students can get, which means plenty irreverent, the band rarely falls short of hilarious in its depictions of the foibles of the enemy. And of itself and its school.

"When you have the band like Stanford has, that always is getting into mischief and is a renegade group, well, the older alumni at Stanford never liked the band," Rose said. "In fact, some really had harsh feelings [toward] the band."

Not to mention how opponents have felt.

Not that the band, the Axe, the tree, or the cannon fired when Cal scores are needed to rile up the competitors.

"It doesn't matter if there's a bowl on the line, or rings or watches, or whatever it might be," former Cal coach Tom Holmoe once said. "There's going to be two teams out there fighting for their teams, their schools, for each other, for what they wanted to accomplish during the season and maybe didn't get a chance to."

For all the tension, shenanigans, and lore associated with the Cal-Stanford rivalry, the game—the Big Game—remains the centerpiece. At least most of the time.

Sometimes, however, the rewards of participating are overwhelmed, even erased, by subsequent tragedy. The Big Game had such a sad circumstance in 1976.

Cal's quarterback in 1975 and '76 was Joe Roth, considered a brilliant NFL prospect, potentially a top-five pick in the draft.

One of the Golden Bears' most popular and talented players, Roth led Cal to a tie for the Pac-8 championship with UCLA. Cal was an offensive juggernaut behind his passing and the all-around play of tailback Chuck Muncie and wideout Steve Rivera. Roth didn't even begin that season as the starter, but by Game 3 he replaced Fred Besana in the lineup.

And Besana went on to play in the pros, so Roth's star figured to rocket much higher.

Roth was a leading Heisman Trophy candidate in '76, but early in the year, a medical exam revealed he had several spots on his lung. Two years earlier, Roth had battled melanoma while playing junior college ball, and a lymph node was removed from his face.

But the cancer had returned, and soon Roth was unable to keep down his meals and was losing weight. Still, he continued suiting up and tried to hide his medical condition.

Roth played in the Big Game even though his body was riddled with lumps, his stamina compromised, his athletic skills diminished. Courageously, he kept a mediocre Cal team close in the game that Stanford won 27–24.

"He never came to me with any of that," said Bob Orr, the Bears' trainer. "I didn't know he was sick."

Few people on the team did, and none knew to what extent. Yet Roth played in two postseason All-Star games, both coached by Cal's Mike White. After the games in Hawaii and Japan, Roth returned home. One month later, he was dead.

Today, a locker stands in Memorial Stadium's dressing room with a blue No. 12 jersey, gold pants, and a Cal helmet in it.

"Words can hardly express the type of young man he was, the courage he had," White said. "I was just in the moment supporting him, being next to him. I was following his inspiration. I've talked with my family about Joe many times since."

The Cal family still draws inspiration from Joe Roth, particularly when the Big Game rolls around.

Not that it takes much motivation to get the Golden Bears or the Cardinal players ready to face off. All either side need do is break out a tape of The Play.

Ah, The Play.

So much lore surrounds that 57-yard miracle (if you root for Cal) or 57-yard travesty (if you root for Stanford) that before even describing just what transpired, it's more appropriate to delve into what followed for three of the main characters.

Such as whatever did happen to that blond quarterback from Stanford named, uh, what was it? Yes, Elway. John Elway.

All the bazooka-armed prodigy did was become the first overall pick in the NFL draft five months later; refuse to sign with the team that selected him, the Baltimore Colts, thus forcing a trade to Denver; take the Broncos to the Super Bowl three times in his first seven years (all defeats); win NFL Most Valuable Player honors in 1987; make two more Super Bowls with Denver, winning them both; retire after that second title; make the College Football Hall of Fame; and overwhelmingly be voted into the Pro Football Hall of Fame in his first year of eligibility.

Yet something still sticks in Elway's craw. Always will.

"It was just a farce. They [the officials] didn't have control of the whole game," Elway said of Cal's theatrics on the Keystone Kops lateral play. "They ruined my last game as a college football player."

Stanford, 5-5 and needing a win to make a bowl game, was behind 19–17 with 1:27 left when Elway did what would become almost routine for him, leading a spectacular comeback drive. A fourth-and-17 conversion on a 29-yard pass to Emile Harry was the most memorable play, and Elway guided the Cardinal to Cal's 18. With eight seconds remaining, Elway called a timeout and Mark Harmon made a 25-yard field goal.

The winning field goal, it appeared.

But there remained just enough time for some Cal trickery that Elway later termed "an insult to college football."

"I don't believe they can take something away like that. I don't believe they can take something like that away from this program," said Elway, whose coaches would protest the result until the Cardinal turned blue. "Something has to be done about the referees, there's no doubt in my mind. It's all right to make a mistake, but somebody should be man enough to stand up and admit it.

"It was a very bittersweet ending. I did not want it to end this way. It's something I'll have to live with the rest of my life."

Kevin Moen has no trouble with that. He's celebrated the greatest athletic moment of his career ever since that wild November Saturday—and The Play.

"Without that play, I would have gone on with my life and just had memories of a nice college football experience," Moen, a Los Angeles businessman, told The Associated Press twenty years after the game. "Now, it's given me a little part of Cal history. . . . Anybody that's involved with sports knows about it. I hear it all the time whenever somebody recognizes my name: 'Hey, he was in The Play!'"

Gary Tyrrell normally might provide a light footnote as the trombone player in the Stanford band. Except that this musician was standing right smack dab in the middle of the end zone when Moen motored into it with the football.

At least Tyrrell had the good sense to not be between the goal lines, where many of his compatriots had surged, thinking the game had ended during Cal's kickoff return.

"It got me more attention than I ever thought I'd get for being in a college band, that's for sure," noted Tyrrell, who became a Bay Area financial officer. "And I feel there's been a real bond with Kevin through the years. He is a class act and a true gentleman."

And a football player, meaning on that unforgettable kickoff return, Moen ran over Tyrrell, who, like his fellow bandmembers, was blissfully unaware of what was occurring on the field. No video clip of The Play ever ends before Tyrrell hits the deck.

"I guess I got flattened, but I got right back up. When I heard the cannon go off, I knew something bad had happened," Tyrrell said.

So what really did happen?

Well, the scoresheet will show this:

—Harmon kicked off from his 15 because Stanford received a 15-yard penalty for excessive celebration following his field goal.

—His squib kick was fielded by Moen at the Cal 46 on the left side. He almost immediately sent an overhand pitch to Richard Rodgers a few yards to his left.

—Rodgers gained about a yard while surrounded and pitched to Dwight Garner at the 45.

—Garner gained 5 yards and got the ball back to Rodgers even though Garner was in the midst of five Cardinal players and was being tackled when he lateraled.

—Rodgers headed to the middle of the field to his right and actually had several teammates nearby. He lateraled to Mariet Ford as the band ran onto the field near the Stanford end zone.

—Ford was at full speed near the right hash mark when he was hit and made a sensational, blind over-the-shoulder lateral to Moen, who also was in full sprint at the 26.

—Moen avoided a potential tackler and every member of the band—until flattening Tyrrell in the end zone.

"I remember looking up at the clock, and I turned to watch all kinds of folks rushing onto the field," Tyrrell said. "I turned around again to find our drum major, and that's when I got plowed over. It looked bad, but it really didn't hurt. I bounced off the Astroturf, picked up my hat and my music, and just kept playing."

And why not? With so many yellow flags littering the field, surely this touchdown couldn't count. Surely, Stanford would be awarded victory. Surely . . .

A quarter-century later, Starkey's description of the lunacy remains the only way to fully describe the scene. Replay the video as many times as you want, but try to accompany it with Starkey's classic description: *"All right, here we go with the kickoff. Harmon will probably try to squib it and he does. Ball comes loose and the Bears have to get out of bounds. Rodgers along the sideline, another one . . . they're still in deep trouble at midfield, they tried to do a couple of . . . the ball is still loose as they get it to Rodgers. They get it back to the 30, they're down to the 20 . . .*

"OH THE BAND IS OUT ON THE FIELD! HE'S GOING INTO THE END ZONE! HE GOT INTO THE END ZONE! Will it count? The Bears have scored, but the bands are out on the field.

"There were flags all over the place. Wait and see what happens; we don't know who won the game . . . We have to see whether or not the flags are against

Stanford or Cal. The Bears may have made some illegal laterals. It could be that it won't count.

"The Bears, believe it or not, took it all the way into the end zone. If the penalty is against Stanford, California would win the game. If it is not, the game is over and Stanford has won. We've heard no decision yet. Everybody is milling around on the field.

"And the Bears, THE BEARS HAVE WON! THE BEARS HAVE WON!

"Oh my God, the most amazing, sensational, dramatic, heartrending, exciting, thrilling finish in the history of college football. California has won the Big Game over Stanford. Oh, excuse me for my voice, but I have never, never seen anything like it in the history. . . . The Bears have won it!"

For once, the hyperbole matched the conclusion of the Big Game.

Chapter 8

Florida "Trivalry": Florida, Florida State, and Miami

With Florida, Florida State, and Miami (not to mention Florida Atlantic, Florida International, Central Florida, and South Florida), there's no shortage of football rivalries in the Sunshine State.

Not to be forgotten is the long shadow just across the border cast by Georgia, the University of Florida's longest-standing rival. No wonder the Big Three of Florida football—the Gators, the Seminoles, and the Hurricanes—can't come to a meeting of the minds regarding their top rival.

In a 2005 *USA Today* poll of sports information directors from the 119 Division I-A football teams, all three Florida schools had different answers when it came to that subject. Even Georgia had to "hedge" a little.

Florida State chose Florida as its biggest rival. Miami identified Florida State, and Florida declined to name anyone, saying only that Georgia was the oldest rivalry among the three opponents. Georgia's sports information director, meanwhile, chose three. Take your pick: Georgia Tech, Florida, or Auburn.

While the Florida-Georgia series goes back some ninety-plus years, the rivalries involving the Big Three of Florida football are relatively young by comparison.

Miami, Florida State, and Florida have made up for lost time in a hurry. Since the 1980s, games between Miami and Florida State, and Florida and Florida State, have usually had an impact on the national championship picture. To a lesser degree so has Miami's series with Florida, which has been played far less continuously throughout the years.

"There had been a big outcry when Florida dropped Miami back in the late eighties," recalled Brent Kallestad, who has covered sports in Florida for The Associated Press for more than twenty years. "And when Steve Spurrier took the coaching job at Florida, he said one of the things he wanted to do is get them back on the schedule. Well, he never did. It sounded nice, but they've only played a couple times in the last twenty years."

The general theory why Florida and Miami have not played more: Because of the highly competitive Southeastern Conference, Florida does not want to load up its nonconference schedule with tough teams.

"The SEC philosophy in a nonconference game has always been to play patsies because the league schedule has been so tough," Kallestad said. "Bobby Bowden's deal at Florida State has always been to play as tough a schedule as possible. So it's a little bit of different philosophy."

In 2002, the Miami-Florida rivalry was reborn following a fifteen-year hiatus. The Hurricanes were ranked No. 1 in the country and the Gators No. 6. The Hurricanes kept their top ranking with a 41–16 victory.

The Miami-Florida clash of 2002 was typical in terms of player personnel. In this case, there were 131 players from the state of Florida involved.

"All of them knew of each other in high school," Miami quarterback Ken Dorsey told *USA Today*. "That's where the rivalry comes from, even though we haven't played each other in a while."

When they do, there's always good anecdotal material. The "Gator Flop," for instance.

In the 1971 game, Florida quarterback John Reaves needed 350 yards to break the career yardage passing record of Stanford's Jim Plunkett.

Although he had had a magnificent day while leading Florida to an insurmountable lead, it didn't look like Reaves was going to get it. Miami was moving close to a meaningless score in the final minute, and it appeared Florida would not get the ball back into Reaves's hands.

Suddenly all but one player in the Florida defense intentionally flopped on the ground, allowing Miami to score a quick touchdown.

That gave Reaves another opportunity to move the Florida offense and he did—with a 15-yard pass.

Reaves had the record, and Florida had the victory, 45–16.

In those years that a round robin is played among the three, the winner gets a trophy, the Florida Cup. Winning the national championship is really what they're aiming for, though.

The Big Three Florida schools have won more than their share. Many more. From 1983 through 2006, the trio combined for nine national championships. Miami won five, while Florida State and Florida won two each.

To put that into context, in a twenty-four-year period, those three schools won more than one-third of the national football championships, leaving the rest to be divided up by the other forty-nine states.

Few teams in college football have had a run like Miami, which won four national titles in a nine-year period from 1983 to 1991 before piling on another in 2001.

There haven't been many years that all three Florida schools weren't ranked nationally at the same time. At one point, the Florida-Florida State clash featured a battle of Top Ten teams for eleven straight years.

Safe to say few intrastate rivals can match that, or match the continuing high quality of three such teams in the same state.

Even in lean years, recruiting in the rich south Florida area makes it possible for any of the Big Three to turn things around in a hurry.

No wonder someone called the three Florida schools "Conference FLA," and prompted one player to say, "Everyone knows the national championship runs through the state of Florida."

Florida, despite a football program that started nearly fifty years earlier, had to play catch-up to its two state cousins on the national stage. The Gators finally won the national title in the 1996 season, then won it a second time in 2006.

For that first championship, the Gators did it in the sweetest way possible, by routing Florida State 52–20 in the 1997 Sugar Bowl.

It was redemption time for coach Steve Spurrier, who had lost to Florida State earlier in the regular season that year. Overall, Spurrier lost eight of fourteen games to Bobby Bowden teams.

While Florida held a 30-19-2 lead in the series with Florida State through 2006, Bowden was personally 17-15-1 against the Gators in that period.

The one time the teams tied in the series also felt like a victory to Bowden. That was 1994, when the Seminoles rallied from a 31–3 deficit to tie the Gators 31–31 in one of the greatest comebacks in college football history.

The rivalry between Florida and Florida State hit its peak when Spurrier brought his pass-happy Fun 'n' Gun offense to Florida to rebuild a scandalous program torn apart by NCAA violations—and to change the offensive philosophy of Southeastern Conference football. Bowden was already firmly entrenched at Florida State, having pulled off a coaching miracle by turning around a sorrowful football program in Tallahassee. The Seminoles had won a total of four games in the previous three seasons, but Bowden soon had them on the high road following his only losing season at Florida State.

The FSU-Florida rivalry turned into a personal duel between Bowden and Spurrier. During their years of competition, the coaches never missed an opportunity to tease each other, and throw an occasional barb—or something stronger.

Hearing reports that Florida State players accepted merchandise from a Tallahassee athletic shoe store one year, against NCAA regulations, Spurrier made his famous statement that FSU stood for "Free Shoes University."

Spurrier was the gadfly that kept the rivalry burning at white heat.

"Spurrier aggravated it," Kallestad said. "He was always complaining about the 'dirty play' of the Florida State players. He was always kind of chippy that way, so he obviously put fuel on the fire. It was tough for Bowden, because he usually pretty much just bites his tongue."

Give Spurrier a microphone and he was very likely to say something derogatory, or nasty, about the Florida State football program. He charged that Seminoles coaches taught their players to purposely injure opponents. In 1996, Spurrier emphasized his point by showing films of Gators quarterback Danny Wuerffel taking "late hits" from Florida State players.

Bowden usually kept his anti-Gators remarks on a more lighthearted note. At a kickoff luncheon one season, Bowden was talking about recent back surgery in Gainesville, home of the Gators. He said the surgery was successful, but there was only one problem.

"I wish somebody would tell me how to remove a Gator tattoo from my buttocks."

Hard to believe now, but it almost took an act of the Florida legislature to bring these teams together. Florida was long established in Gainesville when Florida State, a one-time women's college in Tallahassee, fielded a football team in 1947 after going coed.

Florida wasn't interested at first in starting a series with Florida State. The games with other big-time schools were far more lucrative. Finally yielding to political pressures, the Gators agreed to start a series with the 'Noles in 1958.

The result was a 21–7 Florida win, probably closer than a lot of people expected. And even though Florida went 16-2-1 in the first nineteen games of the series, the Seminoles gave the Gators scary, hard-fought battles.

Of course, it wasn't until Bowden came to Tallahassee in 1976 that the series began to turn in Florida State's favor.

Through the years in this series, the teams have taken turns spoiling each other's national championship hopes and unbeaten seasons; brawled before, during, and after games; and played a number of heart-stopping contests.

None was more exciting than the 1994 game remembered as "The Choke at Doak" or "The Rally at Tallahassee," depending on whose side you were on.

Both teams entered the game at Florida State's Doak Campbell Stadium with 9-1 records.

Florida State, coming off its first national championship but being investigated by the NCAA for the highly publicized free-shoes incident, had taken its only loss against Miami. Florida, which started the season ranked No. 1 for the first time in school history, was upset by Auburn at home on opening day.

Both teams had something to prove, especially Seminoles quarterback Danny Kanell, who had failed his biggest test of the season earlier against Miami.

For the first three quarters against Florida, Kanell looked like he was about to take another flop.

"It was pretty brutal," Kanell recalled.

Going into the final quarter, Florida State trailed 31–3 and many of the Seminoles' die-hard fans had lost faith. They were headed toward the exits to start their postgame tailgating early or listen to the rest of the contest on the long drive home.

Big mistake.

Kanell was a different quarterback in the final quarter, hitting eighteen of twenty-two passes for 232 yards. In one of the most amazing performances in college football history, Kanell led the Seminoles on four straight touchdown drives in the final quarter to pull out the 31–31 tie. Talk about fifteen minutes of fame.

"It was like the perfect storm," Kanell remembered many years later. "One less play, one incompletion, and that comeback doesn't get done."

It was a tie, but a victory in every other sense for Bowden.

The rivals met again in the Sugar Bowl, and this time Florida State didn't wait to dominate. The Seminoles took an early lead and held off the Gators, 23–17.

"I do not want to play them twice ever again," Bowden said after the emotional victory. "It's no fun going into a darn bowl and having to beat your in-state rival."

Bowden didn't have any fun playing against Miami, either.

"You don't know how hard it is to beat Miami," said Bowden, who's had his share of hard luck against the Hurricanes. "I've been playing them for thirty-one years, and they've probably got as good a defense as there is in the country, unless it's us."

Bowden's career record versus Miami (13-18) includes a number of gut-wrenching losses in which the kicking game decided many of the outcomes between two Top Ten teams. A couple of them probably cost him national championships.

In 1983, Miami beat Florida State 17–16 with a field goal as time ran out—and went on to win the national championship.

In 1987, in a game featuring a glittering array of future NFL stars such as Michael Irvin and Deion Sanders, Miami edged Florida State 26–25 in one of the most exciting contests of the series.

In 1991, Miami held on to win 17–16 when FSU missed a field goal attempt, then went on to split the national championship with Washington.

In both 2000 and 2002, Florida State's field goal misses also handed closely fought contests to the Hurricanes.

Not that Bowden didn't have his days in the sun against Miami. On the way to his first national championship in 1993, Bowden's top-ranked Seminoles walloped the Hurricanes 28–10. In 1999, Florida State beat Miami 31–21 on the way to another national title.

Tough as the Miami rivalry has been for Bowden, it hasn't had nearly the animosity created by the Florida series—particularly in the Spurrier years.

"There's nobody we play that we hit harder against and that hits us any harder than Miami," Bowden said, "and yet I haven't seen any bitterness in that rivalry."

What he has seen is a succession of coaches who have marched in and out of Miami without the 'Canes missing a beat. The program started to take off with Howard Schnellenberger in the eighties and continued to fly high through Jimmy Johnson, Dennis Erickson, Butch Davis, and Larry Coker.

Miami got a good head start in the series with Florida State, winning the first five games beginning with a 35–13 blowout in 1951.

It's been a rivalry of dramatic power changes. After the Hurricanes won eight of the first nine games, the Seminoles won the next seven. Through 2006, the Hurricanes led the series 29-22-0.

The game, usually played early in the season now that both teams are in the Atlantic Coast Conference, continues to be one of the most important on either team's schedule—through down years or up.

"You have to win big games like this in order to stay at Miami," Coker once said.

In college football rivalries, they usually don't get much bigger on a national scale than Miami-Florida State. Unless it's Florida-Florida State, of course.

Chapter 9

L.A. Supremacy: UCLA-Southern Cal

Not many rivalries get started with 76–0 and 52–0 routs. If they do, they don't last.

Then again, not many college powers share the same city—their campuses are twelve miles apart—and such a localized fan base as Southern Cal and UCLA. So even with such an inauspicious beginning for the Bruins back in 1929 and 1930, there were few rumblings that the two Los Angeles institutions wouldn't have a future with each other on the gridiron.

The Trojans, under the brilliant Howard Jones, were a powerhouse when the series began. The Bruins barely knew how to align themselves on both sides of the ball and couldn't compete with a Hall of Fame–bound coach who had several legs up in recruiting and game-planning.

"In 1929 and 1930 the USC-UCLA game was like a practice game for USC," said Robert Beaver, who played at UCLA from 1929 through 1932. Wisely, the Bruins took a step back after being crushed in those two games, and the series was halted for five years.

"There is little reason for us to meet until the games are more competitive," Jones said, and he wasn't being smug. He was being realistic.

When the L.A. rivalry resumed in 1936, the Bruins were ready. UCLA had built its program into a West Coast contender, going 30-17-2 in that five-year absence from Southern Cal. The Bruins' claim to being prepared, at last, for another shot at the Trojans seemed valid. And it was.

When Billy Bob Williams—a name more suited to a Texas-Texas A&M game, it seems—scored the first touchdown for UCLA against USC, it was worth celebrating. At least there would be no rout on this day.

Indeed, there would not even be a UCLA defeat. While the Trojans did tie the game 7–7, that's all they could manage. UCLA had done its construction work so well that USC was held to a tie against a team it had smoked so badly in previous meetings.

If that meeting smacked of a Hollywood ending, these schools would provide dozens of climaxes that even the moviemakers would have difficulty concocting.

How apropos for two schools in the shadows of the film capital of the world.

After the 1936 tie, it became apparent that a rivalry was budding in L.A. The coaches, Jones of USC and Bill Spaulding of UCLA, were close friends who wanted to see each other succeed—on other Saturdays, of course—and also wanted to develop UCLA versus USC into a special series. They talked up their teams and each other's, hoping the media would begin regarding Bruins-Trojans on the same level as some of the other great college football matchups.

The next year, Southern Cal won 19–13 in a thriller that helped establish the rivalry.

The Bruins were led by All-American halfback Kenny Washington, one of the great players in UCLA history. Washington could do everything—run, pass, return kicks, tackle. He was a one-man gang that the Trojans couldn't contain.

Still, USC led most of the way, only to see Washington take the Bruins to two late touchdowns and threaten for a third.

"We knew how great a player he is, how dangerous he can be," Jones said of Washington, who would eventually play in the NFL. "But knowing and stopping him were two different things."

The Trojans did hold on, but Jones was a nervous wreck by the end of the contest. Spaulding went to the USC locker room to offer congratulations to his friend, but found the door closed. So he knocked and from inside someone asked who was there.

"Bill Spaulding," the UCLA coach replied. "Tell Howard he can come out now, we've stopped passing."

After another USC rout of UCLA in 1938 came the first meeting between the schools that drew national interest. Washington had been joined by Jackie Robinson in the Bruins' backfield, making for the first all-black tandem in major college ball. Indeed, both had All-American skills and, along with teammate Woody Strode, they formed the first trio of African-Americans on a team.

Although Robinson would courageously make his mark in baseball as the first black player in the major leagues, his football talents were equal to anyone in America. So were Washington's, who would make the College Football Hall of Fame. Which made the final score of that 1939 epic so stunning. Before a crowd of 103,300 at the Los Angeles Coliseum, which had been built for the 1932 Olympics and was then a sports palace, the teams tied 0–0.

Boring? Hardly.

Memorable? Definitely.

The Bruins marched downfield in the dying moments, covering 76 yards for a first-and-goal at the 4-yard line. Washington got the call but was stuffed inside. On second down, Leo Cantor ran for 2 yards. And on third down, inexplicably, quarterback Ned Matthews called the same play. Cantor lost 3 yards.

So Matthews canvassed the players in the huddle about what to do on fourth down. Five of his teammates said they should kick a field goal, the other five wanted to go for the touchdown. Matthews cast the deciding vote to go for it with a halfback option pass by Washington to Bob MacPherson.

Although not going for a field goal and a late lead in such a defensive stand-still was perplexing, the decision to get the ball in Washington's hands—and then have him throw it—was at least logical.

"We were sure of one thing: Washington would have the ball," said Trojans defensive back Bobby Robertson. "So our guys up front were concentrating on him, and the guys in the back, like me, were concentrating on him, too. But I also knew [Washington] might throw the ball: he was a great passer, too."

Robertson broke in front of MacPherson and knocked the ball down, preserving a tie that, in many ways, felt like a Trojans win.

"I considered sending a man in to call for a kick just before we made that first down on the 4," said coach Babe Horrell, who had replaced Spaulding on the UCLA sideline as Spaulding concentrated on his duties as athletic director. "But when my boys made the first down, I changed my mind. After all, these kids were doing pretty well without my help. Anything Matthews did from then on was good enough for me."

The finish was so good that the attractiveness of UCLA versus USC had now reached far beyond the West Coast. Just as Hollywood had done.

In 1942, UCLA finally broke through 14–7 for its first win of the series. Jones had passed away in July 1941, and with him went the Trojans' dominance of West Coast football. He'd led USC to two national titles, five Rose Bowls, and eight conference crowns.

And in 1943, '44, and '45, with wartime travel restricted, the neighboring Bruins and Trojans went at it twice each year. They played early in the season, then finished off their schedules against each other.

Overkill? Not quite. In 1945, the opener, won 13–6 by Southern Cal, drew 81,000 fans. The second meeting, another USC win—the Trojans went 5-0-1 in those three years against the Bruins—drew more than 100,000 to the Coliseum.

Yes, UCLA-USC had hit the bigtime. Which is where the rivalry has remained. Today's coaches certainly recognize that.

"You can feel the energy," said Southern Cal's Pete Carroll, who rebuilt the Trojans into a dynasty that won two national championships (2003, 2004) and played in another (2005). "You can sense it from the media, from the intensity on the practice field, from all the people trying to get tickets. There's an ongoing energy that flows all week.

"If we could fit in 200,000 fans," Carroll continued, "we would."

Adds UCLA's Karl Dorrell, "This one's different because your rival is your next-door neighbor. It's here in Los Angeles, it's everywhere you go. There's either USC or UCLA fans.

"This rivalry would be great if we were both 1-9."

That never has happened. More often than not, one of the teams was playing for a conference title, first in the Pacific-8 and now in the Pac-10. Many times, the game had not only a Rose Bowl berth on the line, but also held national title implications.

And the fact that the schools in most years have finished off difficult schedules by meeting each other added yet another "wow" factor to UCLA-USC.

But perhaps the biggest wow factor of the rivalry has been the great coaches and star players who showcased their talents in it.

Southern Cal's Jones, John McKay, John Robinson, and Carroll have mentored their teams to the top of college football. UCLA's Red Sanders, Dick Vermeil, and Terry Donahue became campus legends.

Heisman Trophy winners Mike Garrett, now the athletic director at Southern Cal, Gary Beban, O. J. Simpson, Charles White, Marcus Allen, Carson Palmer, Matt Leinart, and Reggie Bush showed off their wares. Add to that a galaxy of All-Americans from both sides (Kenny Easley, Anthony Davis, Anthony Munoz, Jerry Robinson, Jonathan Ogden, Troy Aikman, Keyshawn Johnson).

And then there is the lore, which began in earnest in 1941 with the "Victory Bell Caper," which would establish the prize for the rivalry. Unfortunately, it was accompanied by some nasty behavior that went beyond pranks—and almost jeopardized the series.

Several Southern Cal fraternity members decided the bell, which initially sat atop a Southern Pacific locomotive before it was presented to UCLA as a gift in 1939, would look better in USC's possession. So a group of Southern Cal students arranged to "borrow" it. Posing as Bruins fans, they helped UCLA students load the bell onto a truck after the opening game of the 1941 season. One of the Southern Cal students quietly removed the key from the truck. When a UCLA student went to locate another key, the Trojans hastily drove off with the prize.

The bell's whereabouts were still a secret by the final game of the season. And a week after the Bruins and Trojans played to a 7-7 tie in 1941, the students had a scrimmage of their own.

When four Southern Cal students toured the UCLA campus by truck in a display of sheer arrogance, they were hauled off and had their heads shaved. That same day, UCLA students invaded the Southern Cal campus with verbal taunts, looking for trouble. They got it. Southern Cal students were only too eager to shave the heads of UCLA students. Then they dumped them into ponds, along with their vehicles. Later, lawns on the UCLA campus also had "USC" burned into them, presumably by Southern Cal students.

Those episodes overshadowed the more comical ones, such as UCLA students painting the Tommy Trojan statue in Bruins colors.

A truce was ordered, under threat of canceling the games, and the student body presidents from each school met to stem the flow of malevolence. They agreed that Southern Cal would return the bell to UCLA as long as it would become the winner's possession each year after the Bruins and Trojans played.

Perhaps inspired by the bell being up for grabs, the Bruins registered that first win over the Trojans in '42.

That wasn't the end of the high jinks, however.

UCLAns at one point kidnapped Southern Cal's popular mascot dog, Tirebiter, and shaved the letters UCLA on his back. In 1946, the "Great Water Hoax" saw several Los Angeles area newspapers report that the Coliseum field had been flooded by fire hoses carried by Southern Cal students, who wanted to slow down the fleet Bruins runners. There even were stories about fistfights between students of both schools, and the stories spread nationally. But the stories weren't true, the newspapers issued retractions, and the schools eventually concentrated on the field.

Thankfully for the Bruins, the arrival of Red Sanders in 1949 made UCLA a far more formidable opponent. In an odd way, Sanders's work at UCLA benefited the Trojans, because the rivalry gathered momentum and took on the look of other great matchups around the country. Finally, both schools were being regarded on the same level—at least on the gridiron.

Sanders came aboard from Vanderbilt one season after leading the Commodores to their only SEC championship. Considering the powerhouses in the Southeastern Conference (Alabama, LSU, Tennessee, Auburn, Georgia, et al.), what Sanders achieved at Vandy was almost miraculous.

In his eight years at UCLA, Sanders went 66-19-1, in great part thanks to the befuddling single wing offense he ran.

"When people see us coming at them from the single wing, and they haven't practiced against it or played against it very much, it's to our advantage," Sanders explained. "It's what we're comfortable with as coaches, and we know it makes our opponents uncomfortable."

Unfortunately, Sanders often was accused of racism because of his background as a "Southern gentleman." His response always was the same: "Prejudiced? Indeed, I am prejudiced in favor of the player who is the fastest, who can tackle the best and block the best. "

Sanders's players certainly could do that. The Bruins won three straight Pacific Coast championships, and outscored the Trojans 64–7 in winning each meeting from 1953 to 1955.

It was Sanders's 1954 squad that brought UCLA a share of the national title, its only crown. It punctuated a 9-0 season with a 34–0 romp over USC in which the Bruins' 4-4-3 defensive alignment allowed a mere 40 points all season.

"He knew how to handle people," guard Sam Boghosian said of Sanders.

"He was a quiet Southerner with a sharp tongue," added All-American guard Jim Brown. "He treated everyone differently according to what made you tick."

One thing that ticked off Sanders and his team was that it could not go to the Rose Bowl after the 1954 season. A conference rule banned repeat visits, so even though UCLA had the nation's best team, it knew its archrival was headed for Pasadena regardless of the outcome of their Victory Bell meeting.

"That left a sour taste with us," Brown said. "It meant we had to show just which team from L.A. was the best, and that was us."

From opening kickoff to closing whistle, the decisiveness of UCLA's win over an 8-1 USC squad convinced voters nationwide that the Bruins were the class not only of California, but the rest of the college football landscape as well.

"We did the little things," noted lineman Jack Ellena. "Everybody showed up to meetings and practices a half-hour early without being asked. That says a lot about the character of the team."

It was Sanders who once said of the matchups with Southern Cal: "It's not a matter of life and death, it's more important than that." He had become such a prominent figure in the rivalry that a popularity poll by the *Los Angeles Mirror* identified him as the city's most admired man, ahead of all those celebrities in Hollywood.

Tragically, Sanders died in August 1958, in the midst of his coaching prime. Despite a strong roster of football coaches that have succeeded him, no one has equaled the success he had in Westwood.

It would be at Southern Cal where the next Hall of Fame coach in the rivalry would land: John McKay. The witty, innovative McKay came to USC in 1960 and would win AP national championships in 1962, 1967, and 1972 and the UPI title in 1974 before heading to the NFL's Tampa Bay Buccaneers. The Trojans went 127-40-8 under McKay, including 10-5-1 against the Bruins.

McKay also was something of a pioneer in the sport. In 1969, McKay became one of the first major college coaches to start a black quarterback, Jimmy Jones. USC won the conference crown and the Rose Bowl that season.

Two years later, McKay was the first coach to bring a fully integrated team to play at Alabama. Bear Bryant, the Crimson Tide's legendary coach, always credited McKay and that team, led by fullback Sam Cunningham, with leading to the integration of Alabama football.

"He gave USC its finest era in football, a standard by which everything else has become measured," school president Steve Sample once said of McKay.

In 1962, the Trojans brought an 8-0 mark and the nation's top ranking into the game with UCLA, which was having a down season at 3-4. Before that contest, McKay told his team that the Bruins "would be the toughest opponent we have faced."

"Forget their record," he said. "If we had their record and they were undefeated and ranked No. 1, would we give up and let them run through us? Or would we make it the biggest game of our year, a chance to establish ourselves?

"This is USC-UCLA. It never is easy. Nor should it be."

And it wasn't. The Bruins carried a 3–0 lead into the final ten minutes before Southern Cal scored two touchdowns for a 14–3 victory on its way to another national crown.

But it was a trio of games, capped by the 1967 meeting that many consider the classic of all UCLA-USC matchups, that carried the L.A. rivalry toward the very top of its class.

In 1965, each team entered the game 6-1-1 and with a Rose Bowl bid in the offing. The Trojans appeared to be in control—and on the way to Pasadena—with a 16–6 lead and four minutes remaining.

That's when Bruins sophomore quarterback Gary Beban not only solidified his standing as an all-conference player, but also began his legend in the rivalry. Beban led the Bruins to two late touchdowns and a 20–16 victory.

"We pushed them all over the field, but we fumbled on their 1, 7, and 17," McKay noted.

The Bruins also recovered an onside kick to set up the winning touchdown pass from Beban to Kurt Altenberg.

When UCLA beat top-ranked Michigan State 14–12 for its first Rose Bowl victory, it earned the Bruins bragging rights inside Los Angeles and out.

The Bruins were ranked eighth at 8-1 the next year and the Trojans were seventh at 7-1 when UCLA won 14–7. Because of the no-repeat rule, however, USC went to the Rose Bowl.

Those UCLA wins provided a perfect lead-in to the '67 contest, considered by many the greatest the Victory Bell series has seen. It featured perhaps the two best players in the history of each school, Beban and Simpson.

The Bruins entered the game atop the national rankings with a 7-0-1 mark (they tied Oregon State). Southern Cal was ranked third at 8-1 (a 3–0 loss to the same Oregon State team the previous week). Not only would the winner have a shot at the national title, but would also head to the Rose Bowl because the no-repeat rule had been waived.

"They had the best quarterback in the nation," McKay said of Beban. "We had the best running back. They had a great offense; so did we. You sort of knew it would come down to a big play or two."

Beban already had displayed his skills at making those plays, and he was the front-runner for the Heisman. Simpson had thrilled the USC faithful with his scintillating runs and NFL scouts were already drooling over him.

It was as juicy a matchup as sports could provide, and the key participants delivered in style before a sold-out Coliseum and a national television audience.

After Beban led UCLA on a touchdown drive capped by Greg Jones's 12-yard run, the quarterback made a rare major mistake. His pass was picked off by defensive back Pat Cashman, who scooted 55 yards to tie it.

Southern Cal went ahead on Simpson's 13-yard TD run that was set up by Earl McCullouch's 52-yard gain. But in the third quarter, Beban and George Farmer teamed for a 53-yard touchdown pass to make it 14–14.

It had been a courageous performance for Beban, who was bothered by bruised ribs and, at times, was pained simply handing off the ball.

"It was the SC game," he later said. "If I could breathe and stand up and throw, I was going to play no matter how much it hurt."

The hurting would be of another kind later in the game. First, Beban combined with top receiver Dave Nuttall for a tie-breaking touchdown. That was followed by the first of two pivotal plays when Bill Hayhoe, a 6-8 defensive end, secured a glorious place in Trojans history by blocking Zenon Andrusyshun's extra point. Earlier, Hayhoe also blocked a field goal attempt.

"We knew he kicked the ball low," McKay said, "so we put the tallest guy we had in there. It worked. Brilliant coaching."

Still, the Bruins were in front and they hadn't been damaged too much by Simpson, who had a swollen foot. So it was time for the Juice to flow.

Simpson was the quintessential weapon for McKay's I-back formation. He was fast. He was strong. He was smart. He was durable. He could slickly maneuver his way for yards, or power for gains. On the vaunted USC sweep—Student Body Left or Student Body Right—Simpson was as elusive as any target in the sport.

"We wanted to see if he could take it inside," McKay said of how he used Simpson. "We ran him seven straight times in one scrimmage, and that was it. He busted people backward."

He hadn't really busted out in this epic, however. Maybe it was just a matter of time.

With just over ten minutes remaining, Southern Cal was at its 36-yard line. Quarterback Toby Page was ready for a pass play on third down, only to see UCLA's linebackers back in coverage. So he called an audible to "23 blast."

Simpson, who'd carried the ball on the previous two plays, took the ball, sped left through a huge hole, then cut back down the middle. Defenders gave futile chase or flailed as Simpson, who ran a 9.4 100 and was also a track star, motored past on his way to a 64-yard score.

"When I looked up after I made my block," said fullback Dan Scott, "all I saw was a lot of guys falling on the ground as No. 32 was running to the end zone. Best sight I've ever seen."

Almost as good was Rikki Aldridge's extra point that provided the difference, 21–20.

Simpson finished with 177 yards and two touchdowns on thirty carries. Beban wound up with 301 yards and two scores.

Although Beban would become UCLA's only Heisman winner, edging out Simpson, Southern Cal went on to beat Indiana in the Rose Bowl for the national championship.

And Simpson would run off with the Heisman the next season, when he led the Trojans to a 28–16 win over the Bruins. He then headed to the NFL, to the Hall of Fame—and, of course, to infamy.

McKay and UCLA coach Tommy Prothro developed quite a rivalry. Like McKay, Prothro was a Hall of Fame coach who also went on to work in the NFL. His first Victory Bell game was in 1966, when a 14–7 win helped Prothro to some Coach of the Year honors. He went 41-18-3 through 1970, when he made the big step—professionally if not geographically—to coach of the Los Angeles Rams.

Prothro, who always had a briefcase with him on the sideline—a quirk that he never explained—was 2-3 against McKay. In 1969, with a Rose Bowl berth on the line, Jimmy Jones hit Sam Dickerson for a 32-yard touchdown play with 1:32 left, giving USC a 14–12 win. Prothro's normally disciplined team was victimized by a fourth-down pass interference call late in the game in a matchup of a pair of 8-0-1 teams ranked in the top six in the nation.

Prothro finished off his stint with the Bruins in style, though, with a 45–20 romp in 1970, the most points in regulation time scored by UCLA in the rivalry.

When Prothro headed to the pros, he was replaced by Pepper Rodgers and the fashionable offense of the time, the Wishbone. Although McKay didn't exactly despise that offense, he was smart enough to stick with the I-back attack and recruit for it. It was rare that USC didn't have a top tailback, a strong and mobile offensive line, and an intelligent, versatile quarterback.

Which made for some intriguing matchups with UCLA and the flamboyant Rodgers.

"We always believed we could stack the line and stop that Wishbone," McKay said. "It usually comes down to the athletes you have on the field, not schemes. But we were confident in what we were trying to do against anyone."

Particularly in 1972, when USC cruised to a 24–7 win over UCLA en route to another national crown, and in '73, a 23–13 victory. Both years, the Trojans would send nine men up to the line of scrimmage to deal with the Wishbone, which cracked under such pressure.

McKay's final season with the Trojans was 1975. The Bruins won the teams' annual matchup 25–22 under Dick Vermeil in one of the sloppiest games in Victory Bell history. Then McKay tried his hand at the pros, where he issued perhaps his most famous one-liner.

When asked about his team's execution after yet another lopsided loss by his expansion Buccaneers, he replied: "I'm all for it."

McKay died in 2001. At a memorial service in his honor, it became clear what he meant to all Trojans everywhere.

"He was one of the greatest football coaches of all time," Garrett said. "He made us all play beyond ourselves. He was a man we could look up to."

Former Trojans quarterback Pat Haden read from a letter he wrote in tribute to McKay.

"I went to the Coliseum a few days ago, and it wasn't quite the same," Haden said. "To me, that memorable site and you are inexorably connected. It was your stage for sixteen years, what La Scala was for Caruso, the L.A. Memorial Coliseum was for John Harvey McKay."

The stage would change (in alternate years, at least) in 1982 when the Bruins moved out of the Coliseum. Local officials were pushing to get the NFL's Raiders to move down the coast from Oakland, which would have put three tenants at the outmoded facility. So UCLA chancellor Charles Young struck a deal to play in the Rose Bowl, where the Bruins have remained—and with a true home-field advantage.

"I wasn't there for the early years we played at the Rose Bowl, but I know it was a big deal to have it as our home field when we played USC when I was at UCLA," said Troy Aikman, the top overall pick of the 1989 draft, a three-time

Super Bowl winner with the Dallas Cowboys, and an NFL Hall of Famer. "I can't imagine having to play every year at a stadium both teams share, especially in that kind of a rivalry, a great rivalry."

The first Victory Bell game at the Rose Bowl was the last of a trio of rip-roaring finishes in which the total margin of victory was five points.

UCLA won the 1980 game when star running back Freeman McNeil caught a pass tipped by USC cornerback Jeff Fisher, the future coach of the Tennessee Titans, and rambled 50 yards for the winning TD in the final minutes. The next year, the Trojans blocked Norm Johnson's field goal attempt with 29 seconds remaining and USC escaped with a 22–21 victory. And in '82, perhaps inspired by truly being the home team in their own stadium, the Bruins stopped USC's two-point conversion try to edge the Trojans 20–19. UCLA then won the Rose Bowl.

The move to Pasadena for their home games not only created a true home-field edge in alternating years for the Bruins, it also led to a series of power changes in the series with the Trojans. UCLA won three in a row (1982 to 1984), then Southern Cal lost only one of the next six matchups. That was followed by the longest winning streaks in the rivalry: for eight straight years, the Victory Bell's stand would be painted blue for UCLA wins (1991 to 1998); then, for seven in a row, the stand got the red treatment for Southern Cal victories (1999 to 2005).

Most of the Bruins' victories in their winning string came under Terry Donahue, who went 151-74-8 in twenty seasons at the helm, including 10-9-1 against the Trojans. UCLA's 24–20 win in his finale pushed Donahue past break-even. It was especially rewarding because Donahue's Bruins were only 6-4 heading into the game, while USC was 8-1-1 and ranked eleventh.

Donahue left college football as the winningest coach in Pac-10 history. He spent so much time in Westwood that John Robinson, who took over at USC the same year Donahue became coach of the Bruins, left the Trojans for the NFL and then came back—only to lose his last three meetings with Donahue.

"He's a great coach and a great guy," said Robinson. "I don't think many people at USC will miss him not coaching them, though."

Donahue left to work in television and eventually wound up as an executive in the NFL.

"It's been a wild and wonderful ride," he said of his two decades as UCLA coach—and more than a quarter-century at the school overall. "It's been more than one person should ever get in a lifetime."

During UCLA's eight-year winning streak—almost unfathomable in a rivalry between such esteemed programs with such strong coaching staffs and recruiting bases—the Bruins won by seven points or fewer six times.

Most notable in the streak: a 38–37 win in 1992 when a 5-5 Bruins team survived as Rob Johnson's two-point conversion pass was knocked down by Nkosi Littleton, and the first overtime game in series history, a 48–41 double-OT affair in 1996, Bob Toledo's first season replacing Donahue.

In '92, the Trojans fell behind by seven points when UCLA's John Barnes hit star receiver J. J. Stokes for a 90-yard touchdown play with 3:08 to go. It was the most sensational and biggest play of a stunning performance for the sophomore wideout, who finished the game with a school-record 263 yards on only six receptions. He scored three touchdowns.

"I was looking for their corners, they were never around," Stokes said. "I was surprised at how open I was." Barnes also threw TD passes of 57 and 29 yards to Stokes, plus a 59-yarder that set up another score.

When Johnson scored his third touchdown of the game, a 1-yard sneak with forty-one seconds remaining, the Trojans opted to go for the win. "Never thought about it," USC coach Larry Smith later insisted when asked about kicking the extra point for a tie.

Littleton had a feeling the two-point try would go to tight end Yonnie Jackson.

"I saw him come right by my face and I wasn't going to let him go," Littleton said. "Johnson tried to look me off, but he threw it behind him a little bit and right into my hands."

Donahue called it "the most emotional game I have ever been in. We came back like I've never seen before. Barnes's performance ranks as good a quarterback performance as I have ever seen.

"The third quarter was theirs, the fourth quarter was ours. J. J. Stokes took control of the game, he played off the charts. I thought it would be a low-scoring game. I never envisioned any offensive display like this. Our whole season was riding on this game."

Barnes was an unlikely hero, hardly in the mold of a Beban or Aikman. He attended Saddleback Community College, Western Oregon State College, and UC Santa Barbara before winding up at UCLA, but behind three other quarterbacks.

All of them got hurt, and Barnes stepped in to rescue a lost season—and win the biggest game of his life.

"Coach Donahue had told me my chances of playing were slim and none," Barnes said of his, uh, recruitment. "It's just kind of funny how things work out. I never thought I'd be here a year ago."

Nor did Smith think the Bruins would be in the game, and eventually win it, against his Trojans, who entered with a 6-2-1 mark.

"We gave up too many big plays," Smith said. "I feel very angry, the team is angry. We had a shot, and we blew it. We have nobody to be mad at but ourselves."

The Army mule stands guard at the Army-Navy game. (Ken Rappoport)

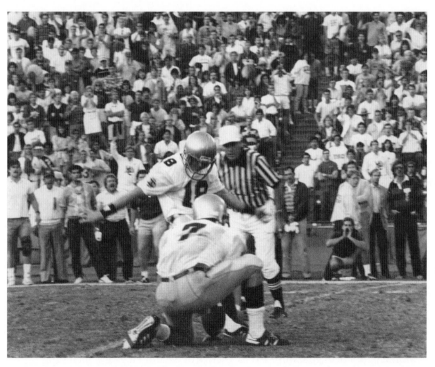

John Carney kicks a 19-yard field goal at the end as Notre Dame beats Southern Cal 38-37 in their 1986 thriller. (Notre Dame Sports Information Office)

Yale's Stone Phillips eludes a Harvard tackler in "The Game," which traces back to the very beginnings of college football. (Yale Sports Information Office)

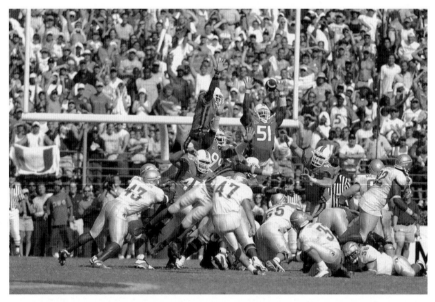

Florida State's field goal flubs led to a series of Miami victories, including this 28-27 final in the thrilling 2002 "Wide Left" game. (Miami Sports Information Office)

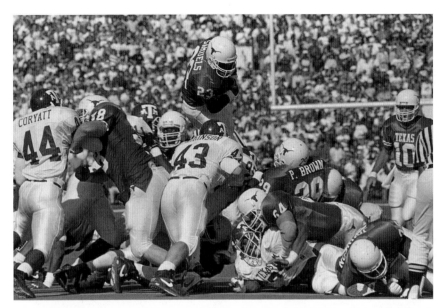

It's over the top for Texas as the Longhorns beat Texas A&M 28-27 in a battle of bowl-bound teams in 1990. (University of Texas Photography Department)

The Lehigh-Lafayette game, shown here at Lafayette's scenic Fisher Field, is known as the "Most Played Rivalry." (Lafayette Sports Information Office)

Lindsay Scott races down the sidelines to the winning TD as Georgia beats Florida 26-21 in their memorable 1980 game. (Georgia Sports Information Office)

Not even Hurricane Katrina could stop the Bayou Classic clash between Grambling and Southern. (Grambling Sports Information Office)

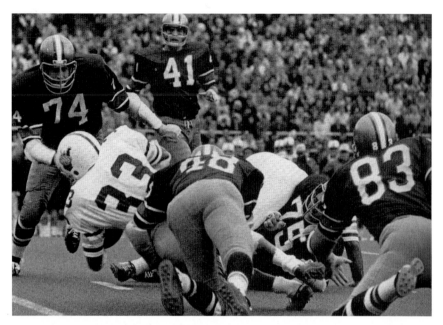

The 1970 game between Pitt and West Virginia featured a miracle finish for the Panthers. (Pitt Sports Information Office)

The Williams bench erupts as Ken Dilanian recovers an Amherst fumble on the Williams 12-yard line to preserve the first perfect season in the Ephs' football history in 1989. (Bill Tague/Williams Archives)

The big prize for this small school rivalry: Wabash players hold the Monon Bell after beating DePauw. (Wabash Sports Information Office)

Arizona vs. Arizona State: They play for the Territorial Cup, the oldest intercollegiate rivalry trophy in America. (Ben Rider/UA Athletics)

It's always full throttle when Tennessee meets Alabama in one of the South's most heated rivalries. (Tennessee Sports Information Office)

"Give them a lot of credit, they made one more big play than we did—they stopped the two-point play."

Four years later, there'd be another shootout in Pasadena.

Neither team was going anywhere in 1996. Southern Cal came in at 5-5, which was better than UCLA's 5-6 record in Toledo's initial season. What the new coach needed was something dramatic and successful against the Bruins' biggest foe.

He got more than he bargained for. As did Robinson.

The Trojans moved into a 38–21 lead with eleven minutes to go when Matt Koffler found speedy freshman R. Jay Soward for a 78-yard touchdown pass.

"I thought the game was ours," Koffler said. "I thought we had it in the bag."

Instead, as had become its custom in the 1990s, Southern Cal went into the bag.

Bjorn Merten's 47-yard field goal with 6:12 remaining was followed by a 42-yard UCLA drive and Keith Brown's 1-yard touchdown run with 2:49 left.

The Bruins gambled on an onside kick that failed, and the Trojans looked safe. But LaVale Woods fumbled, and UCLA stormed downfield in a mere forty-eight seconds. The Bruins needed six plays to cover 56 yards, and Skip Hicks scored on an 11-yard run.

When Merten made the extra point, it was tied. Thanks to NCAA rules that had eliminated ties, the game headed to an extra session for the first time.

"I thought we got into USC's head, five straight losses and all," said UCLA quarterback Cade McNown, who ran for two touchdowns and passed for 356 yards and a score. "We got into a zone in the second half. We made so many big plays it's hard to pick out one or two."

Let us help.

How about when Travis Kirschke blocked a 41-yard field-goal attempt by Adam Abrams in the dying seconds? Or Hicks going 25 yards for the decisive touchdown on the first play of the second overtime? Or Anthony Cobb's interception of Koffler's fourth-down pass, the final play of a wild day in the Rose Bowl.

"It's quite a feat to beat our crosstown rival six [straight] times," Toledo said. "I'm the happiest guy in the world."

And Robinson?

"It just seems like nightmarish things happen to us," he said." My team played an outstanding game, but that's just the way it went."

It was the way it seemed to go during that period for the Trojans against the Bruins, who were ringing their rival's bell with incredible regularity.

The last time the Trojans had taken possession of the Victory Bell, in fact, was with their own miraculous comeback. In 1990, they won 45–42 on a 23-yard pass from Todd Marinovich to Johnnie Morton with sixteen seconds remaining.

Where was some of that magic?

The Trojans wouldn't find it in the next two years. The string of losses to UCLA reached eight, and Robinson already was gone—with an 0-5 record against the Bruins in his second go-around at Troy—when USC broke through.

Oddly, it was under one of their least-successful head coaches, Paul Hackett, and with one of their least-accomplished squads (4-6 heading in) that the Trojans finally snapped the losing streak against UCLA. And, perhaps even more oddly, it was the first of seven straight wins in the series for Southern Cal.

"This city is about this rivalry in football," Hackett said before the '99 matchup. "Eight years we've come up on the short end. I don't know if there is anything more important than just breaking this streak, regardless of all the other things that are involved.

"Do you want to be the team that kept the streak going? Do you want to be the team that broke the streak? We've been talking about it for a year. Eight is enough."

To ensure that, they turned to Chad Morton, their tailback and biggest talker. Weeks earlier, Morton, the younger brother of 1990 hero Johnnie Morton, had guaranteed the streak would end. And with 91,384 fans at the Coliseum, he had a lot of people to please.

So he rushed for 143 yards in a sloppy affair (twenty-five penalties), while senior QB John Fox, who had been benched, then returned to the starter's role, and freshman receiver Kareem Kelly combined for two scores.

"You wouldn't believe the pressure that was on me since I made the guarantee," said Morton, who was carried off the field as fans ran out of the stands as if Southern Cal had just won the national championship. "This week, I didn't sleep at all, but the biggest thing was that I backed it up.

"The team was so fired up when I said it, and they backed me up, and coach backed me up. Now it's probably the best feeling in the world."

Now, could the Trojans make it last? Indeed. But they couldn't save Hackett's job.

USC carried a 3-7 record into the Victory Bell extravaganza against a 6-4 UCLA squad in 2000. For the seventh successive year, no Rose Bowl spot was in the offing for either side, but the game was one of the most exciting in the long, celebrated series.

Young quarterback Carson Palmer had a huge game with 350 yards and four touchdowns, providing a glimpse of the Heisman talents he would display in 2002. In the dying moments, helped greatly by a pass interference penalty against the Bruins, he guided Troy 47 yards into field-goal position.

"That was a terrible defensive display," Toledo said. "We let USC have the ball too much, and they had too many conversions. I thought we would be in overtime, we were already planning it, then we had the pass interference and then they kicked the field goal.

"We've got to live with this for 365 days. I read that some people thought this game meant nothing, but it means a lot to me, no matter what people think."

At least Toledo would be back at his spot for the next game with USC. Hackett wouldn't be so fortunate.

To replace the fired coach, Garrett hired Carroll, who had very limited success as head coach with the New England Patriots—and virtually none in one aborted season leading the New York Jets. While Carroll was lauded by players and media around the NFL as a good guy and a "players coach," there were many critics of Garrett's decision.

Emphasis on *were*, because it turned out to be a stroke of genius by the USC athletic director. Not only was Carroll perfect for the college game as a leader, teacher, and recruiter, but he also put together a staff that, year after year, would be paid the highest compliment in the profession—by being raided.

Carroll's first Victory Bell experience couldn't have been more positive: a 27–0 blanking of the Bruins. The Trojans were off and running, and not just past UCLA but past *everyone.*

Southern Cal extended its winning ways against the Bruins through 2005 as Carroll loaded up his team with top recruits from throughout California and elsewhere in the nation. Southern Cal won two national titles and played for a third. It handed its archrival humbling 52–21, 47–22 and 66–19 defeats.

And in 2006, with the Trojans perched for yet another shot at the national crown, the Bruins decided that no great rivalry can be, well, great, if it is so one-sided.

"I think we're a pretty good team right now," Carroll said of his 10-1 squad as it headed to Pasadena to meet a disappointing [6-5] UCLA team. "We have a great opportunity. We have a great game coming up, a great matchup in a game we love to play in. We can't wait to get started. We'll play anybody, anywhere."

Cocky? Perhaps. But Carroll and the Trojans had earned that right with their stellar performances.

"The history of all sports says yes," Carroll said of the plague of overconfidence in such a scenario. "The history of this football team says no. We haven't had problems with that. That is not a factor I'm concerned about at all."

As for the Bruins, well, they'd won two straight after losing four in a row, and they already had a bowl berth (Emerald against Florida State) in hand. Still, their résumé paled in comparison to those other L.A. guys. Especially when the two schools were on the same field.

"It's been very frustrating. It makes you sick," Bruins cornerback Trey Brown said. "It's been way too long, especially for our seniors that have been here and worked so hard through their careers.

"What better way to send them off than by beating USC. They haven't had a chance to do so, and we have another opportunity. It's great."

It could be great if the Bruins could provide some sort of challenge. They certainly had the motivation after the whipping USC laid on them the previous year—a loss reminiscent of those first two meetings way back when.

"I remember thinking as I stood in the tunnel, 'I don't ever want to feel this again,' " Bruins center Robert Chai said of the 66–19 debacle. "I don't want anyone on this team to forget what that felt like.

"All year long, you talk about this game. You talk about it at the beginning of the season, talk about it during the season, talk about it during summer training. You talk about USC, that you want to beat them. And unfortunately the past couple of years, we haven't done the job."

To do the job and grab back that beloved bell, the Bruins needed, according to many, a miracle. What they got wasn't quite so extraordinary. But it was enough for one of the biggest surprises in UCLA-USC annals.

The Bruins unnerved Southern Cal quarterback John David Booty and his potent offense with a powerful defensive performance. Although the Trojans moved the ball well nearly all day, they either committed penalties, turned the ball over, or were overwhelmed by UCLA's energized defense.

There was some ugliness before the climax. Both teams huddled on the field during a TV timeout, with players jumping up and down, waving their arms, and whooping it up in what amounted to an intimidation dance-off. Both sides were given unsportsmanlike conduct penalties.

UCLA held a 13–9 lead in the fourth quarter when Booty engineered the kind of march that usually led to victory. The Trojans reached the Bruins' 20 with seventy seconds to go, and nearly everyone at the Rose Bowl (and those watching on national TV) expected a last-minute touchdown and yet another USC victory.

"We'd worked so hard and done so much, we just couldn't let that happen," UCLA's Eric McNeal said. Then he made sure it didn't.

McNeal deflected Booty's pass into the air, then pivoted and caught it. A sensational, game-clinching play, the kind USC had been manufacturing for so long against UCLA.

The Trojans' streak was over, and their shot at the national title was gone. USC had scored at least 20 points in sixty-three straight games, an NCAA record. The Bruins held the Trojans to merely nine points. As Dorrell, his staff, and Bruins fans everywhere celebrated, defensive end Justin Hickman led his teammates into the UCLA student section.

"I feel great for our players," Dorrell said. "They've had to endure a lot. We believed in ourselves. We were fortunate to be the ones on top.

"I didn't believe it until the clock hit zero. All we wanted to do was stay close and get a chance to win."

The Bruins got their chance, and they won. Paint the bell stand blue—for now.

Chapter 10

World's Largest Outdoor Cocktail Party: Florida-Georgia

Generally known as "The World's Largest Outdoor Cocktail Party" because of the festive celebrations surrounding the game, maybe we should call Florida-Georgia "Mardi Gras East."

The action starts long before kickoff as loyal fans of the Gators and Bulldogs begin their annual pilgrimage to Jacksonville, Florida, for the neutral-site contest at Alltel Stadium (formerly the Gator Bowl).

As it becomes "The World's Largest Outdoor Cocktail Party," the area around Alltel Stadium also becomes "The World's Largest Outdoor Parking Lot." Some call it "RV City." The lot directly across from the stadium starts filling up with RVs and motor homes as early as a week before the game. Needless to say, it's choked to overflowing by game time.

A sea of colors fills the area, predominantly red and black for Georgia's fans, blue and orange for Florida's. The vehicles are decorated from top to bottom with flags, stickers, and other team paraphernalia.

There might be signs like ALLIGATOR ALLEY to denote a large section of Florida fans, and BULLDOG BOULEVARD for Georgia's. Despite the sharp division, there is always a festive spirit among the tailgating fans as smoke from barbecues infiltrates the air and beer (and other alcoholic beverages) flows freely.

RV City isn't the only place for celebration. The game takes over the city of Jacksonville, with hotels booked solid for months—in some cases a year—in advance. With free entertainment in the downtown area leading up to the game, Jacksonville becomes Party City, USA.

In the days before the game, it's mostly one big happy family with the emphasis on partying. That all changes on game day, when fierce loyalties separate the fans.

The 84,000 tickets are split right down the middle, giving both sides an equal voice in the proceedings. It wasn't always that way.

"In the fifties, Florida had most of the tickets to the game," recalled Georgia football historian Loran Smith. "When Vince Dooley came here, we started winning games and things began to change. Our athletic director demanded that we not only get half of the tickets, but we get half of the good seats. Florida ran the game and took the best seats. They gave us the lesser locations for years. Athletic director Joel Eaves demanded equity and got it, rightfully so."

It is one of a handful of neutral-site games in the country; at least that's what it's called. Smith doesn't think it is a true neutral site like Army-Navy in Philadelphia, or Grambling-Southern in New Orleans.

"It's in a Florida city and the town is against us," he said, "but we've had our moments."

Dan Magill, who started as the Georgia sports information director in 1949 and later became a tennis coaching legend at the school, points out that only the Army-Navy game has been played in the same neutral site (79 in Philadelphia) more than Florida-Georgia in Jacksonville (74).

"It's the biggest game on the road for Georgia fans," said Magill, now curator of the ITF Collegiate Hall of Fame on the Georgia campus.

The game is not the only motivating factor for fans, particularly those from Georgia. They like to take advantage of the usually balmy Florida weather and make a vacation trip out of the jaunt from Athens to Jacksonville.

"We have a big intrastate rival with Georgia Tech," Magill said, "but our fans really love to go down to Florida and spend the weekend."

The fans aren't the only ones to enjoy the scenario.

"There was no game I enjoyed scouting more than that one," said longtime Georgia coach Vince Dooley. The Gators-Bulldogs rivalry has "bowl festivity with big-game intensity," he added.

At the heart of all the serious fun surrounding the game is serious football that has impacted the Southeastern Conference divisional races through the years. Since the SEC's first title game in 1992, Florida has represented the East on seven occasions and Georgia twice. That representative often has been determined by the Florida-Georgia result.

When Heisman Trophy winner Steve Spurrier returned to his alma mater to coach Florida and eventually win a national championship, the rivalry moved to a new level of intensity—and hostility. Spurrier was an equal opportunity rabble-rouser, also causing a good deal of friction with his other top rival, Florida State.

The high point for Spurrier against Georgia—the Bulldogs would call it the low point—occurred in their 1995 game at Sanford Stadium in Athens, Georgia.

Because of construction on the Gator Bowl, the game was moved to the campus sites for two years. The Bulldogs had a proud history at their home field known as "Between the Hedges." No opponent had ever scored as much as 50 points there, but this wasn't Georgia's day. The Bulldogs were on their way to an embarrassing defeat, losing to Florida by 28 points in the closing minutes.

When Spurrier realized his Florida team had a chance to be the first visitors at Georgia to hit the 50-point mark, he went for it. With less than two minutes left, Spurrier called for a pass to complete a 52–17 rout.

Georgia fans likely never forgave Spurrier's running up the score. But it wasn't the first—or last—time Spurrier would embarrass an opponent like that.

As Pepper Rodgers, Spurrier's former coaching opponent and colleague, once said: "Embarrassment is part of the game to him."

Spurrier has a long memory, at any rate. Facing Georgia always made him see red. He still remembered bitter losses to the Dawgs as a player, including the 27–10 thrashing in 1966 when he was considered the best quarterback in college football.

Spurrier had an awful day. He was intercepted three times, more than he had been collectively picked off in Florida's first seven games. Trailing 10–3 at the half, Georgia rallied with 24 straight points in the second half to hand the seventh-ranked Gators their first loss of the season.

As a starter, Spurrier was 0-3 against the Bulldogs. Spurrier more than made up for this in the twelve years he coached at Florida, beating the Bulldogs eleven times. The Georgia game was always circled in red letters on Spurrier's calendar. Recalled Smith:

"Spurrier picked the game to win for two reasons: One, it had such a strong bearing on the conference championship, and two, he developed this fierce hate for Georgia because they beat him when he was a player."

The game was so important to Spurrier that he scheduled an open date before he played Georgia so his team would be well rested.

"And that really helped him," Smith said. "Of course, he coached when we had two coaches, Ray Goff and Jim Donnan, who had a hard time beating him. So Spurrier really had the advantage. But he strengthened that advantage by having the open date."

Florida's recent domination—fifteen of seventeen games through 2006—is polar opposite of the way the series started. It began in 1904 or 1915, depending on whom you believe.

Georgia claims it won the initial game in 1904 by a 52–0 score. Florida insists it didn't have an official football team until 1915, the year Georgia won 39–0, and the Bulldogs merely beat a club team in 1904.

So there's a slight discrepancy in the schools' record books. Ask Georgia how the series stands and the answer is 46-37-2 in its favor. Ask Florida and it's 45-37-2. At any rate, the Bulldogs dominated early, winning the first seven games (six by shutouts) and thirteen of sixteen, with one tie.

The series is replete with memorable outcomes, one more surprising than the other. Historically, the game has been one marked by furious fourth-quarter rallies. At one point, eleven of thirteen games were won in the last period, sometimes on a play drawn and sent in on a napkin.

In 1976, Florida held a 27–13 halftime lead before Georgia scored 28 straight points for a 41–27 win. Remembered as much as the rally was an unfortunate decision by Gators coach Doug Dickey. With Florida leading 27–20 in the third quarter, Dickey decided to go for a first down on fourth-and-1 from his 29. Georgia stopped Earl Carr short of the needed yard and scored three straight times for the victory.

"It was the greatest comeback I've seen," said Magill, who started watching Georgia football in 1929 when the Bulldogs dedicated Sanford Stadium with a victory over Yale.

The 1976 win also featured one of the greatest individual performances Magill had seen in Georgia football history.

"Ray Goff, who was later head coach, was the big star," Magill recalled. "He was a big husky quarterback, just as good a runner as he was a passer."

That day, Goff rushed for 184 yards, including three touchdowns, and passed for two more. He was chosen Quarterback of the Week by The Associated Press.

In 1993, Georgia trailed by a touchdown late in the game but was driving for a score. Quarterback Eric Zeier completed a touchdown pass with five seconds remaining—but hold on. Officials said Florida safety Anthone Lott had called a timeout before the ball was snapped, nullifying the play.

The Bulldogs were forced to re-play the down. This time, a pass interference call against Lott gave Georgia yet another down to try to score. But Zeier's pass fell incomplete, allowing the Gators to escape with a 33–26 triumph.

For sheer drama, it's hard to top the 1980 Florida-Georgia game. "That was the most memorable game for me," Magill said.

And for many others at Georgia.

With star freshman running back Herschel Walker their big offensive threat, the Bulldogs had visions of a national championship. Coming into the Florida game, Georgia was ranked No. 2 in the country behind Notre Dame. Both were the last unbeaten major-college teams in football.

With a pristine 8-0 record, Georgia was a seven-point favorite over Florida, 6-1 and ranked No. 20 in the country.

Walker, who finished with 238 yards, helped the Bulldogs rush to a 20–10 lead after three quarters.

Suddenly Florida came to life. The Gators scored 11 points on a touchdown, two-point conversion and a field goal, and led 21–20 with less than seven minutes left.

"By then Florida was outplaying Georgia," the *New York Times* reported. "Its defensive line was bottling up the Georgia attack, except for Walker's escapades."

It looked bad for Georgia when Florida punted out of bounds on the Bulldogs' 7-yard line with just ninety-five seconds left.

It looked worse when Georgia quarterback Buck Belue, finding no receiver open, ran and lost a yard. Then Belue had a pass dropped by his receiver.

Now it was third down, with 1:04 to play.

Belue went back to pass, but was forced out of the pocket and had to scramble.

"I think when Belue scrambled, we may have relaxed a bit," said Florida coach Charlie Pell.

Receiver Lindsay Scott had raced out on a simple curl pattern and was open, although ringed by Florida defenders. Scott frantically waved his arms. Belue connected with a pass at the 35.

"He spun, slipped through the ring and took off," the *Times* said.

Scott didn't stop until he had reached the end zone to cap a memorable 26–21 victory for Georgia.

It was memorable for Scott in other ways. He had lost his starting job for two weeks because he was late for a Sunday team meeting, and only got it back for the Florida game.

"I don't think there was any question Florida had the game," Georgia coach Dooley said. "But no matter how bad it gets, you've got to hold on and never give up. I guess when you are winning, you will need those kinds of good things to happen to keep winning."

In losing, Pell thought his Gators showed "a tremendous amount of courage. There were several times I can count that a normal team would not have stood up and fought back, but ours did. The difference in being No. 2 in the nation and No. 20 is knowing how to make the last play."

The victory kept the Bulldogs in line for the national championship, which they eventually won with a 17–10 decision over Notre Dame in the Sugar Bowl.

Scott's catch "was the most important play in Georgia history," Smith said. "We don't win that game, we're obviously not going to win the national championship."

Smith had another reason to remember that game: He was accidentally run over by Dooley in the process of Scott's touchdown play.

"Vince had a unique style, he was really into the game," Smith said. "He had a lot of body language, he twisted and turned. His body went into contortions and you'd think he was out of control. But that was just during the play, when the game got tense. Vince really gyrated with every play. Then, as soon as the play was over, he was back under control. When he had to be in on a decision, he was calm, he was ready."

As Smith recalled, Dooley's sideline antics reached a peak in that 1980 Florida game when the coach saw Scott break into the clear on his touchdown run.

"I had run towards the end where Lindsay scored," Smith remembered. "[Dooley] came down the sideline running with Lindsay and just ran right into me and knocked me askew. He didn't even know he did it."

Smith had seen this behavior pattern by Dooley over the years. Working in the sports information department at Georgia in the seventies, Smith came up with an idea to do a video of Dooley as a presentation for his one hundredth victory.

"I put a photographer on the opposing sidelines and trained on him. We played Clemson before we played South Carolina in my memory. But, anyway, I got the video I wanted and we played it unbeknownst to him. We opened his TV show when we played South Carolina for his one hundredth win.

"And that's when people realized he wasn't stoic. His image had sort of generated, making him appear stoic. So people were amazed that he was into the game as he was. I played it before the Athens Touchdown Club and they roared, they were on the floor."

The controversies are sometimes remembered as much as the games in this bitter rivalry.

Officials from both schools were concerned when fans stormed the field to tear down goalposts at the end of games in 1984 and 1985. Some consideration was given to moving the game out of Jacksonville, but officials came up with a better solution: tighter security.

Of more concern to school officials is the game's commonly known slogan as The World's Largest Outdoor Cocktail Party. It's credited to a Florida newspaperman who reportedly came up with the phrase in the 1950s after he saw a drunken fan offer a drink to a policeman.

Lighthearted as the remark was meant to be, it has been anything but funny to officials of both schools, particularly in light of recent alcohol-related deaths of students. Hoping to downplay the alcoholic image, Georgia and Florida both refuse to acknowledge the game as The World's Largest Outdoor Cocktail Party. Instead they just call it the "Georgia-Florida Game" or "Florida-Georgia Game," depending on which school is the home team that particular year. They have also asked networks that broadcast the game not to use the "cocktail" expression on the air.

Call it what you will, but when the final gun goes off, the Florida-Georgia clash just translates to high-quality football in a high-profile environment by two historic programs. In Smith's mind, the rivalry has surpassed the fabled Georgia-Georgia Tech series by many yards, particularly after Georgia Tech left the Southeastern Conference.

"When Tech went out of the SEC, that took some of the luster off that game. I don't think the real Georgia man would say that's the most important game on the schedule."

Because of the importance of new conference affiliations, fresh football rivalries are springing up all the time in America. That certainly holds true for the SEC.

"If you look at the SEC East, you have more than one rival," Smith said. "For us, Tennessee is big, South Carolina is big. It comes down to, if you beat Florida and Auburn early in the season, you have a good chance to win."

But in terms of fan appeal, few of these rivalries surpass the environment and excitement of the Georgia-Florida game, Smith points out.

"TV loves it," he said. "It makes for a really big weekend."

Chapter 11

The Most-Played Rivalry: Lehigh-Lafayette

Howard Foering is one of the legendary names in the Lehigh-Lafayette rivalry, but you won't find him listed in a media guide. You would more likely find his name in *Ripley's Believe It or Not!*

When the Lehigh graduate attended the 100th game of the rivalry, in 1964, it marked the ninety-first time he had watched the teams play. Repeat: ninety-first time.

It didn't go unnoticed in the press box. Upon hearing of Foering's fanaticism, one sportswriter remarked with a straight face: "I wonder where he was the other nine games."

That's the kind of lionhearted loyalty inspired by the rivalry between the Leopards of Lafayette and the Mountain Hawks (also known as the Engineers) of Lehigh.

Foering's feat is only surpassed by the sustaining record of the series itself—the "Most Played Rivalry," as it is generally called. It's the longest consecutive series in college football history.

When Lafayette and Lehigh met in 2006, it marked the 142nd game of the series. To put it in perspective: Harvard and Yale started their ancient rivalry in 1875—nine years earlier—and have played 19 fewer games.

Of course, Lehigh and Lafayette did double up some seasons, playing as many as two games and even three in the early years of the rivalry.

It wasn't a bad idea. They saved on travel expenses, because the schools are located just thirteen miles apart in the Lehigh Valley region of eastern Pennsylvania. In the early days before automobiles, special trains from the Lehigh Valley and Jersey Central lines, along with trolleys, were run between the towns for the games.

And if familiarity breeds contempt, as they say, then these top-level private schools are practically a mirror image of each other. Along with the football players they recruit, they also battle for superior students for their elite academic programs.

And the competition doesn't end there. There is continued, good-natured ribbing between the students throughout the year. Reads one Lafayette bumper sticker: LEHIGH—BECAUSE NOT EVERYONE CAN GET INTO LAFAYETTE.

Long after graduation, it still goes on.

Ann Kline, Lehigh Class of '81, was playing tennis once with a woman literally wearing her heart on her tennis outfit. LAFAYETTE was printed as loud as can be on her shorts.

"So you had an inferior education," one woman said to her.

"You must have gone to Lehigh," replied the Lafayette grad.

Suffice to say, there are no football scholarships at either school. Like the rest of the teams in the Patriot League, the students pay their own way to play Division I-AA football.

The academic demands on the players at Lehigh and Lafayette, many of them engineering students, haven't seemed to impair the quality of their play. In the Patriot League's twenty-two-year history, Lehigh has won seven conference titles and Lafayette six.

The most memorable games in the rivalry? For starters, try Lehigh's 37–30 double-overtime victory over Lafayette in 1995 that gave the Mountain Hawks the Patriot League championship outright.

You could make a case that it was the most exciting game in the rivalry's history because it was the first time the teams took their grudge match into over-time. The overtime was made possible that very year by a Patriot League ruling, as it was for NCAA schools across America.

And it was capped by one of the most memorable plays in the rivalry, a catch by Lehigh's Brian Klingerman in the back of the end zone as fast-closing darkness descended on Goodman Stadium. It is known in Lehigh lore as "The Catch."

"I'm obviously biased about this, but that was probably the greatest game of the Lafayette-Lehigh rivalry," said Nick Martucci, who was a freshman playing defensive end for Lehigh that day. "It was a back-and-forth game."

Lehigh trailed 30–14 midway through the fourth quarter. The Mountain Hawks needed to score twice and convert the two-point conversion both times to prevent a second straight loss to Lafayette.

A tough assignment. But not impossible by any means, Martucci said.

"We had a game earlier that season against Columbia when we came back" from a big deficit, Martucci said. "So ever since that game, we always had a positive attitude about being able to pull things out in a tight game. Coach [Kevin] Higgins, all he talked about that year was believing. He would say, 'You got to believe.' "

Besides, the Lehigh seniors couldn't bear going out with another loss to Lafayette.

"We talked on the sidelines," Klingerman said. "The year before, Lafayette had thumped us pretty good [54–20] and we talked about those seniors having to go out and remember that as their last game. We said, 'We can't let this happen.' "

So Lehigh rallied to tie in regulation 30–30. A key point in the comeback came when tight end Dave Muren took a short pass over the middle, broke two tackles, and went in for a touchdown in the fourth quarter.

"That was kind of the spark that we needed," Martucci said. "At that point, we said, 'All right, this game is definitely not over.' "

After one overtime, it was still 30–30. And turning very dark at Goodman Stadium, which had no lights.

"It was getting pretty dark at the start of the second overtime," Klingerman recalled. "The referees had actually told us that they would probably not let another overtime happen, since it was getting so dark."

What little light there was emanated from the scoreboard. The teams played on that side of the field to make use of the lights. "They turned the scoreboard lights up as high as they can go to help brighten the field," Martucci remembered.

Lehigh had the ball first in the second overtime and drove toward the Lafayette goal line. The ball sat on the Lafayette 14 when Lehigh went into the huddle. Quarterback Bob Aylsworth looked at Klingerman and called a familiar play.

"It was one of the favorite plays for Bob Aylsworth and myself," Klingerman said. "It was an option route, depending on what the defense gives you. I had the option of doing an 'out' or just curling or taking it to the post."

The huddle broke and Klingerman lined up on the right side. Lafayette noticed. The Leopards had a man on the Lehigh wide receiver, plus a safety over the middle in case Klingerman decided to cut to the inside.

"The defense didn't give us an ideal" situation to run that play, Klingerman remembered. "But Bob and I knew when we called that play what we wanted to do and what we had to do to get the ball in the end zone.

"We had run this play hundreds and hundreds of times in practice and summer camps. We just ran the play again and he put the ball in a perfect spot, where they couldn't get it and I was really the only one who could."

Klingerman made a spectacular one-handed catch in the back of the end zone, and had no trouble seeing the ball—or the goal post.

"The goal post was right in front of me. I went basically in the middle of it. And there were fans lined on the end zone, right over the goal line, so it was one of those things that I definitely knew I was in bounds."

The Mountain Hawks' defense then stopped the Leopards to clinch the victory, which had a double meaning. "Not only did we beat Lafayette," Martucci said, "but we prevented them from getting a share of the championship."

The entire Lehigh team sprinted onto the field along with thousands of others. "It was a madhouse," Martucci said.

Small wonder. The rivalry has a history of wild, often violent, celebrations.

"In my sophomore year the night before the Lehigh-Lafayette game they showed a video of near-riots from an earlier game," Martucci recalled. "The students were trying to rush the field and take the goal posts down. The cops came and they were spraying pepper spray."

A tale of excessive celebration in this rivalry: Kline was pledging for a sorority. It was her job to get a piece of the goal post after the game. She did, but she was maced by the cops. She said it was worth it; the next year they had guard dogs at the game. "I would much rather be maced than attacked by those dogs," she said.

Klingerman had heard about the disturbances at Lehigh-Lafayette games, and personally experienced them while on a recruiting visit to Lehigh in his senior year of high school.

"There were tons of police all over, but it was just chaos after the game, students swarming the field trying to tear the goal post down. And I remember my buddy saying to me, 'You've got to go here—this is awesome.' And that was kind of the final decision for me. That put the icing on the cake to go to Lehigh."

It didn't hurt that Lehigh also won, Klingerman said.

Authorities for both schools have gone to great lengths in recent years to keep things under control. They have even started a game extra early, at ten o'-clock in the morning, to keep pregame partying to a minimum.

Martucci said during the week leading up to the game, "the campus is crazy. It's just pretty much a weeklong party, and it's a tough job for coaches to keep players away from that. In fact, we would go over and stay in a hotel the night before the game just to get away from the campus, and get everybody calm and focused on the game."

Hard partying isn't the only activity for the students prior to the Lehigh-Lafayette game. Many have directed their energies to more creative pursuits in the buildup.

Klingerman recalled that one year an airplane flew over the campus with a banner announcing, "Zippy says that Lafayette sucks." There were also leaflets scattered all over campus: "Come see Zippy on Saturday."

Klingerman had no idea who Zippy was. "An alumni or somebody had paid for an airplane to fly overhead. Each school tried to one-up the other with pranks and those sorts of things," he said.

For as far back as one can remember, devilish pranksters have been a part of the scene in this colorful, no-holds-barred rivalry.

Take the Lehigh students who one year invaded the Lafayette campus and gave the manicured field a chemical treatment. When crowds started arriving for the big game, they were shocked to see the word LEHIGH burnt in a huge patch on the field.

In the 1930s, Lehigh students detached the sword from the Marquis of Lafayette, the proud campus statue at the Easton, Pennsylvania school. When the university finally got the sword back, it made sure the same thing wouldn't happen again. Administrators enclosed the statue in a protective crate that deterred any interlopers from doing their dark deeds.

Perhaps the most creative of the pranks came to light—literally—in the 1950s when students tried to preignite each other's bonfire before the game.

A Lehigh student, obviously an engineering major, developed a remote-control model airplane that was supposed to explode into flames upon contact. However, the device fizzled and failed to ignite when it reached Lafayette's woodpile.

The Lafayette students resorted to more old-fashioned means, shooting flaming arrows at their Lehigh target. The Lehigh students were prepared and put out the fire with buckets of sand and blankets.

Both sides have been firing shots at each other, in more ways than one, since their first meeting on October 25, 1884.

Lafayette already had two years of intercollegiate football under its belt, having played (and lost) its first game to Rutgers in 1882.

Theodore L. Welles, who had played with the Wilkes-Barre Academy and the Princeton freshmen, introduced football to Lafayette in 1880. After two years of intramural play, Lafayette made its move into the intercollegiate ranks. Welles was team captain, cook, and bottle washer.

"We had no regular trainer or training table, and all the training received was an endeavor to make the players keep good hours, refrain from beer and other intoxicants, and get out to practice and run after practice for two to three miles a day around the circular track on campus," Welles once wrote. "This latter practice gave us good wind and hardened us up in a very effective manner."

For Lehigh, the Lafayette contest was its very first football game. Only three of the undergraduates had played football before, including Richard Harding Davis, the team captain. The others had to learn the game in the three weeks of practice leading up to the meeting with Lafayette.

"We knew so little of the game that only one man had strips on his shoes and the rest of us slid over the worn grass as though we were on roller skates," said Davis, who introduced the sport at Lehigh.

At least the Lehigh team was well suited in other ways. Davis and his teammates had prevailed upon the Lehigh administration to fork out $52 for eleven brown-and-white jerseys.

The final score was no surprise: Lafayette 50, Lehigh 0. For Davis, it was forgettable for more than one reason.

"My chief recollections of that first game consist of my personal encounters with the spectators and Easton policemen, who had an instinctive prejudice to Lehigh men that was expressed by kicking them in the head when one of them went under the ropes for the ball," said Davis.

Davis, a future journalist, novelist, and playwright, not only arranged for the game and played in it, he also covered it for the student newspaper.

In the second game with Lafayette played that year, Davis scored Lehigh's first touchdown. Lafayette won by 30 points, 20 less than the first game, and Davis conceded, "We improved ever so slightly."

By the late 1880s, Lehigh had improved more than slightly. From 1888 through 1891, Lehigh boasted a nine-game unbeaten streak against Lafayette. Hard to believe now, but there was actually some sentiment that the series should be discontinued because of Lehigh's sudden dominance.

"Year by year became just so many triumphs for Lehigh, until she can now afford to leave Lafayette out of the regular schedule," Davis wrote in 1891.

Good thing no one listened to him, although a squabble over a player's eligibility forced the cancellation of the 1896 game—the only year the series has not been played since the beginning. Naturally, it became known in Lehigh-Lafayette lore as "The Year They Didn't Play."

The player in question was Lafayette's George Barclay, who had played professional baseball. After hearing of Barclay's professional status, even if it was in another sport, Lehigh immediately canceled its two scheduled games with Lafayette.

Barclay will be remembered in sports annals for an entirely different reason: he is credited with devising the first football helmet.

If Lehigh had to pick a season not to play Lafayette, 1896 would have been the one. That year, the Leopards went 11-0-1, shutting out ten opponents and laying claim to the national championship under coach Parke Davis.

The Engineers weren't having too much luck with Lafayette in this period at any rate. In the twelve games played from 1895 through 1901, Lehigh only won once. Lafayette also dominated a bit later in the twentieth century with ten straight victories from 1919 through 1928. By this time, Jock Sutherland was working his coaching magic at Lafayette before going onto glories at Pitt. Sutherland's 1921 Lafayette team claimed the school's second national football title.

It was just before this Lafayette supersize streak that Lehigh made a statement. In 1917, the Engineers posted the biggest rout in the series, 78–0. The 1918 game, a 17–0 victory for Lehigh, produced a legendary run by Raymond B. "Snooks" Dowd.

Give or take a few yards, Dowd supposedly ran a record 115 yards for a touchdown. How so, you ask?

According to observers, Dowd first ran the wrong way, circled his own goal posts, and went the right way for his game-winning TD. Down through the years, the run has taken on mythic proportions, placed at anywhere from 49 to 160 yards by various sources.

The 1921 national championship notwithstanding, Lafayette backers had to be more pleased with Sutherland's record against Lehigh: 5-0. Until he took over the coaching job, Lehigh had won three straight and six of seven over Lafayette.

"The students, alumni, everyone, were continually bringing this game before me," Sutherland said. "The same inquiry was repeatedly made. 'Can we beat Lehigh?' Nineteen fifteen had been the last time Lafayette had triumphed, and this was 1919. I surely wanted to win this game, as I understood what it meant to Lafayette."

Sutherland turned out some good, even great, teams at Lafayette. But even when his teams weren't great, they were good enough to beat Lehigh. In 1924, Lehigh was undefeated and heavily favored over an inconsistent Lafayette team. No matter. Lafayette triumphed in a 7–0 thriller as Frank Chicknoski scored the only TD of the day from three yards out.

A rain-soaked field kept the scoring down, but not the noise. Lafayette was forced to go to a huddle for the first time that season because the players couldn't hear the signals above the sound of 15,000 roaring fans that jammed the Lafayette stadium.

Herb McCracken continued Sutherland's success, particularly over Lehigh. In 1926, the year Lafayette won another national championship, the Leopards walloped the Engineers 35–0 behind Mike Wilson, one of the great players in Leopards history. It wasn't until 1929, after ten straight defeats to their archrivals, that the Engineers finally beat a Lafayette team. And it wasn't until five years later, 1934, that they could do it again.

"Everybody took their hats off to Lehigh," wrote the *Easton Express*.

That's not all they took. The Lehigh fans also took the goal post and the Lafayette College flag. They didn't get the sideline markers, which had been wisely removed by Lafayette before the game was over.

That 13–7 Lehigh victory started a string of three straight over Lafayette before the Leopards broke the spell with a vengeance. For fifteen games, from 1937 through 1949, Lafayette did not lose to Lehigh.

Right in the middle of that success was Frank Downing, a quarterback from Brooklyn, New York, with a flair for winning big games. Downing quarterbacked the Lafayette team from 1947 to 1949.

"I was no Joe Namath, but I was a quarterback," Downing said with modesty. "I happened to arrive on the scene when I could hit the barn door at ten yards. The other guys competing with me could only hit it at five. So I was a cog in the wheel. We wound up pretty good."

Downing's claim to fame:

"I may have been the only quarterback in the history of the rivalry that beat the Lehighs three times in a row."

"The Lehighs": that's how Lafayette students refer to their rivals. There's a story attached to it.

"When I played, every year on campus before the Lehigh game we had a bonfire," Downing said. "It wasn't outlawed then. A guy named Danny Hatch was our inspirational pep rally speaker every year for the Lehigh game. He was like Mr. Chips, a skinny, old guy. He had been there forever, and he always taught math class.

"He would start out talking about the old days. You know, 'We beat them in 1893, we beat them in 1894, and tomorrow we're going to beat them over there in Bethlehem.' The way Danny would finish up his pep talk, every time he would mention Lehigh, he would say, 'Beat the Lehighs.' Not Beat Lehigh, but 'Beat the Lehighs.' And that's sort of been the tradition. It's carried on now. The kids all yell, 'Beat the Lehighs.' "

Downing was a product of the Brooklyn school system. Downing's school, Brooklyn Technical High School, was an elite academic school, one of the few in New York's five boroughs that required an entrance exam to get in.

One of Brooklyn Tech's rivals was Brooklyn Prep, featuring a back by the name of Joe Paterno. Downing and Paterno became friends. Many years later, Downing would join the famous Penn State coach in a coaching capacity.

As a student, Downing was headed to Lafayette. "Our coach at Brooklyn Tech was a Lafayette College guy, so he steered many of us to Lafayette," Downing recalled.

Downing served in the Army for a year before playing three solid seasons for the Leopards.

"I arrived, wet behind the ears, and I wound up as quarterback of the team, and we had a pretty good team," Downing recalls of Lafayette's 1947 season.

The Leopards were 6-3 that year. What made it a success was a 7–0 victory over Lehigh.

Downing recalls his first experience with the Big Game: "I hadn't caught onto it, but that week leading up to the game, there were bonfires and speeches. And we go over to Bethlehem, and we were going along pretty well, winning by seven points. We got a drive going, and I'm in the huddle, an eighteen-year-old kid, and I call a pass play. Our captain calls a timeout. He said, 'We're not throwing any more passes. We have this game in our hip pocket. You're trying to inflate your statistics or something? We'll have none of that throwing a pass.' So we ran the ball and we won the game (7–0) and we were all happy."

They were also happy the following year when they beat the Lehighs 23–13 and finished 7-2. But the Leopards were saddened when coach Ivy Williamson left for Wisconsin after the 1948 season.

Clipper Smith, a former pro coach, took over. With a senior-studded lineup led by Downing at quarterback, everything looked promising for the Leopards in 1949. Until they played their first game, that is.

By the time they faced Lehigh in the last game of the season. Lafayette had inexplicably managed but one victory in seven outings.

"It was one of those woulda, coulda, shoulda teams, which means we were not winning many games, but losing them by hairbreadth margins," Downing said.

Downing knew a victory over Lehigh would somehow make things right. It was his last college game, and he could go out a winner against Lafayette's fiercest foe.

But a week before the game, Smith decided to replace Downing at quarterback with Gordie Fleming. It raised some eyebrows—Fleming was a halfback playing out of position. It seemed a desperation move.

Downing was given the job of preparing Fleming, his roommate and ex-Brooklyn Tech teammate, for the game.

"I spent the whole week prepping this guy to be a quarterback," Downing said. "And he was a darn good athlete, better than me."

Downing was down, to say the least. Going back to his freshman year in high school, he had never been benched.

"We're going over to the game in Bethlehem in a bus and I'm saying, 'Boy, this is a great way to finish up my football career, sitting on the bench.' "

With a 6-2 record, Lehigh was favored over the 1-6 Leopards. The Engineers looked the part, rushing to a 12–0 lead in the first half on touchdown runs by Dick Gabriel and Joe Scannella.

At this point, Fleming came running over to the sideline, grabbed Downing, and pulled him over to Coach Smith. Downing had no idea what was happening.

"Do you want to win this football game?" Fleming asked the Lafayette coach.

"Sure, I do," Smith said.

"Well then, Clipper," he said, pointing at Downing, "you better put him back at quarterback and let me get back to running back."

Which is what Smith did. With Downing directing the attack, the Leopards scored three touchdowns in the second half for a stunning 21–12 upset. A 19-yard pass from Downing to Jack Savage set up the go-ahead score for Lafayette.

"We drove back to Easton that night one happy bunch of guys," Downing said. "Even though we didn't have much of a season, we beat the Lehighs."

That was the end of Lafayette's domination in the series for a while. Lehigh won the next three games with teams coached by William Leckonby, one of the most successful coaches in the Engineers' history.

Leckonby was on board when Lehigh beat Lafayette in two of the series' most exciting games, in 1952 and 1961.

In 1952, Lehigh pulled out a 14–7 victory in the closing minutes on a 23-yard touchdown pass by John Conti, a reserve sophomore quarterback who weighed 165 pounds soaking wet. Lehigh's defense was the star of the day, stopping Lafayette three times inside the Engineers' 5-yard line.

In 1961, Leckonby's final year as the Lehigh coach, the Engineers defeated Lafayette 17–14 on a 20-yard field goal by Andy Larko with six seconds to play.

Fast-forward to 2005 for another Lehigh-Lafayette beauty: Jonathan Hurt caught a pass in the end zone in the closing seconds to give Lafayette a 23–19 victory and its second straight Patriot League championship.

The victory was in the midst of a Lafayette revival following seven straight losses to Lehigh from 1995 to 2001.

"It was the third Lafayette victory in four years, so that was very meaningful," said Joe Finnen, longtime public address announcer for Lafayette, who took the job in 1966.

It was especially meaningful because in the nineties, Lafayette had considered dropping out of Division I-AA and changing to a Division III program. That would have ended the series with Lehigh.

"But after taking a good hard look at it, they decided to stay where they are," Finnen said. "That was greeted enthusiastically by all the athletic observers around here."

Good thing for the football program that Lafayette stayed put. With a 49–27 victory over Lehigh in 2006, the Leopards earned a share of the Patriot League championship with their rivals.

That gave Lafayette a 75-62-5 lead in a series where winning records aren't paramount heading into the big matchup.

Indeed, the 1964 game was also memorable, but not because of the quality of the teams. Lafayette and Lehigh had the grand total of one solitary victory between them. But this was the historic 100th game in the rivalry.

A standing-room-only crowd of 19,000 descended on Fisher Field (capacity 13,500) in Easton, and excitement was in the brisk fall air. Many former greats and legendary alumni, including superfan Howard Foering, of course, were back for the weekend at Lafayette.

Foering, an energetic ninety-six-year-old with a white mustache, sat in a Lehigh section nineteen rows up. He had seen his first Lehigh-Lafayette game in 1886, two years after they started the rivalry. Not a fond memory: Lehigh was shut out twice that year by Lafayette.

Among the ninety games he had already witnessed, two stood out in his memory: Lehigh's 66–6 victory in 1890 and the 78–0 rout in 1917.

In a salute to the series, the band played "Happy Birthday." Then the rivals played football, and as if decreed by some heavenly council, Lehigh and Lafayette battled to a 6–6 tie.

Most of the excitement for the day was saved until the end. Lehigh dug in and stopped Lafayette on four downs with the ball inches from the goal line as the teams played the fifth tie in the series.

Then, as today, there were no trophies but the Most Valuable Player award at stake—and bragging rights for another year.

For anyone who has played in a Lehigh-Lafayette game, that's quite enough.

Chapter 12

The Bayou Classic: Grambling-Southern

Not even Katrina could blow away the Bayou Classic.

The bands played on and the show-stopping football rivalry between Grambling and Southern went ahead without missing a beat in 2005. In the wake of the crippling storm, the two historically black Louisiana schools merely picked up and moved their traditional game to Houston.

Neither rain, nor sleet, nor hurricane could stop them from delivering one of the greatest shows on turf.

Houston's Reliant Stadium was the appropriate choice to replace the Louisiana Superdome in 2005. For one thing, it wasn't far from Louisiana. Like New Orleans, the Texas town had a big stadium to accommodate the huge crowds. Plus, Houston was a lifesaver—literally—for New Orleans in the aftermath of the most devastating storm in U.S. history.

"When we were in crisis in this state," said Dr. Angela Weaver, a Grambling official, "it was the city of Houston that was the first to extend a helping hand to our citizens."

It was a pickup for all concerned, including the 53,214 who showed up for the game. As far as the contest itself, Grambling did more knocking down than picking up in beating its longtime rival, 50–35.

In 2006 it was business as usual for Grambling and Southern. They returned to the Superdome for another Bayou Classic—and a classic in its own right. Southern nipped Grambling 21–17 after making a goal-line stand in the final minutes.

Talk about a close rivalry; that result tied the all-time series 27-27. After the 2006 season, Southern was leading the Bayou Classic 17-16.

Classic name, classic games in one of the most flamboyant rivalries in black college football.

It's a weekend of furious activity that includes a battle between Grambling's Mighty Tiger Marching Band and Southern's "Human Jukebox"—in short, an excuse for a big party surrounding the annual football tussle.

Doug Williams, who starred in the Bayou Classic for Grambling and then won a Super Bowl with the Washington Redskins, doesn't think anything matches Grambling-Southern.

"The Super Bowl is a great game," said Williams, the MVP and first black quarterback in the NFL's title game, in January 1988, "but it's really a business thing. The Classic is a family affair. You can see your brothers, your cousins, your friends at the Bayou Classic. Everybody's having fun and everybody's a football fan."

To be sure, other great rivalries between historically black schools dot the football landscape. Some of the best: Bethune-Cookman and Florida A&M (the Florida Classic); Grambling and Prairie View A&M (the State Fair Classic); Tuskegee and Alabama State (the Turkey Day Classic); Alcorn State and Jackson State; and Texas Southern against Prairie View A&M.

Most of these are in-state rivals. In the case of the two Louisiana schools, it's the team from the south (Southern) against the team from the north (Grambling), about two hundred miles apart. Few rivalries among historically black colleges and universities have had the staying power of the two Louisiana schools.

Through good seasons and bad, and economic problems at black schools across America, the rivalry flourished in the twentieth century and into the twenty-first. At the end of the tunnel there was always the bright light of the Bayou Classic.

The series was raised to a higher level with the start of the Classic in 1974, when a crowd of 76,753 filled the Louisiana Superdome for the so-called "Black Super Bowl." The Bayou Classic was an immediate hit, selling out year after year.

Of the thirty-three Bayou games played through 2006, thirteen featured crowds of over 70,000.

When the late Eddie Robinson first arrived on the Grambling campus in the 1940s to coach the football team, he had less ambitious goals. He just wanted to turn around a football program that had gone through hard times under five previous head coaches.

"We didn't have much to look ahead to," Robinson said, "but even less to look back on."

Robinson could only dream about fashioning football programs like those at Tuskegee Institute in Alabama; Bluefield Institute in West Virginia; Wiley College in Texas; Kentucky State; Morgan State in Maryland; Florida A&M; and, of course, Southern, in Baton Rouge. These programs gave black football its foundation in the 1920s and '30s, many years before their players changed the landscape of the NFL and made a social impact in America.

At Grambling in the 1940s, a psychology of failure hung over the football program, so much so that all Robinson could think about was putting together a winning season. And beating Southern, of course.

"They were the big school and the most powerful in the Southwestern Athletic Conference (SWAC)," Robinson said of the team coached by the legendary Arnett William "Ace" Mumford, one of the early giants of black football. "It was unheard of for us to beat them. When they came to play you, you were supposed to be whipped."

Mumford coached twenty-five years at Southern, producing eleven SWAC champions and four Black College football titles. His .733 winning percentage (169-57-14) emphasized Southern's dominance in the state of Louisiana and black college football in general.

Before the heat was turned up on the series, Southern hardly looked upon Grambling as an equal football rival—or an equal in anything.

Southern University was noted by some as the Harvard of the black colleges in the South. It was created by an act of the Louisiana legislature in 1880 and was firmly rooted in Baton Rouge since 1914, as solidly as the oaks that shade its yawning campus hard by the Mississippi River.

Grambling, founded in 1901 in a bucolic wilderness of northern Louisiana, was a quasi-public institution for many years. It wasn't until the 1940s that Grambling attained the status of a four-year college.

For many years, the Grambling-Southern game took on the tone of a class war: the supposedly more-sophisticated, better-educated blacks of Southern versus the country blacks from Grambling's rural area.

"To some degree, there might have been some jealousy on their part because of our high academic standard," said Ulysses Dean Jones, Southern associate athletic director in the 1970s and one-time All-American under Mumford in 1940. "We were the other school, the parent school. Grambling was just a two-year college then. That jealousy probably did exist when I was here in 1937."

Nevertheless, both schools in their own way represented educational opportunities for blacks that otherwise would not have existed in Louisiana at that time.

As a native of Baton Rouge, Robinson was well aware of the played-upon social distinctions. It only motivated him more to beat Southern.

"Southern used to treat Grambling like the little brother," Robinson said. "There were times when Southern was not interested in playing us. They'd play

Wiley, Prairie View, stop over and play us a practice game a day or two before their big game, and work the plays. They'd beat us, of course."

The starting point of the Grambling-Southern series was the 1930s. Brice Taylor was the Southern coach who put Grambling on his regular schedule, with really nothing to gain.

"Taylor said he would play us just the same," remembered Dr. Ralph Waldo Emerson Jones, then president of Grambling College. "It was mighty nice of him. We only had a few men and we did the best we could."

Southern, which started its football program in 1915, eleven years before Grambling, had no problems against the Tigers in the early years of the series. It started with a 20–0 Jaguars win in 1933, and Southern won two more games by shutouts in the thirties. The combined score of the first three games: 93–0.

It wasn't until Grambling finally won a game under Robinson in 1947 that things began to look better for the Tigers' football program.

"The first time we beat them, it was a happy day for us," Dr. Jones said. "I was lifted higher than the sky. I felt we had reached the zenith of our sportsdom when we finally beat Southern."

Jones was educated at Southern, but crossed over to Grambling and started a football program there in 1926. He wasn't the only one who made the transition. Emory Hines had been an offensive line coach at Southern before taking the head coaching job at Grambling from 1935 to 1940. This type of football cross-breeding only added more fuel to the rivalry.

"When I first came to Grambling, just about everyone working at the school at that time was from Southern University," Robinson said.

Robinson remembered fierce battles and bad blood between the rivals in the early days.

"I lost my first game in 1946, but when we came back and beat them the following year (21–6), they were really upset," Robinson said.

For Robinson, it was one of the biggest victories in a career that spanned nearly sixty years and a college-record 408 victories.

"As far as games go, that 1947 game was really the Big Game for Eddie Robinson," pointed out Collie Nicholson, Grambling's longtime sports information director. "They came into Grambling highly touted, the SWAC champ, and we beat them with two long touchdown runs. It was something they thought could never be done."

The Tigers were hoping to be invited into the SWAC. It didn't help their cause any when a huge fight broke out in the 1948 game won by Southern. That caused a disruption in the series that lasted eleven years.

"People were concerned," Robinson said. "They wouldn't let us into the SWAC."

So the Tigers went to the Midwest Conference, where Robinson produced an undefeated, untied team in 1955.

It wasn't until the 1959 season that the Tigers were finally extended an invitation to join the SWAC.

In 1960, Grambling lost to Southern but still gained a share of the SWAC title. In 1965, Grambling won its first SWAC championship outright with Robinson's son, Eddie Jr., playing a key role at quarterback.

In the 1960s, Grambling's profile was raised considerably with a television film, *One Hundred Yards to Glory*. It depicted Grambling's success in sending players to the NFL, starting in the 1940s with Paul "Tank" Younger, a fullback who was the first player from a predominantly black school to sign with an NFL team. After Younger made an impact in pro ball, NFL teams began looking more and more to the black colleges for talent.

The names of players produced by black schools sound like a Hall of Fame list. In fact, it is: Walter Payton (Jackson State); Jackie Slater (Jackson State); Ken Houston (Prairie View); Deacon Jones (Mississippi Valley State); and future Hall of Famer Jerry Rice (Mississippi Valley State).

Under Robinson, Grambling produced more than its share of football greats. The following, all Hall of Famers, just scratch the surface of more than two hundred players that Robinson sent to the pros from Grambling: Willie Brown, Buck Buchanan, Willie Davis, and Charlie Joiner.

Southern has had its share of standouts, including Hall of Famer Mel Blount and wide receiver Harold Carmichael.

No wonder the Grambling-Southern rivalry has produced a series of so many competitive games, with the teams fighting for every inch of the 100-yard turf. Sometimes, like the 1969 game, they were surrounded by controversy and separated by an official's ruling.

Just before the half, Grambling fullback William O'Neill leaped into the end zone from the 1-yard line, but fumbled. The official ruled no touchdown, although Robinson insisted he had "broken the plane" of the goal line.

"It was our understanding that if you broke the plane, it was a touchdown," Robinson said, "but they wouldn't give us that score, and as a result we lost the game (21–17). We were upset with what happened in 1969."

The '69 game marked a turning point in the rivalry for another reason: It was witnessed by a huge overflow crowd.

"They were sitting all over the place; it was unreal," said Louisiana newspaperman Buddy Davis. "The Grambling stadium sits in a bowl and they had fans all over the place, sitting on the embankment overlooking the stands. Even the governor of Louisiana was sitting on the embankment with the fans."

It served as a motivating force to move the game to more spacious surroundings.

"We had 27,000 people squeezed into a facility built for 18,000," Nicholson said. "We were determined never to play a Southern game in our stadium if we could help it. The towns of Grambling and Ruston ran out of gasoline. People had to stay the weekend. There was no food, no room for anybody. People were sleeping in their cars."

By the 1970s, while the Grambling-Southern rivalry was creating tremendous interest on both campuses, it was not producing a lot of revenue.

"We weren't making any money playing Southern on campus because we didn't have enough seats," Robinson said. "People would come and break down the fences because they didn't have seats available to them."

Following a 1972 cancellation at Southern because of student unrest, the game was moved to Shreveport in 1973 at Robinson's urging. It attracted a crowd of 40,000 to a much larger stadium, and was fast becoming the No. 1 attraction in black college football.

"Starting in Shreveport," Robinson said, "the rivalry took on a different look altogether."

Another year, another packed house. This time it was Tulane's Sugar Bowl. Playing before 80,000, Grambling whipped Southern 21–0 for its fifth straight victory in the series.

In 1974, the game was moved into the Louisiana Superdome and the Bayou Classic was born. There, a sellout crowd watched Grambling's 33–17 victory as the Tigers continued their domination in the series. Their winning streak grew to eight with a 55–20 rout in 1977 behind Williams's quarterbacking. In '78, the Tigers made it nine in a row over their archrivals for their longest winning streak in the series.

But Southern dominated with eight straight victories from 1993 to 2000.

By then, big-city crowds were an exciting way of life for Grambling. The Tigers had taken their game to the people, playing in urban areas around the country, and usually selling out.

Nicholson, Grambling's visionary sports information director, had grabbed a page from Notre Dame to promote his team. In the 1920s, Knute Rockne set up games across the country with major powers, many of them in big cities such as Chicago and Los Angeles. Playing Southern Cal before huge crowds, it got the attention Notre Dame needed for national recognition. And college football gained ground in the national consciousness as well. Likewise, Nicholson set up games for Grambling in Yankee Stadium and the Houston Astrodome. The Tigers also played in Washington, D.C., and even in Hawaii and Japan as they built their reputation far and wide.

"Here I was, a kid from old Zachary [Louisiana], playing in Japan, Hawaii, and Washington, D.C.," Williams said. "And it was all because of Collie's mighty pen."

Of course, Nicholson brought along Grambling's fabulous band for colorful halftime shows. The band not only traveled with the football team, but Nicholson got it gigs at the Super Bowl as well.

"They were going to places since the late 1960s," Louisiana newspaperman Buddy Davis said in a 1970s discussion of the high-flying Tigers. "They went to Miami while all the other teams in the SWAC were still playing in their backyards," The joke then, still valid: If football is ever played on the moon, Grambling will be one of two teams in the game.

Like the other SWAC teams, Southern was swept up in Grambling's far-reaching ambitions. Reluctant at first to move games off campus, the Jaguars were soon enjoying a financial windfall as a result of their high-profile contests with Grambling in New Orleans.

Since taking up residence in New Orleans, the Grambling-Southern rivalry has become more than a football game. It's become a socio-cultural phenomenon. Robinson once described it as "the biggest black happening in the United States, if not the world."

The "happening" includes a battle of two of the best college bands in America. From the night before to halftime to post-game, they compete at the same intensity level as the football teams. The Grambling band has made worldwide tours to promote the school name internationally. The Southern "Human Jukebox" band has been ranked the best college band in America by a national newspaper.

Attendance was down in 2006 for a variety of reasons. It was the combination of the teams' poor records and the fact the New Orleans population was tragically reduced significantly after Hurricane Katrina, according to Grambling sports information director Ryan McGinty.

But the rivalry still hadn't lost its luster.

"It's the Super Bowl with a soul shake, an Ali fight with marching bands," was the way one writer described the Bayou Classic once upon a time.

When the last note is played, fans are already making plans for next year's game as they scatter to points all over America, just as the coaching staffs might be looking ahead.

"I'm just so happy to have this rivalry," said Robinson, who retired after the 1997 season with a 408-165-15 record, including 23-23 versus Southern. "It's the greatest thing that ever happened for black football."

Chapter 13

Backyard Brawl:
Pitt-West Virginia

It happens every football season: the badges, stickers, and T-shirts blossom on the campus of the University of West Virginia.

Beat the Hell Out of Pitt, the badges might exclaim. The T-shirts are of similar persuasion. One of the more popular items in past years has an arrow on the front pointing under the arms with the words, Under the Arm-Pitt expressed in bold red letters.

No holds barred.

"We both have our little snide T-shirts," said Pitt sports information director E. J. Borghetti, whose father, Ernie, played for Pitt from 1959 to 1963.

There are no subtleties in the Pitt-West Virginia football rivalry. No love lost, either.

Marino Paranzenzo, longtime *Pittsburgh Post-Gazette* sportswriter, once recalled: "It's a small state trying to beat a bigger state. I have been down to West Virginia and the feeling is very much anti-Pitt.

"Once they were playing the national anthem and someone yelled, 'Beat the hell out of Pitt' in the middle of it. Everyone was standing at attention and out of this quiet came this loud scream. It was unreal.

"Another time, I was in a West Virginia diner and someone was screaming, 'Beat Pitt.' This was *six or seven* weeks away from the game. I mean, the hate is really something down there."

Jack Fleming, the late Pitt radio announcer who grew up in Morgantown in a home within sight of the football stadium, was introduced to the rivalry at an early age.

As the Pitt players took the field, the story goes, Jack's mother said to her young son: "That's Pitt. You hate Pitt now. You will hate Pitt tomorrow. You will hate Pitt your whole life. And you will hate Pitt after you die."

When Don Nehlen was brought in to coach the West Virginia team in 1979, one of his main missions was to stop Pitt, which had been a thorn in the Mountaineers' side.

"The people who hired me wanted me to beat Pitt and didn't care if we lost to the others."

After ninety-nine games through 2006, Pitt led the so-called "Backyard Brawl" 59-37-3.

"It was lopsided for many years," notes Beano Cook, onetime Pitt sports information director and longtime commentator on ESPN. "It developed into a good rivalry because West Virginia has been winning a lot lately, and now they're playing at the end of the year. West Virginia has replaced Penn State [now in the Big Ten] on the Pitt schedule."

According to Cook, Russ Frank of the *Pittsburgh Press* is credited with calling the game the Backyard Brawl.

"It wasn't called that when I was SID [in the fifties and sixties]," Cook said.

The Brawl has featured some of the most thrilling games and biggest names in football history. For starters, try Dan Marino, Mike Ditka, and Tony Dorsett for Pitt, and Sam Huff for West Virginia. All National Football League Hall of Famers.

The Hatfields and McCoys of college football go back a long way together. Theirs is one of the sport's most enduring—and most spirited—rivalries, thanks in large part to played-upon social distinctions.

"Pitt people make a lot of the West Virginia 'hillbillies' and 'moonshiners' and look down their noses at them," Shorty Hardman, longtime sports editor of the *Charleston Gazette*, once recalled. "This has infuriated the West Virginians very much."

Casimir Mylinski, the former Pitt athletic director, once explained it another way: "The students at Pitt feel that West Virginia doesn't come up to the Pittsburgh academic level. West Virginia, I guess, is considered one of those rural schools in Appalachia and Pitt is the city slicker that West Virginia would love to beat the daylights out of. They fight like mad when we play each other. Anything goes . . . a broken arm doesn't mean anything."

The schools are roughly ninety miles apart and share a hardworking, blue-collar mentality.

Two prime examples: Huff, an All-America lineman and all-pro linebacker, is from a small mining town in West Virginia. Dorsett, a Heisman Trophy–winning halfback before starring in the NFL, is the product of a Pittsburgh-area steel mill family.

These teams have been battling each other in football since 1895 (an 8–0 WVU win), but it wasn't until Jock Sutherland came roaring into Pitt in the 1920s that the rivalry really picked up steam.

It was then that Sutherland's monolithic teams sparked fires of outrage in West Virginians. Not only did Sutherland beat the Mountaineers on the field, but also in the recruiting war for players. During these innumerable victories, Sutherland snatched such greats as Marshall Goldberg, Gibby Welch, and Ray Montgomery away from West Virginia territory. To lose to Pitt was one thing for Mountaineers fans. But to see their own state-bred stars delivering the knockout punches was something else.

This thievery by Sutherland was more than just a minor irritation to Mountaineers fans, especially in Goldberg's case. "It just broke everyone's heart in the state when Sutherland got him," Hardman remembered. The impact was even more dramatic when Goldberg fulfilled his promise of greatness, spearheading some of Pitt's best teams as part of Sutherland's "Dream Backfield" of the 1930s.

It took some time, but West Virginia eventually reversed the recruiting trend. The Mountaineers subsequently mined some diamonds of their own in western Pennsylvania, virtually in the shadow of Pitt's ivy walls, which explains their rise to power in the 1950s and 1960s, and their success against the Panthers during this period.

This crossfire of recruiting activity has been one of the most combustible elements of the Pitt-West Virginia rivalry. The players from both sides are usually familiar with each other from high school, and a strange, intoxicating element of reverse state pride is sometimes present. Notes one observer: "The West Virginia players who are from Pennsylvania really delight in beating Pitt. You know, 'You didn't recruit me, so we'll really show you.' The bitterness of this rivalry is really something else."

There is a game within a game matching the recruiting success of each coach. During the 2005 season, Pitt coach Dave Wannstedt said he felt the Panthers "owned" western Pennsylvania recruiting, a remark not taken lightly by West Virginia coach Rich Rodriguez. Showing the deep competitive feelings of the rivalry, Rodriguez not so politely disagreed. He came back with derogatory remarks about Pitt's recruiting. These verbal jabs were only natural and not unexpected, considering these coaches' histories. After all, they have a deeply personal attachment to the Pitt-West Virginia rivalry, Wannstedt having played for the Panthers in the 1970s and Rodriguez for the Mountaineers in the 1980s.

Pitt, although holding a huge edge in victories in the series, historically has had to rise to the occasion for the West Virginia game. And the times when the Panthers took their rival lightly, it has cost them dearly.

The 1959 game may have been the biggest upset of the series. A mediocre West Virginia team that never won another game that season beat Pitt 23–15.

"Pitt had a lot of talent on that team," said Tony Constantine, a noted West Virginia football historian and sports writer. "Afterward, the Pitt coaches told the West Virginia coaches that only one of the West Virginia players, guard Bill Lopasky, was considered good enough to make the Pitt squad."

In 1976, Pitt was a prohibitive favorite, but West Virginia gave the eventual national champions one of their biggest scares of the season before losing 24–16. After the last West Virginia score, with a few minutes left, Pitt used up the time by giving the ball to Dorsett on every play. By the time Dorsett finished his career at Pitt, he had led the Panthers to a national title and broken Goldberg's school career rushing record.

The Pitt-WVU rivalry began in 1895 when Pitt was known as Western University of Pennsylvania and West Virginia was nicknamed "The Snakes." The game took place on the infield of a harness racing track in a section of Morgantown. With touchdowns counting four points, West Virginia scored an 8–0 victory.

There were some disruptions in the early part of the rivalry. Because of World War I and a national flu epidemic, West Virginia did not field a team in 1918. A dispute over financial guarantees caused a three-year lapse in the series from 1940 to 1942. The Brawl has been an annual event since 1943.

At one time, the rivalry was a three-way affair including Washington and Jefferson, a school located in Washington, Pennsylvania, between Morgantown and Pittsburgh. But W&J, which played in the 1922 Rose Bowl game, de-emphasized football in the early 1930s and dropped out of competition.

Pitt holds a big margin over West Virginia primarily because of two forceful periods in the history of this rivalry.

From 1904 through 1921, West Virginia played Pitt eleven times and failed to win one game. The closest the Mountaineers came to a victory was the 1909 game when the teams played to a scoreless tie. From 1929 through 1946, the Panthers won all fifteen meetings, mainly on the strength of Sutherland's magnificent teams.

Pitt's 1937 squad was generally considered to be Sutherland's best. The austere Scotsman was football's ultra-perfectionist and his grim demeanor reflected his game plan: a powerful, uncompromising ground game based on the finest blocking and most determined running. The Panthers' powerful offense, a double-wing attack, was nicknamed the "Sutherland Scythe."

Led by Goldberg, an exquisite blocker as well as ball carrier who was equally dangerous at halfback or fullback, Pitt was always formidable and very often frightening.

Goldberg's sublime presence enhanced one of the deepest backfields ever seen in college football. Featured in the "Dream Backfield" were Goldberg, Dick Cassiano, John Chickerneo, and Harry "Curly" Stebbins.

They weren't the only capable runners for Pitt in those days. Sutherland could also call upon Frank Patrick, John Michelson, Bill Stapulis, Bobby LaRue, and Ben Kish to power the double-wing "Scythe." Up front, Pitt had such stalwarts on the line as Frank Souchak, Bill Daddio, Tony Matisi, Al Lezouski, and Steve Petro.

This 1937 Pitt team went 8-0-1, its only blemish a 0–0 tie with Fordham and its "Seven Blocks of Granite" line featuring the great Vince Lombardi. The Panthers were national champions that year, but that wasn't their only mark of distinction. Pitt was invited to play in the Rose Bowl, then the top bowl game in America by far, but turned down the invitation.

"The vote was 17–16," Goldberg once recalled of the team decision to reject the Rose Bowl. "There were a few reasons, one being what happened to us the year before."

The season before, Pitt played in the Rose Bowl and routed Washington 21–0 to complete a 9-1 season. The players understood they would be paid $100 each for expenses, and outfitted with a new suit.

"We got nothing except a sweater and a pair of pants," Goldberg recalled.

Goldberg said Sutherland cashed in some bonds he had and the other coaches tossed a few bills into a pot. The Pitt players wound up with a grand total of $2 each, which they quickly dissipated at the Santa Anita racetrack.

West Virginia had brilliant talents in early eras such as fullback Ira Errett "Rat" Rodgers (considered to be one of the school's all-time greats) and center Russ Bailey, but did not truly come into national prominence until the 1922 season, when the Mountaineers went undefeated.

It was during this season that they beat Pitt for the first time since 1903 with a team that produced a list of honored players, including halfback Nick Nardacci, tackle Russ Meredith, and guard Joe Setron.

The coach of these early West Virginia teams, Dr. Clarence Spears, started what is generally recognized as the "golden era" in football at Morgantown. From 1922 through 1925, Spears and later Ira Rodgers combined for a 33-3-2 record through a heady period that featured two consecutive victories over Pitt and, in general, equal footing for the Mountaineers with their troublesome rivals.

Spears brought a flair to coaching, introducing new color in the figurative as well as the literal sense at West Virginia. When he first arrived in Morgantown from Dartmouth in 1921 and learned how long it had been since West Virginia beat Pitt, he decided a psychological lift was needed. So he ordered gray jerseys to be worn for the Pitt game instead of the usual school colors of gold and blue.

In Spears's first year, West Virginia came close before succumbing to the Panthers 21–14. But then the Mountaineers beat Pitt in 1922 and 1923. West Virginia not only wore the gray against Pitt, but other teams as well for several years before returning to the traditional colors.

The 1922 Pitt game, incidentally, is among the most cherished victories in West Virginia's football history. Mountaineers press guides applaud it as one of the school's top-ten all-time victories. Not surprisingly, three other triumphs over Pitt share a place in that elite group.

West Virginia literally waited until the last minute in 1922 to break its long winless streak against Pitt. The Mountaineers won on a 39-yard field goal drop-kicked at the end by Armin Hahrt, a freshman back from Dayton, Ohio. "The boot surprised almost everybody because few people knew he could dropkick the ball," Constantine noted.

West Virginia made it two in a row over Pitt with a 13–7 victory the next year, but the Mountaineers' success over their bitter rival stopped as soon as you could say, "Jock Sutherland." During Sutherland's euphoric reign at Pitt from 1924 through 1938, West Virginia was able to only manage one victory in fifteen games—a 9–6 triumph in 1928. Typical of Pitt's domination during this time was a 40–0 triumph in 1927 spearheaded by All-American halfback Gibby Welch, a product of Parkersburg, West Virginia, one of the many famous turncoats in this rivalry.

In that game, Welch set a Pitt record by returning a kick 105 yards for a touchdown. That was before the college rule was changed to limit a run to 100 yards, no matter where it started.

West Virginia went through a succession of five coaches while Sutherland was the Pied Piper at Pitt. It wasn't until the 1950s that the Mountaineer football program really had stability and this was supplied, finally, by Art "Pappy" Lewis. He stayed ten years and coached some of the most glamorous teams in West Virginia history. That included a Sugar Bowl club in the 1953 season that counted Huff, tackle Bruce Bosley, halfback Joe Marconi, and quarterback Freddy Wyant among its members.

But just because the Mountaineers had some of the best teams in their history didn't always mean they could beat Pitt. And vice versa.

After all, it is the "Backyard Brawl."

In 1955, the Mountaineers went to Pitt Stadium with a 7-0 record and ranked in the nation's Top Ten. The Panthers were 5-3 and heavy underdogs, but All-American wide receiver Joe Walton caught an early TD pass and Pitt was on its way to a stunning 26–7 upset over the Mountaineers before a capacity crowd of 58,000 that included scouts from the Sugar Bowl and other bowls. It was the second straight year Pitt prevented West Virginia from having an unbeaten season.

"Pitt got the bid to the Sugar Bowl," Constantine remembered. "Pitt fans tore down their own goal posts at both ends of the field before the game ended. West Virginia scored on the last play of the game, and had to run the ball for the extra point because there were no goal posts to kick at."

It was payback time for West Virginia in 1959. It is doubtful that a Mountaineers squad ever won against greater odds, whether against Pitt or any other team. There simply was no comparison in talent. Pitt had beaten such opponents as Notre Dame, UCLA, and Duke, and West Virginia was not considered in the class of any of those elite teams.

But Danny Williams played the finest game of his career at quarterback for West Virginia with his handling of the option play and his timely passes, scoring one touchdown and throwing for another. The Mountaineers intercepted five passes thrown by Pitt quarterback Ivan Toncic, and Dick Herrig returned one 30 yards for the clinching touchdown as WVU upset Pitt, 23–15. "His performance," remembered Constantine of Williams, "won him a place in Pitt's all-opponent team."

The Mountaineers then reverted to form, losing their remaining five games, including a trouncing by Penn State—a team that Pitt would handle easily later in the year.

The 1965 game was not so much a surprise who won, but how many points were scored: 111. West Virginia had 63 and Pitt 48 in one of the zaniest games in college football history. There have been lots of lower-scoring collegiate basketball games, one sportswriter pointed out.

West Virginia quarterback Allen McCune had a field day against Pitt, completing eighteen of twenty-three passes for 320 yards. He threw touchdown passes of 14, 15, 17, 59, and 72 yards.

Sophomore halfback Garrett Ford chipped in with touchdown runs of 5 and 58 yards while Pitt coach John Micholsen shuddered. "I've never seen so many perfect plays," he said in a low moan. "They were going for the home run all the time."

So were Micholsen's Panthers, it seemed. In all, fifty-two passes were thrown in the game and the teams gained a total of 1,071 yards from scrimmage—just sixteen short of the all-time collegiate record. Sighed Micholsen: "Just the fact that the defense is out there ordinarily would prevent anything like that."

The 1970 game featured a miracle finish for Pitt. West Virginia held a seemingly safe 35–8 lead at the half. A rout for the Mountaineers? Guess again.

Back came Pitt to win 36–35, grinding out yardage on long drives. "They were patient," Constantine remembered. "They just took it three, four yards at a time. It appeared that Pitt started trying to control the ball to avoid further humiliation at its own homecoming game, then learned it could gain consistently with power football."

Poor punting by West Virginia helped the Pitt cause. The Mountaineers' offense did not wake up until after the final Pitt touchdown, which came on a 5-yard pass from Dave Havern to Bill Pilconis. Then a drive by West Virginia to get close enough for a field goal died with a fumble after a completed pass near the Pitt 30.

The mood in the press box changed as quickly as the complexion of the game did, Hardman remembered: "In the first half, West Virginia writers would be cheering and carrying on and Pittsburgh public relations director Dean Billick had to get on the address system to tell everyone to keep some decorum in the press box. But when Pitt came back to win it, Billick was leading the cheers for the Pittsburgh writers. Then it was all right to cheer in the press box. . . ."

The West Virginia fans, many of them drunk on liquor and all of them furious, attempted to storm the Mountaineers' locker room after the game.

"They were all outside the dressing room," Hardman remembered, "trying to get their hands on West Virginia coach Bobby Bowden. Police had to restrain them. If they hadn't, they might have killed him."

Bowden lived with the nightmare of that loss for many years. He still thinks about it today, calling it "the most embarrassing loss in my entire coaching career."

Those same fans that wanted to kill Bowden no doubt would have kissed him after the 1975 game, won 17–14 by West Virginia in another storybook finish associated with this thrill-a-minute rivalry.

Pitt, led by the ubiquitous Dorsett, was heavily favored. But somehow, the Mountaineers managed to hang with Johnny Majors' Panthers. And the Mountaineers got the ball with seventeen seconds left after forcing Pitt to punt. A pass gained 26 yards, the receiver going out of bounds to stop the clock with four seconds remaining.

Then sophomore Bill McKenzie, a walk-on, kicked a 38-yard field goal as time ran out. He never saw the ball go over the crossbar, having kept his head down as kickers are supposed to do. But he knew that he had scored when his teammates swarmed all over him in jubilation.

The game stuck with Bowden long after he had moved on to Florida State.

"A lot of times the Florida writers will ask me to tell them what my favorite games have been, and I always remember the West Virginia-Pitt game of 1975," he said. "That was one of the most exciting games. Number one, it was my birthday, number two, my son Tommy caught several key passes in that game. And then McKenzie kicked that field goal as time ran out."

The Brawl has inspired some incredible individual performances, such as Kevan Barlow's spectacular day for Pitt in the 2000 game.

"The year prior to that, Kevan had an uncle who was killed in a shooting in a Turkey Day pickup football game—very tragic," Borghetti recalled.

A year later, inspired by his uncle's memory, and knowing what happened just 365 days earlier, an emotional Barlow rushed for 272 yards and four TDs to lead Pitt over West Virginia 38–28 in the last college football game played in Pittsburgh's Three Rivers Stadium. The performance broke a West Virginia opponent rushing record set by Syracuse's Larry Csonka.

"Not only playing a rival, but knowing the emotion he was playing under, was something that always stuck with me," Borghetti said.

Some other memorable moments in the series:

—In 1982, Marino surpassed Dorsett as Pitt's all-time total offense leader, and the Panthers held on for a 16–13 victory when a field-goal try by West Virginia hit the crossbar as time expired.

—In 1983, the Mountaineers topped the Panthers 24–21 as quarterback Jeff Hostetler drove his team 90 yards for the winning score in the closing seconds.

—In 1989, West Virginia took a 31–8 lead into the fourth quarter before Pitt staged a furious, last-ditch rally to tie the game 31–31 on a 42-yard field goal by Ed Frazier.

—In 1994, West Virginia came out on top 47–41 as Chad Johnson fired two touchdown passes in the final ninety-two seconds.

Then the Brawl to top all Brawls in 1997.

That was the year Pitt was trying to rebuild its program under Walt Harris, who had replaced Johnny Majors as coach. From 1990 to 1996, the Panthers had just one winning season and a 24-53 record in that time.

"We felt going into the ['97] season that we had to get to a bowl game to get the program jump-started again," Pitt quarterback Pete Gonzalez told the *Pittsburgh Post-Gazette*. "There were some ups and downs and we took our fans on a wild ride, but it all came down to the Backyard Brawl, and so failure in that game wasn't an option."

In 1996, Pitt had gone 4-7, with embarrassing losses to Ohio State (72–0), Miami (45–0), Syracuse (55–7), and Notre Dame (60–6).

"We had hit rock bottom," Borghetti said.

In 1997, the Panthers were determined to turn things around behind Gonzalez, newly installed as starting quarterback.

With a 4-3 start that included an upset victory over Miami and a school-record 470 yards passing in a double-OT win over Rutgers, Gonzalez developed the nickname of "Pistol Pete."

But the Panthers were unable to keep the momentum going, and only a late-season upset over Virginia Tech gave them a chance to salvage a winning season and a bowl bid. There was still one game to go—against West Virginia.

With a 5-5 record in a roller-coaster season, Pitt was a 12-point underdog to a Mountaineers team loaded with future NFL players.

But it didn't matter to the Panthers, who took a 21–10 halftime lead. Pitt was still in control in the fourth quarter, 35–25, after Gonzalez fired a TD pass to Juan Williams.

Pitt had a 10-point lead with less than ten minutes remaining. A winning season and a bowl bid seemed all but assured—to everyone else but the Panthers, that is.

"Nobody on our sideline thought it was over because that's the way that season went," Gonzalez said.

He was correct.

Back came West Virginia on a touchdown pass by Marc Bulger and a field goal by Jay Taylor with 1:18 left in regulation to tie the game at 35.

The teams battled through a first overtime, then a second, still locked at 35.

Then in the third OT, the Mountaineers went ahead 38–35 on a stunning 52-yard field goal by Taylor.

Things didn't look good for Pitt, particularly after Gonzalez was thrown for a 10-yard loss that set up a fourth-and-17 on the West Virginia 32.

Game over? Season over?

Gonzalez felt differently. "I just knew something good would happen."

It did. The Pitt QB completed a 20-yard pass to Jake Hoffart, then a couple of plays later hooked up on a 12-yard TD strike with Terry Murphy.

Final: Pitt 41, West Virginia 38.

The victory launched Pitt into a bowl game and put the Panthers on the right track again.

How sweet it was for Pitt, not only gaining bowl-eligible status, but also beating West Virginia in the process.

"It was a special victory for us in many ways," Borghetti said. "Pitt had a proud seventies and a productive eighties, but the nineties weren't very kind to

Pitt football. West Virginia really dominated the series. West Virginia was certainly a favorite at home—and they had already solidified their postseason."

Two years later, Pitt started on a run of five straight bowl games.

"I've told people that Pete Gonzalez's touchdown pass to Terry Murphy in the third overtime was Pitt's most significant touchdown pass in fifteen-plus years, when Dan Marino threw the winning touchdown pass against Georgia in the final minutes of the 1982 Sugar Bowl," Borghetti said.

Ho, hum, just another Backyard Brawl thriller.

One West Virginia coach has called the Pitt-WVU series "the Blue Collar Super Bowl, the mills against the miners."

Yes, and so typical of football teams that are located so close to each other, familiarity breeds contempt—and competition.

Chapter 14

The Biggest Little Game in America: Williams-Amherst

Even before the first snap in the first game of their series, Williams and Amherst had already forged a furnace-hot rivalry.

It had nothing to do with football, everything to do with a felony.

To begin at the beginning, circa 1820: Zephaniah Swift Moore, the second president at Williams College, didn't think the school could survive in the rural area of northwest Massachusetts. Too isolated, he said.

So he quit his job and headed sixty miles southeast to a more heavily populated area to found a new school, Amherst College. Adding insult to injury, he brought along students and faculty members, even books from the Williams library.

Thus, when Williams and Amherst began playing football in 1884, the rivalry was already forged in the white heat of animosity. Amherst athletic teams were known as the "Lord Jeffs." To the Williams camp, however, they were known as the "Defectors." Still are.

"We hold it against them every chance we get," said Williams sports information director Dick Quinn.

He's not kidding. One year at the Williams-Amherst game, the Williams band presented the Amherst band with a $1.8 billion library fine for Moore's "overdue" books.

Talk about carrying a grudge.

"They're less than popular around here," Quinn said of Amherst. "They even stole our color, purple, and their first building was an exact replica of one of our buildings."

The Lord Jeffs have also robbed the Ephs, pronounced "EE-fs" and named after college benefactor Ephraim Williams, of unbeaten seasons. In 2002, Amherst's 45–35 victory marked the third time the Lord Jeffs had spoiled an unbeaten season for Williams.

The Ephs have played undefeated-season spoilers as well in this series dubbed, "The Biggest Little Game in America." When Williams nipped Amherst 23–20 in an overtime thriller in 2001, it marked the seventh time the Ephs marred an unbeaten season for the Lord Jeffs. At the same time, the Ephs concluded their campaign with a perfect record.

Unlike many of the big college rivalries, Amherst-Williams is as basic and pure as it gets. It's Division III football, which means no athletic scholarships, no trophies, and no playoffs or bowl games. They play strictly for pride.

"This is our Super Bowl," said Pat McGee, former defensive lineman for the Lord Jeffs. "The fact that we don't get to participate in the playoffs makes this game that much more special. This is it."

Dick Farley, the most successful coach in Williams history, explains the rivalry in another context.

"It's as much a social occasion as it is a game," he said. "The alumni still want us to be successful, but they spend more time tailgating and chatting with old friends than they do watching the game. It's a social and cultural happening."

In 1955, Quinn points out, the game drew the nation's attention on the NBC Radio Game of the Week, with Brooklyn Dodgers announcer Vin Scully as the play-by-play man.

Now alumni around the world can watch the game on closed-circuit TV. It's shown to some fifty markets in America and as far away as Hong Kong. Williams-Amherst alumni often get together and rent a venue, splitting the cost.

"They're now playing the game at noontime, so it could be brunch in L.A. and lunch in New York," Farley said.

Farley calls it a "friendly and respectful" rivalry.

"I say a friendly rivalry because a lot of these people live in the same area, they work in the same hospitals and law firms. There's something about the game of football—you can knock the hell out of each other for two, three hours, and then shake hands, sit down, and end up being friends for the rest of your life with the guys that you played against."

Despite their status as small colleges—no more than a couple thousand students each—they have produced some big-time football players. Williams's Jack Maitland played for the Baltimore Colts and Amherst's Doug Smith for the Miami Dolphins.

Another former athlete who graduated from Williams: George Steinbrenner.

Steinbrenner, the principal owner of the New York Yankees, was one of the country's top track-and-field hurdlers of his day. He also was the sports editor for the Williams student newspaper. As such, he predicted a rout of Amherst in 1951. He was right on the money: Williams crushed Amherst 40–7.

The schools have produced high-profile names off the field as well. U.S. President James Garfield and baseball commissioner Fay Vincent both went to Williams, and President Calvin Coolidge to Amherst.

As two of the ten teams in the New England Small College Athletic Conference (NESCAC), Williams and Amherst play only eight games in a season plus a scrimmage against a conference opponent. The reason: college administrators prefer to emphasize academics rather than athletics.

Be that as it may, NESCAC is home to some of the longest-standing rivalries in college football. The Williams-Amherst rivalry stands at the top of NESCAC with 121 games played through 2006.

There are also some "tri-valries" featuring three schools.

For a while, Wesleyan was a significant part of the "Little Three" rivalry with Williams and Amherst. Williams usually plays Wesleyan in the seventh game of the season before tackling Amherst in the season-ender.

"It's the Second Season," said Renzie Lamb, former assistant football coach at Williams. "We come to the end of our first six games and it's two more games against our traditional rivals. So that kind of gives us the benefit of a focus."

Wesleyan, though, hasn't won the Little Three since 1970. "They've had more success in developing NFL coaches," said Quinn, identifying Bill Belichick of the New England Patriots and Eric Mangini of the New York Jets.

Due in large part to longtime coach Farley, Williams holds a sizable edge in the series (68-48-5 through 2006). In seventeen years as Williams's head football coach, Farley posted a 114-19-3 record with five undefeated seasons and he landed in the College Football Hall of Fame. More important, as far as Williams was concerned, Farley's teams boasted a 14-2-1 record against the Lord Jeffs. One of Farley's main priorities when he came to Williams was to reverse the trend against Amherst, which had won six straight in the series.

He immediately did that, and then for some time after that. Under Farley, Williams beat Amherst eight straight years before a scoreless tie in 1995. Then Farley's teams won four more to make it thirteen games in a row without losing to Amherst.

"It was quite a run," Farley said. "They were a little [less talented] than we were. But a lot of the games were kind of a flip of a coin. People were saying, 'What can you attribute your success to?' and I just said good fortune and good kids."

There was no problem getting the players up for the game, as Farley remembers. "We used the [phrase], 'Sixty minutes to play and a lifetime to remember.' In some ways, I think they didn't want to be the ones to drop the success rate."

Before arriving at Williams, Farley admittedly didn't know much about the school, or the rivalry with Amherst. Farley was more familiar with the University of Massachusetts, which he competed against as a Boston University athlete. At BU, Farley was on the track and football teams.

"I grew up in the Boston area, so I knew the Boston College-Holy Cross rivalry, I knew Boston University-Boston College, I knew Harvard-Yale," Farley said. "The thing I didn't recognize until I got here was that Amherst was founded by a guy who was not happy at Williams. Even Harvard-Yale doesn't have that, literally a guy leaving one school to go start another as president. Not as a player, not as a coach, but as president."

After a couple of years in professional football and a couple more as a high school coach, Farley found his way to Williams by way of a newspaper ad. "Williams was looking for a track coach and an assistant football coach. I had done both sports for four years at BU and I thoroughly enjoyed both activities."

Farley didn't know it at the time, but he had a connection at Williams in athletic director Bob Peck. Peck had been the AD at Boston University and knew Farley's name.

Welcome to Williams, Dick.

In his first fifteen years at Williams, Farley was head track coach in the winter and spring, assistant football coach in the fall. When football coach Bob Odell retired, Farley took over in 1987 and remained in that capacity through the 2003 season. He went out a winner with a 14–10 victory over Amherst. "Not a bad way to end it," he said.

It wasn't the end for Farley, however, as he stayed on at Williams as assistant track coach and director of club sports.

Not only did he leave a legacy as a winner, Farley also always left them laughing.

Quick with a quip, Farley once noted about a slow-footed player: "In a race with a pregnant woman, he's third."

Some other Farleyisms:

—"If you can't play here, you can't play anywhere. There's no Division Four."

—"Nothing good happens after midnight."

After losing his first three games at Williams, Farley went the next 128 without losing back-to-back contests. When he left football, it was with the sixth-best percentage in the sport's history at .849. And some of the athletes who played for Farley, such as Scott Perry and Ethan Brooks, did go on to the NFL.

Farley wasn't the only coaching giant in the rivalry. Like Farley at Williams, Jim Ostendarp also made his impact at Amherst. He coached football there from 1959 to 1992 and fashioned a career record of 168-91-5 at a college known primarily for academic excellence. He turned out unbeaten teams in 1964 and 1984 and four players for the NFL.

When he retired, the Baltimore native held the record for most coaching victories in the history of New England small-college football. He never forgot the school's priorities, though.

When ESPN wanted to televise the 100th game of the Amherst-Williams series in 1985, he declined. "We're in the education business, not the entertainment business," he said.

Ostendarp had a unique perspective on the rivalry because he had coached at Williams from 1955 to 1957. Once settled at Amherst, he felt he had found his destiny. Asked by a reporter if he ever thought about going to a bigger school, Ostendarp replied, "Where would you go after Amherst?"

Not that things were always quaint and peaceful there.

Early accounts of the rivalry vibrate with malicious, hard-hitting play. Most of the games in the early days amounted to free-for-alls with little regard for rules, or feelings. Fighting between the teams was common. Reporting on the 1891 game, the *Williams Quarterly* noted, "Amherst slugged whenever opportunity offered."

In their first meeting in 1884, Williams built a 15–2 lead before the game was called because the Amherst players had to catch a train. Ensuing games were closer and uninterrupted by travel issues.

In 1906, Amherst and Williams were locked in a scoreless tie on a snow-covered field before a player described only as "Beach of Amherst" ran 99 yards for a touchdown in the final quarter.

At least that's what everyone thought. Beach's footprints in the snow revealed that he had stepped out of bounds on the way to the goal line. Williams was denied the TD and the game ended in a 0–0 tie.

There was no love lost, and little hospitality, as the rivalry stormed through the twentieth century. After the 1928 game, the *Williams Record* complained that the Lord Jeffs subjected the Ephs "to the danger of pneumonia and colds by allowing only three towels to the whole squad and coaches."

That same game, a 40–15 victory for Williams, was memorable for another reason. The Amherst coaches, in a desperation move, sent in one of their own players dressed in a Williams uniform in hopes of confusing the opponent. However, he was caught red-handed and red-faced by officials and ignominiously forced to strip off his jersey in full view of the entire stadium.

Such mischievous behavior in this rivalry, especially in modern times, is usually reserved for the fans.

Some remember the 1952 game for the dramatic Williams torch parade down Route 2. Students roused school president James Phinney Baxter out of his house to join the fun. At the center of things was a scaffold where an Amherst ghost hung in effigy. It wasn't long before the ghost went up in flames.

In 1967, Williams students came out with buttons that said, "Calvin Coolidge went to Amherst," a political commentary presumed to be an insult.

And then there are the traditions that have made the Amherst-Williams rivalry so unique. At Williams, for instance, there is "The Walk." If Williams wins the game at home, players walk down Spring Street in Williamstown to St. Pierre's barbershop singing the school's fight song. They cram into the tiny, four-chair shop, and celebrate with cold drinks and cigars. No telling how many heads might be shaved.

"Walking up to St. Pierre's, it's just the greatest feeling in the world," said Graham Goldwasser, a former Williams linebacker.

Close shaves haven't been confined to barbershops in this series. There have been plenty on the field, including a classic in 1942.

Williams had one of its best teams in history that year, loaded with All-Americans, All-East, and All-New England selections. Riding a thirteen-game winning streak, Charley Caldwell's Williams team was ranked No. 1 in the East and was a heavy favorite in a battle of unbeatens.

That didn't mean a thing to the Lord Jeffs, who pulled off a 12–6 upset in one of the series' most memorable games.

Following a scoreless first half in the game at Amherst, Williams went ahead in the third period on an 18-yard touchdown pass from Bob Hayes to Bill Schmidt. The try for the extra point went wide, but the 6–0 lead going into the fourth quarter looked like it might be enough for a Williams victory, especially with the way the Ephs were playing defense.

But Amherst came back on a 14-yard touchdown run by Frank Koebel that left the game tied at 6–6 when "Automatic Joe" Mills missed the extra point.

"His try went wide and the spectators seemed resigned to a tie," the *New York Times* reported.

Not Amherst. The Lord Jeffs purposely kicked the ball out-of-bounds to the Williams 35. The Lord Jeffs' defense held, forcing Williams to punt.

The Ephs did, but what a strange punt it was.

"Just as Tom Powers essayed to make the punt, a strong blast of wind arose, and the ball virtually went straight up and returned to the ground, only five yards from the line of scrimmage," the *Times* said.

Ball on the Williams 40. Two plays yielded 10 yards. Then Amherst's Roland Smith connected with Bob Agnew for the winning touchdown.

In 1967 came another classic. Williams preserved an unbeaten season and clinched the Little Three title with a 14–10 victory on Charlie Bradbury's 46-yard TD pass in the closing minutes.

In 1971, things weren't going so well for Williams against Amherst. The Ephs trailed 6–0 late in the first half and couldn't get on track offensively. Lamb had scouted Amherst and noticed the Lord Jeffs having trouble playing against the wishbone offense. He suggested to Odell that the Ephs switch to the wishbone, which they had been practicing all of the prior week.

Dave "Cha Cha" Reimann, a little-known backup runner who played mostly on the scout team, became a star that day in one of the great zero-to-hero stories. He scored on touchdown runs of 60 and 14 yards as Williams came back to beat Amherst 30–14.

"He couldn't believe how tired he was," Quinn remembered of Reimann. "You know, in practice they usually run six, seven yards."

For plentiful thrillers in this rivalry, there was no period like the latter part of the twentieth century and the beginning of the twenty-first.

Start with 1989, when a lot was at stake for Williams. In more than one hundred years of football, the Ephs had never had a perfect season. But now they were on the verge of one, and how sweet it would be to accomplish the feat with a victory over their archrivals.

It would not be easy. Nor should it ever be in a great rivalry.

Amherst was only 4-3, but always a dangerous opponent for Williams. As per his custom, Williams assistant coach Lamb appeared for a weekly pregame luncheon with the media to talk about the game.

As coordinator of the defense at Williams, Lamb pointed out that Amherst did not have a very good running attack. Lamb said that Amherst would not be able to run on Williams because "we're too good up front."

Big mistake.

"That was Wednesday at noon," Lamb remembers. "On Friday, the *New York Times* comes out with a preview by William Wallace."

The headline on the story, according to Lamb, screamed: AMHERST CANNOT RUN AGAINST WILLIAMS.

"Dick Farley hit the roof," Lamb said. "He says, 'This is going to be on every bulletin board in Amherst. We are in deep trouble.'"

Deep trouble, indeed. Amherst scored a quick touchdown—on a running play no less—for a 7–0 lead. After a Williams fumble by quarterback Chris Hevesy, the Lord Jeffs scored again on another running play.

"Five minutes into the game, they have two running touchdowns and it's 14–0," Lamb said.

Lamb was in the press box communicating with the coaches on the field.

"The kids were in shock," Lamb said.

Lamb was more confident. "We just made some adjustments. We just tightened up [on defense] a little bit, we played good pass defense. I mean, we *were* a better team."

Back came Williams to tie on a TD run by Hevesy in the second quarter and by Lars Hem in the third. With 7:32 to play in the third quarter, Brian Taptich kicked a 27-yard field goal to give Williams its first lead of the game, 17–14.

Amherst still had some life left. With just a couple of minutes to go, the Lord Jeffs drove downfield. With 1:33 remaining, Amherst had the ball on Williams's 9-yard line. But three plays later, Williams's defensive end Ted Rogers stripped the ball from Amherst quarterback Stephen Bishop and Ken Dilanian fell on the fumble.

"And that was the end of the game," Lamb said. "And let me tell you, I was happy, Dick was happy, the team was happy."

Lamb wrote a note to *Times* writer Wallace.

"I told him it was a great article and everything he wrote came true," Lamb said. "It had a happy ending."

The 1995 "Mud Bowl" was memorable more for the weather than for the excitement. A hard rain had turned the field into virtual quicksand, completely bogging down the offenses. The result: a 0–0 tie.

"That was the best Williams team I've seen," said Quinn, who had started working for the school in the 1980s.

Williams was a three-touchdown favorite over Amherst, so the tie almost felt like a loss to the Ephs.

"It doesn't take away the 0–0 tie, but I told the guys it took an act of God to beat them," Quinn said. "The field was like playing in clam chowder."

The Mud Bowl was followed by "The Drive" in 1996, when Williams went 98 yards for a touchdown in the final five minutes to upset Amherst 19–13. The rally, capped by Mike McAdam's TD run, spoiled a perfect season for the Lord Jeffs.

McAdam had quit the team the year before. "He said he was burned out," Quinn recalled, "but the next winter he saw the coach and told him he wanted to come back."

Farley told McAdam he was welcome back, but he'd better work out and be in shape. McAdam made good use of his second chance. He started every game and scored that winning TD against Amherst.

In 1997, the teams played what is considered the all-time classic in the series and actually one of the greatest college football games played on any level.

"It's one of the big shows on the New England Sports Network (NESN)," Lamb said. "Whenever they have some free time, you know, two hours to fill, they play that game. They've played that game seven or eight times a year since 1997."

Just like Cha Cha Reimann, this story centered on a virtual unknown who came out of the shadows to be a hero. In this case, Colin Vataha, son of former NFL player Randy Vataha.

On the Friday before the Wesleyan game, the next-to-last contest of the season, the Williams players were playfully kicking the ball around when Farley noticed this freshman booming 40- and 50-yarders.

It caught the attention of Farley, who was in need of a consistent field goal kicker. Only one problem: Farley subsequently found out Vataha had never kicked in high school because of an ankle injury. Still, he showed promise, and Farley invited Vataha to work on his kicking game with the coaches in practice.

"We started to do that on Monday the week before the Amherst game," Farley said. "We did it all week."

The year before, Williams spoiled Amherst's bid for an unbeaten season with a late rally. The Lord Jeffs were unbeaten in the first seven games of 1997 and determined not to let Williams spoil things again.

Just like in the previous year, the Lord Jeffs led going into the fourth quarter. And just like in the previous year, the Ephs came back to make a game of it. Williams even moved ahead 45–38 in the closing minutes.

"It was one of those things going back and forth," Farley remembered of the thrill-a-minute contest featuring alternating quarterbacks for Williams.

Back came the Lord Jeffs. With 1:49 left, Rich Willard fired a 34-yard TD pass to Matt Hall to cut the Williams lead to 45–44. The Lord Jeffs lined up for the tying extra point. But Hall, the kicker, crossed up Williams by throwing an unexpected two-point conversion pass to Todd Haggert that gave Amherst a 46–45 lead.

"I don't think there was any panic," Lamb said. "We brought the ball up the field. What happened was, I think Amherst was so excited after they got their two-point conversion and they were finally ahead, that they weren't as focused as we were."

The Ephs went into their two-minute drill, catching passes and running out-of-bounds to stop the clock. After one such play, a Williams receiver was hit by an Amherst player on the sideline. Amherst was penalized 15 yards.

On the Williams sideline, Farley was thinking touchdown rather than field goal.

"We didn't really want to get to Vataha to kick the ball," Farley said. "To be honest with you, we were hoping to score a touchdown because we didn't want to put him out there under all that pressure."

But a pass failed; it could easily have been intercepted by Amherst.

Farley had no choice.

"Then we sent Vataha out to kick," he said.

There were two seconds left. Vataha, who had been successful with extra points and field goals earlier in the game, kicked a 27-yarder this time for a 48–46 Williams victory.

"He just went out there and hit it like a nine-iron," Lamb said of Vataha. "He was too young to know about the rivalry, too young to be nervous."

Be that as it may, Vataha had stepped into the spotlight of the Biggest Little Game in America.

"I think it's a battle between brothers," Lamb said. "There's no hate when brothers fight, just competition."

Chapter 15

The Monon Bell: Wabash-DePauw

They won't draw 100,000 or more fans to their game. The national media will pretty much ignore them. Rarely are any national championships on the line.

All of which gives the Wabash-DePauw football rivalry just a little more charm, just a bit more intrigue. And, yes, still as much relevance as any of those Division I "Big Games" and Battles for the Whatever.

Wabash is the men's college of less than 1,000 students in Crawfordsville, Indiana. The Little Giants (sometimes called Cavemen) wear red and white. They play in the North Coast Athletic Conference.

DePauw is the coeducational school of more than 2,000 students in Greencastle, just twenty-eight miles away. The Tigers wear black and gold. They are members of the Southern Collegiate Athletic Conference.

Enough of the details. Now onto the Battle for the Bell.

The two Division III schools have been at it since 1890, when DePauw won the first meeting 34–5. That victory was so decisive that Wabash forfeited the next year.

Over the ensuing one hundred years, then into the second century of the series, Wabash built a 53-51-9 overall record (through 2006). Since the Monon Bell became the prize in 1932, DePauw is up 35-34-6.

Ah, the Monon Bell.

A gift from the railroad that serviced both towns, the Bell has become more than a trophy awarded to the winner of the annual matchup. It is something of a Holy Grail for the two schools from similar towns in the same area of the Hoosier state.

"It is the biggest game for both teams, for every player, and it stays with you forever," said Pete Metzelaars, a former Wabash star who went on to a solid career in the NFL—a true rarity for players from these schools. Metzelaars actually was a basketball star in college, leading Wabash to its only national title in 1982.

"I still remember how badly it hurt to lose the Bell game. It's one of the great rivalries in all of sports, and I've seen a few of them in the NFL. I think the Monon Bell game will always be with me, a big part of me."

And just to remind Metzelaars, plus the thousands of others who have attended either college, there is a song to spice matters even more. "The Ballad of the Monon Bell" debuted in 1985, written by several DePauw graduates and recorded by Jim Ibbotson, a member of the Nitty Gritty Dirt Band—and a Tigers alum.

The song in part:
Long before the cannonball traveled through her towns,
The state of Indiana owned the jewel of the crown.
The train, they called the Monon, the stories they still tell,
The Cavemen and the Tigers playing for her bell.

So in late fall, at Blackstock Stadium in Greencastle or Byron P. Hollett Little Giant Stadium in Crawfordsville, they face off for the right to not only ring the Bell, but also to own it for a year.

"That week is very similar to what it's like on any other college campus during a rivalry week," said Wabash sports information director Brent Harris. "I start hearing from alums two to three weeks before, and the week of the game I get e-mails and phone calls and even visits from alumni all the time.

"On Thursday morning each week, we have a gathering with a speaker, but the week of the Bell game, the football captains and coaches speak at the chapel. The Bell is up front and the guest of honor is up at the front. It's a major event."

Various alumni groups from each school have events leading up to the game, not all of them in the neighborhoods of DePauw and Wabash. They range from the Monon Bell Stag, attended by both sides, to a blood drive to see who can donate the most pints of blood.

And there are Monon Bell parties all over the nation, from less exotic places such as Indianapolis to as far away as Los Angeles. Those gatherings have become more commonplace—and likely more intense—ever since the DePauw-Wabash game has been available on satellite feeds and nationwide radio broadcasts.

"One of things we have with the national TV broadcast, we have alumni parties in forty to fifty cities, all of them a cooperative effort," Harris notes. "It's a mini-rivalry unto themselves in those cities, with a mini-version of the Monon Bell they might exchange depending on who wins. I've heard stories from people who have gone to these parties and it's like being in the stadium."

There was one employee of UCLA's information department who was an alum of DePauw. When Harris was exchanging messages with her on another subject, she closed her note with "Go DePauw, Beat Wabash!"

She then headed to a party to watch that game in the morning—in Los Angeles.

A sports information director from another school in the conference was traveling with his team and got a chance to sneak a few peeks at the game while on the road. The Bell carries that much allure, even for nonparticipants.

"It's a big rivalry, sure," Harris said, "but it's amazing when you look behind the scenes at how the two schools work together."

Yes, but working together is not what opponents do when they get on the field. They try everything to outperform each other. Wabash and DePauw certainly have found ways to do that for more than one hundred years.

Wabash didn't get its first win until 1894. The next year, the Little Giants were accused by the *DePauw Weekly* of bribing the referees. That led to some ill feelings, enough so that the series experienced a three-year hiatus from 1897 to 1899.

The schools sort of made up for it with two meetings to celebrate the new century. They split in 1900, and DePauw swept in 1901.

Several games in the early years were notable, but one was historic.

In 1903, Wabash suited up an African-American player, Sam Gordon. DePauw refused to play and remained in its locker room until several Methodist ministers from the school intervened. As did Civil War General Lew Wallace.

They urged the Tigers to reconsider, to forget the "color line" and stick to the spirit of sports. They did, and Wabash won 10–0.

DePauw was more adamant about not facing a team with a black player the next year. Wabash had its most powerful team and was routing everyone on the 1904 schedule. But not DePauw, whose president, Bishop Hughes, canceled the Thanksgiving Day game because the Little Giants' Bill Cantrell was black.

In general, Wabash and DePauw met annually from that year on, with one major exception. The 1910 game was called off after Wabash's Ralph Wilson died in a game against St. Louis. Wilson was buried under a tombstone in a Crawfordville cemetery: "Ralph Lee Wilson, 1891–1910. Did Wabash Win?"

Wabash was 4-0 when it canceled the rest of its schedule.

The 1920s might have been Roaring everywhere else in sports, but not for the Tigers' offense in this series. After the Tigers won 3–0 on a 52-yard drop-kick field goal by Harold Galloway, Wabash strung together six wins. DePauw scored a total of, well, zero points in those half-dozen contests.

Under coach Pete Vaughan, the Little Giants were Goliaths during that streak—they also won 13–7 in 1927—and the seven successive wins over their archrival represented the longest Wabash string in the series.

DePauw would go ten years without a loss to Wabash (1955 to 1964), with two ties included.

In 1932, the rivalry took on its three-hundred-pound trophy, which immeasurably ratcheted up emotions. A DePauw alumnus named Orien Fifer wrote to the *Indianapolis News* suggesting that this growing rivalry needed an award to identify it, much in the same way the Old Oaken Bucket (Indiana-Purdue) or Little Brown Jug (Minnesota-Michigan) made other series memorable.

The Bell, which sat atop the locomotive of the Monon Railroad that connected the two towns, became the prize. And from the beginning, it was coveted.

The '32 contest was a classic. Crawfordville and Greencastle were inundated by a blizzard, even making travel on the Monon line precarious. Blackstock Field was under about a foot of the white stuff, so just getting the turf clear to play the game was a major challenge.

DePauw coach Gaumy Neal, who played at Wabash as an undergrad, had an idea.

"I went to the student body and asked for help," he said. "We supplied the equipment, the shovels and the wagons, and they worked almost until game time to clear the field. It was a great contribution by the DePauw students."

Unfortunately, although most of the snow had been removed, the field froze on the eve of the contest. It was icy for much of the game.

DePauw was a power that year behind running back Don Wheaton, one of the all-time greatest Tigers. But Wheaton would be victimized by the weather and the Wabash defense on this day.

In the most exhausting of conditions—a bonfire was built on the Wabash sideline to keep the players as warm as possible—Wheaton continually was thwarted. By the third quarter, it became clear that any team managing to score would own the Bell.

It wasn't until the dying moments that either side truly threatened. And it was not the Tigers and their star runner, but the visiting Little Giants.

With about three minutes remaining, Wabash reached the DePauw 1-yard line for a fourth-down play. Opting not to attempt a field goal, the Little Giants went for the touchdown.

"Coach Vaughan always taught me that it was wise to keep a play, an ace in the hole, so to speak," said quarterback Stuart Smith. "That I had done."

Rather than have the fullback carry the ball, as most teams would do and most everyone expected, Smith called for Red Varner, one of the trailing halfbacks, to run off left guard. It was a brilliant call, except for one thing: the awful footing. "One could have driven a freight train through that hole," Smith said.

But Varner slipped to the ground back on the 4-yard line. And the game ended 0–0.

That left the prized Bell in DePauw's possession because the Tigers had won the previous year's meeting. And in 1933, they truly owned it with a 14–0 victory by the greatest of all DePauw squads.

Neal's squad was unscored upon in '33, winning every game. It is considered among the most powerful small-college teams in history and is the last to win every game by shutout.

While the action on the field remained taut, exciting, and entertaining, the shenanigans involving the Monon Bell were equally noteworthy.

Both schools always have had a code of honor where the Monon Bell is concerned: You can steal it, but no weapons can be used, it can only be taken during football season, and it must be returned before the kickoff of DePauw-Wabash.

It's hard to say when the Bell was first "borrowed" by one set of students or the other—most observers believe the first time it disappeared was in 1941. Wabash owned it, and when the Bell went missing, there was little consideration that perhaps DePauw's students had taken it. Instead, the folks at Wabash figured after three weeks of searching that it was already melted into scrap after being stolen by some actual crooks.

But it turned up with Tiger paws all over it, if you will. That eventually led to the schools often hiding the prize when it came into their possession.

The two most memorable Bell legends are from 1965 and 1967.

In '65, Jim Shanks, a sophomore at Wabash, impersonated a delegate from the U.S. information service in Mexico City. Shanks visited the DePauw campus and got an audience with school president Dr. William Kerstetter. In character, Shanks made a convincing argument that the Greencastle college needed more students from Mexico.

Kerstetter quickly agreed that two scholarships should go to Mexican students interested in attending DePauw. Then Shanks was given a tour of the school, pausing to take photos. One of the pictures was, naturally, of the Monon Bell, which Shanks promised to bring back to Mexico and to display prominently.

The Bell was hidden away under some barrels in a maintenance building, but athletic director James Loveless agreed to show it to Shanks. The interloper took a few pictures and soon left the campus.

Of course, Shanks would be back, with three accomplices, but Greencastle police stopped them. However, while that was going on, another group of Wabash students grabbed the booty as "Operation Frijoles" was a rousing success.

The Monon Bell remained in Crawfordsville until just before game time, when Wabash dean of students Norman Moore returned it. But the Little Giants marched off with it later in the day thanks to a 16–6 win. And their fans ran around the DePauw stadium wearing sombreros and ponchos.

Two years later, after DePauw—which was the dominant team in the rivalry from 1955 to 1970—had won back the Bell 9–7, came the Mud Bowl.

Having been burned in '65, the DePauw students were determined not to have the Bell fall into Wabash hands again. So a group of them secretly took the clanger and buried it, three hundred pounds and all, near the north end zone of Blackstock Stadium. For the next eleven months, no one other than the perpetrators knew where the Bell was.

They didn't count on a snowstorm turning the ground into a quagmire on game day, though. So in the third quarter, the Bell was dug up out of the mud, blunting somewhat the effect of where it had been hidden.

The Little Giants didn't seem to mind the mess, though, after a 7–0 victory.

All kinds of superb memories have been created on the field, too. In 1994, for instance, the first two plays of the game were kickoff returns for TDs. Wabash got a 94-yarder, then DePauw immediately returned the favor. But the Tigers missed the extra point, making it 7–6 without a play being run from scrimmage. Wabash won that one 28–24.

In other years, one of the teams would be in the running for the postseason and its chief rival would ruin those chances. In 1981, DePauw won 21–14, snapping the Little Giants' twenty-four-game unbeaten streak and knocking them from the playoffs. Nick Mourouzis, the new Tigers coach, had printed T-shirts that read "40-40-8," and he passed them out after his team evened the all-time series.

If two games stand out as absolute classics, they were the thrillers in 1960 and 2001.

The '60 matchup came in the midst of DePauw's stunning 8-0-2 run against its archrival. And the Tigers were favorites over a Wabash squad that had one mere victory all season, although DePauw had managed just two wins and a tie.

Just to prove how little the records mean in the series, the teams staged a wild one. Wabash built a 13–6 lead and had the ball, but the Little Giants fumbled. Their defense, so staunch all game, held on three downs and forced a punt.

Except the Tigers had no intention of punting. Coach Tommy Mont was enough of a gambler that he called for a fake, and DePauw completed a pass for the first down.

He wasn't done. As the Tigers moved toward the end zone, their option offense finally clicking, Mont had quarterback John Rubush roll out with the choice of running in for six points, or throwing if he was bottled up. And he was bottled up like a Pepsi.

So just before the defensive charge reached Rubush, he flipped a lateral to Dan Blunt for a diving score, making it 13–12.

With the Bell already in their charge amid a five-game undefeated string against Wabash, it made sense for DePauw to kick the extra point and take the 13–13 tie and the Monon Bell back to Greencastle.

Well, maybe it made sense to a lot of others, but not to Mont. And not to Tigers fans.

The NCAA had added a rule allowing teams to place the ball on the hash mark at the 2-yard line and run a play for two points. Mont had been asked before the season whether that was a strategy he would employ.

"Yes, I would," he said. "Why not, if you can win a game?"

So now, would he stick by that philosophy with the biggest game of the season on the line? Or would he take the tie?

"No choice there," Mont would say. "Any coach who settles for a tie in this series doesn't deserve to be coaching in this series."

Some reports claimed Mont walked toward the grandstands and asked the fans what they wanted him to do. Others say he'd already told his Tigers they would go for the win.

Wabash's coaches apparently discounted any thought of Mont going for the deuce. They sent their kick team onto the field, hoping for a block to preserve a one-point victory.

DePauw lined up in kick formation, but with Rubush as the holder. The quarterback took the snap, rolled out with the kicker as his trailer on the option, and leaped into the end zone.

The Tigers mobbed each other. The Little Giants stared at each other dejectedly. Final score: DePauw 14, Wabash 13.

Of course, the Little Giants had their special moments, too. None was better than in 2001.

DePauw needed a victory for a winning record, while Wabash was 7-2 heading into the final game. The Little Giants got going quickly and led 14–0, but the host Tigers tied it in the third period. Wabash once more went on top, but DePauw was determined. The Tigers simply had very little time to do something.

What they did was march 61 yards in nine plays, led by quarterback Jason Lee. Taking the ball with 1:22 to go, devoid of timeouts, DePauw got completions of 16, 22, and 17 yards from Lee. Matt King's TD run and the extra point tied it 21–21.

A mere fourteen seconds remained as Wabash prepared to receive the kickoff, with overtime—for the first time in the rivalry—on the horizon.

"That's what happened to us last year," receiver Kurt Casper told the *Crawfordsville Journal-Review*. "We had a nine-point lead with nine minutes to go and we choked it away. Our team motto is, 'We Believe,' and so I think no one gave up. Even until that last play, I think everyone knew we were going to do it."

Blind faith, perhaps. But faith nonetheless.

Freshman Eddie Garza returned the kickoff to the Wabash 39. That left 10.2 seconds.

Jake Knott, who was having a big game—he finished with 381 yards passing and four touchdowns—threw to Casper over the middle at the Little Giants' 48. Wabash called a timeout with all of 2.7 seconds remaining.

The call by coach Chris Creighton, working his first Monon Bell game, was a doozy. Some might term it a desperation pass, but there was a design to it.

Knott would roll right and throw the ball deep to 6-foot-5 tight end Ryan Short, who would be stationed at the DePauw 4. Creighton and his staff reasoned that on what certainly was the final play of regulation, the Tigers would have their defenders at or behind the goal line, knowing a completion anywhere but in the end zone would not be enough for Wabash.

But Short was not supposed to catch the ball. Instead, facing the line of scrimmage, he was going to tip it backward into the end zone, hopefully to Casper.

"I knew Casper would be there, but you really don't think it's going to work," Short said. "We believe, but for *that* to really work, it's just like a dream."

Dream on, Wabash.

The ball settled in Casper's arms. In the end zone. With the clock at 0:00.

Final, thanks to The Catch: Wabash 27, DePauw 21.

"I looked around and saw Phi Psis, Sigma Chis, alumni, faculty, staff, everybody hugging each other," said assistant coach B. J. Hammer. "Time stopped for a minute or two. For that couple of minutes, everything—the September 11 tragedies, the problems we've all had this fall—was gone. And all that was there was the Monon Bell ringing."

As it should be.

Chapter 16

Best of the Rest

Forget about the Little Brown Jug.

Never mind the Old Oaken Bucket.

How about the Territorial Cup?

The Territorial Cup?

Why, yes, the Territorial Cup actually is the oldest intercollegiate football rivalry trophy in America, outdating the more famous Little Brown Jug and Old Oaken Bucket by quite a few years.

It's the prize that goes to the winner of the Arizona State-Arizona series, one of America's most bitter and enduring football rivalries. This one has everything: politics, power plays, and punch-outs. Reason enough to rank it No. 18 among our great college football rivalries.

The Cup was originally awarded to Tempe Normal School (now Arizona State) in 1899. That's ten years before the Jug came into prominence and twenty-six before the Bucket made its debut.

The Jug, a gray plaster crock that Michigan coach Fielding Yost once used to carry drinking water for his players, was first awarded to the winner of the Minnesota-Michigan series in 1909. The Bucket, said to have been a drinking vessel for Morgan's Raiders of Civil War days, was first awarded in the Indiana-Purdue series in 1925.

Arizona and Arizona State have had their own Civil War for quite a while—and for good reason.

In the late fifties, Arizona State hoped to reach university status, but was rebuffed by a power group led by lawyers from the University of Arizona.

Not to be denied, the Arizona State camp got its proposition on the general ballot and touched off one of the most bitter and expensive political campaigns ever seen in the state. Frank Kush, the Arizona State coach, remembered putting up Arizona State posters only to have them immediately torn down by irate University of Arizona alumni.

In the year of the 1958 election, Arizona State took its hard feelings to the football field and thoroughly swamped the Wildcats 47–0.

One unhappy Wildcats fan probably summed up the feelings of many others when he said: "State's real argument was that their football team had kicked hell out of us, so they deserved to be a university."

Perhaps. But the voters nevertheless passed Arizona State's proposal to become a full-blown university by an overwhelming two-to-one margin.

That wasn't the only good reason for Arizona State to hate the University of Arizona, at least on an athletic level.

Going into their 1968 "Duel in the Desert," Arizona had an 8-1 record and State was 7-2. The winner of the game gained a berth in the Sun Bowl.

At least that was the deal ASU had agreed upon. Arizona coach Darrell Mudra had other ideas. He gave an ultimatum to the Sun Bowl committee to take his team regardless of the outcome of the ASU game, or the Wildcats would not appear in the Sun Bowl.

The power play worked, but Mudra had to be somewhat embarrassed when ASU clobbered his team 30–7 in what became known as the "Ultimatum Bowl."

Despite bad feelings at ASU, something good came out of it for the Sun Devils: their very own bowl game.

Community leaders established the Fiesta Bowl in 1971 so that ASU would have somewhere to play in the postseason when it was ignored elsewhere. The Fiesta Bowl, of course, eventually became part of the highly lucrative Bowl Championship Series (BCS) to decide the national champion.

Both Arizona and Arizona State opened their doors in the 1880s and started playing football around the turn of the twentieth century. Arizona dominated the rivalry early on and Arizona State came on strong in the second half of the century. From 1965 to 1981, the Sun Devils won fifteen of seventeen games.

The rivalry has been filled with long power swings and a series of heartbreaking upsets—none more upsetting to ASU than the 1986 game. The Sun Devils had already wrapped up a berth in the Rose Bowl with a 9-0-1 record. At home in their final regular season game, ASU figured to add the Wildcats to their list of victims.

Surprisingly, the Wildcats crushed the Sun Devils 34–17 in a game that featured a stunning play by Chuck Cecil. Cecil picked off a pass by Jeff Van Raaphorst in the end zone in the fourth quarter and raced the length of the field for a clinching TD.

Arizona students put the topping on the upset when they handed Arizona State students a "gift" of black roses.

In such an antagonistic rivalry, it's only natural that players' emotions unfortunately sometimes result in brawls. Such was the case in 2001 when the teams came to blows after Arizona players danced on ASU's midfield logo following a victory at Sun Devil Stadium.

Nor is there any love lost in the rivalry between Mississippi and Mississippi State, No. 19 in the rankings.

The teams play for a trophy called the "Golden Egg" and the game itself is referred to as the "Egg Bowl." The Egg, which resembles an old-fashioned football more than it does an actual egg, made its debut in 1927 as the winner's trophy. The two student bodies agreed to reward the trophy in hopes of preventing the kind of riots that overshadowed the 1926 game. That year, Mississippi ended a twelve-game losing streak with a 7–6 victory in Starkville. The Ole Miss fans, thrilled with their first victory over their hated rival in thirteen years, celebrated by charging the field and taking down the goal posts in a frightening show of crowd hysteria.

The rivalry has had a way of making heroes out of both coaches and players. In 1975, Mississippi State coach Bob Tyler came out of a hospital bed despite suffering from an excruciating kidney stone. He remained on the sideline throughout the entire game in Mississippi State's 13–7 loss to Ole Miss, then quickly went back into the hospital for more tests.

As for players' performances in this spirited series, it would be hard to forget Mississippi's Arnold "Showboat" Boykin in the 1951 game. All he did was score seven touchdowns, a record for Division I football, as Ole Miss buried State 49–7.

Archie Manning and his son Eli, now the New York Giants' starting quarterback, were two of the foremost names associated with the rivalry. Archie, an all-everything at Ole Miss, was the more famous. But even he never had the success that Eli did against Ole Miss's greatest rival. Eli's biggest game in the rivalry came in 2003, the series' one hundredth game, when he led Ole Miss to a 31–0 win over Mississippi State. Eli was 2-1 against Mississippi State while his father was 1-1-1.

Fierce state pride also highlights several other intrastate rivalries. Some of the more prominent: Washington-Washington State (No. 22 in our ranking); Georgia-Georgia Tech (No. 23); Oregon-Oregon State (No. 24); Toledo-Bowling Green (No. 25); Oklahoma-Oklahoma State; Virginia-Virginia Tech; Montana-Montana State; Cincinnati-Miami (Ohio); South Carolina-Clemson; and North Carolina-Duke.

Doyt Perry coached at Bowling Green for many years and considered Toledo "the most important game on our schedule."

"An important thing was the close proximity of campuses. We probably had more kids from Toledo than anywhere else, at least when I was coach. Some of these kids played with or against some of the Toledo players while in high school. So there was no real problem in getting the kids up for the game."

The game that Perry likes to remember: when his Bowling Green team routed Toledo 39–0 in 1955 and started a string of twelve victories in the series.

"We're twenty miles apart, just down I-75, and the rivalry goes on with all sports, not just football," said Dave Meyer of the Bowling Green sports information office. "We're competing for the same players all the time, the same coaches, the same families. The location is very similar."

Bowling Green led the series 36-31-4 through the 2006 season.

After 106 games, Montana and Montana State were still pretty much the worst of enemies—at least athletically.

"We don't like each other," said Renee Valley of the Montana sports information office. "Of course, that's because we're intrastate rivals, and just in season when we're playing them in any sport."

For some of the fans, the rivalry really touches a nerve.

"I've heard that some people [from Montana] will not even stay in Bozeman [where Montana State is located]. Those are the hard-core Montana natives."

Montana, a liberal arts college located in Missoula, is about three hundred miles from Montana State, an engineering and agricultural school. Montana led the series 66-35-5 through 2006.

"We're still going at it hot and heavy," Montana State assistant coach E. J. Arnold said of the rivalry with Montana. "We're still playing each other the last game of the year."

Among interstate foes, big names and dominating personalities have been the feature of the Alabama-Tennessee series. It is one of those rare rivalries identified by the time of year it is played—"The Third Saturday in October"—even thought that may not always be the case.

"Sometimes it misses the mark," said Haywood Harris, longtime sports information director at Tennessee. "Every once in a while, we play the fourth Saturday."

The rivalry got its spark in 1928 on a memorable 98-yard kickoff return for a touchdown by Gene McEver, a Tennessee fullback known as the "Wild Bull." The play, one of the most storied in Volunteers history, helped Tennessee pull off a monumental 15–13 upset over the Crimson Tide.

"Somehow, the Major [coach Robert Neyland] had us convinced that we were going to win," McEver said. "I don't know how we did it."

It was a huge coming-out party for Neyland, Harris points out.

"Alabama was so good, there was talk of going to Alabama coach Frank Thomas and asking him to cut the third and fourth quarters in case things got out of hand, in order to spare Tennessee humiliation."

Among coaching figures, Neyland was the giant in Tennessee football annals, as was Bear Bryant at Alabama. Bryant was a legendary player before he became a Hall of Fame coach. And a most courageous player at that. Once he took the field for Alabama against Tennessee despite a broken leg.

Both coaches turned out too many All-Americans to mention. One of them, Tennessee's George Cafego, remembered that when Neyland came to Tennessee in the 1920s, "he was told that the team he had to beat was Alabama. If you want to go anywhere, do anything, you had to beat Alabama. That was the rallying cry on campus, that was all you talked about all summer."

Neyland put together an 11-5-2 record against the Crimson Tide before Bryant swung the momentum Alabama's way starting in 1958. In twenty-three games against the Volunteers, he was 16-5-2.

"I feel like three-fourths of the Alabama nation would rather beat Tennessee than Auburn," said Crimson Tide center Antoine Caldwell. "I didn't really understand until after we won that game [6–3 in 2005]. It seemed like the whole city was elevated. We just realized how big a deal it is to beat Tennessee."

As Bryant once said about the rivalry that started in 1901:

"You found out what kind of person you were when you played Tennessee."

It's not often that a tie is cause for celebration, but it was in 1965 at Tennessee because it came in the midst of a four-game losing streak to Alabama.

"Alabama was driving for a winning field goal and Kenny Stabler [Alabama quarterback] threw the ball out of bounds, thinking it was third down, not fourth, and we salvaged a tie [7–7]," Harris recalled. "That was a great tie for us."

The series has generally been a model of respect—except for one period in the early 2000s when Alabama was involved in a recruiting scandal.

"Tennessee was charged with bringing it to the attention of the NCAA and there was so much hard feeling," Harris said. "But generally the series has been a standard for courtesy and good feeling between the fans of both schools who respect each other's football histories."

A few states to the west, Kansas and Missouri strap 'em on for another historic "border war." This one began in 1891, making the rivalry the oldest west of the Mississippi and fifth oldest in college football.

Everyone, from freshmen fanatics to the leaders of the universities, gets psyched as the teams prepare to play for the "Indian War Drum." Before one such contest, the Kansas chancellor was heard to proclaim:

"We'll put Missouri's Tigers so far in the tank, they'll never come out."

The 1956 game provided a happy finale at Missouri for longtime coach Don Faurot, who was credited with inventing the split-T formation. The game seemed destined to end in a 13–13 tie until Kansas coach Chuck Mather called for a daring reverse deep in Jayhawks territory. Missouri offensive tackle Chuck Mehrer broke through to nail the ballcarrier for a safety, handing Missouri a 15–13 win.

At a cocktail party that evening, one Missouri alumnus uttered the immortal line to Faurot:

"Well, Don, you lose some, you win some, and every once in a while, one washes up on the beach."

In 1960, Kansas spoiled Missouri's only chance for a national championship. In a touch of irony, the Jayhawks eventually forfeited that 23–7 victory because they used an ineligible player. Missouri coach Dan Devine paid Kansas back many times for that 1960 upset, including a crushing 69–21 defeat of the Jayhawks in 1969. Pouring it on with an Orange Bowl bid in the offing, Devine was enjoying every moment. Kansas coach Pepper Rodgers said he was trying to give Devine the "peace sign." However, the Missouri coach only returned "half of it" from the opposite sideline.

Not all the top rivalries come in pairs, of course. Some come in threes, as earlier noted with the Florida-Florida State-Miami troika.

The Army-Navy rivalry has a third side to it as well, with Air Force. The trio plays each year for the Commander-in-Chief's Trophy, the winner decided on its record against the other two. Through 2006, Air Force led the series with sixteen trophies, Navy had nine, and Army six. There was no clear-cut winner the other four years in the series, which started in 1972.

A couple of other threesomes: Maine's Bates, Bowdoin, and Colby, who play for the CBB Trophy, and Central Michigan, Eastern Michigan and Western Michigan, who compete for the Michigan MAC Trophy.

Such trophies, jugs, and buckets are part of the charm of college football. Everyone, it seems, has a rival he wants to beat—whether it's the Battle for the Bones between Memphis and UAB, Battle for the Bell between Marshall and Ohio, or the Battle for the Boot between Arkansas and LSU.

As former UCLA coach "Red" Sanders once said of the rivalry with Southern Cal: "It's not a matter of life and death—it's more important than that."

Chapter 17

Best of the Past

When Notre Dame resumed its series with Army in 2006, no one expected it to be competitive like the old days. It wasn't—Notre Dame won 41–9.

But at one time, the Army-Notre Dame series was as compelling as, well, a Knute Rockne pep talk. From 1913 to 1947, it was at its storied height, playing many of the games in big-city stadiums to accommodate the huge demand for tickets.

You want historic contributions?

Try the forward pass, which Notre Dame unleashed against Army in 1913 in a manner that college football had never seen.

Famous players?

How about Notre Dame's "Four Horsemen" or George Gipp? Or Doc Blanchard and Glenn Davis, Army's "Mr. Inside" and "Mr. Outside"?

Famous moments?

Will "Win one for the Gipper" do?

Great games?

A titanic scoreless tie in 1946 when both teams were vying for the national championship.

Yes, these all were part of the famed Army-Notre Dame series before it was discontinued in the nineties. It might be renewed now and again, as it was in 2006, but clearly it's just not the same.

The furious and fabulous Army-Notre Dame rivalry of old was one of many that burned brightly once upon a time. Now, no longer.

Blame the changing map of football: teams dropped big-time programs, took on less ambitious schedules, were realigned in a conference, switched to different conferences, and changed from independents to league affiliations.

All this and more has contributed to the changing landscape of college football in America through the years.

Before going to the sidelines, the Fordham-New York University series was known as the "Battle of the Bronx." Indeed. The rivalry became such a draw that it had to be moved to big-time venues like Yankee Stadium and the Polo Grounds. Crowds of 80,000 were not uncommon.

The 1920s and 1930s were the flaming days of the "Violent Violets" (NYU) and the "Seven Blocks of Granite" (Fordham) featuring a player by the name of Vince Lombardi.

A New York jeweler, Lewis J. Madow, put up money for the Madow Trophy, which went to the Most Valuable Player in the NYU-Fordham clash. The trophy was the forerunner of the Lambert Trophy, which annually goes to the best football team in the East.

The rivalry, started in 1899, reached fever pitch after the First World War and really took off in the twenties when Chick Meehan came from Syracuse to coach NYU and Major Frank Cavanaugh came from Boston College to Fordham.

Before Meehan arrived at NYU, he was involved in another of the East's top early football rivalries: Syracuse-Colgate.

Until the rivalry was discontinued after the 1982 season, Colgate-Syracuse was one of the most colorful in football. The Red Raiders dominated early with the so-called Colgate "Hoodoo," a part of American football lore. From 1925 to 1937, Syracuse was unable to beat Colgate. But when the Orange started improving dramatically and later competing for national honors in the 1950s, Colgate was really no match for Syracuse.

That was never the problem between Oklahoma and Nebraska. But since their conference, formerly the Big Eight, became the Big 12 in 1996, the Sooners and Cornhuskers have met on an irregular basis because of their realignment into separate divisions.

Bad news for the schools, which had built up a tremendous rivalry and huge fan base, particularly in the seventies when the Big Eight championship usually hinged on the outcome of their games—most of which were televised nationally.

That included the battle of 1971 for the Big Eight championship and national title that was billed the "Game of the Century." It was all that, and more.

The Thanksgiving Day showdown matched the nation's top-ranked team (Nebraska) against No. 2 (Oklahoma).

Filled with continuing highlights and heroism, the game's most spectacular moment occurred within the first four minutes when Nebraska's Johnny Rodgers returned a punt 72 yards for a touchdown.

"I don't know what I did or what I was thinking about," Rodgers would say after the game. "The return was set up to the right, but I saw a hole to the left and cut back. I do remember seeing Joe Blahak up ahead and thinking he would get a block for me."

Rodgers's score made it 7–0 Nebraska, but even though the Huskers' boasted the nation's No. 1 defense, it was a day for the offenses.

The teams traded the lead four times, including a rally by Oklahoma in the fourth quarter that gave the Sooners a 31–28 advantage on a 16-yard TD pass by Jack Mildren.

There was still time for the Huskers to make a comeback. Although they were 74 yards away, they were confident they could do so.

"We wanted to use up as much of the clock as possible," Nebraska quarterback Jerry Tagge said. "We didn't want them to have time to score again."

Using up nearly six minutes of the clock, Nebraska steadily moved downfield and capped the rally with Jeff Kinney cracking over from the 2-yard line for his fourth TD of the afternoon.

Final: Nebraska 35, Oklahoma 31.

Game of the Century, indeed.

It could never be topped, but the teams made it close with yet another battle of No. 1 versus No. 2 in 1987. This one was won by Oklahoma's second-ranked Sooners over the top-ranked Cornhuskers, 17–7. The game was regarded as "Game of the Century II" in the series.

Before Penn State changed its independent status and joined the Big 10 in 1993, Pitt was the biggest rival on the Nittany Lions' schedule (with Syracuse also in the mix).

Now Penn State plays neither on a regular basis. But there was a time when a Penn State-Pitt battle—or Penn State-Syracuse—often determined Eastern supremacy in college football. Sometimes they helped influence national rankings, but, in the case of Pitt-Penn State, state pride in the "Battle of Route 22" was often just as important.

Perhaps Pitt's most significant victory in the series, which started in 1893, occurred in 1976. Tony Dorsett, Pitt's Heisman Trophy winner, ran for two touchdowns and 244 yards to lead the Panthers to a 24–7 victory on the way to the national title.

It was one of the most emotional games in the series, and featured a bit of sideline drama. FBI agents were brought in to guard Penn State coach Joe Paterno and his players following death threats by a crank caller.

The 1966 game was important to both teams for a reason other than the national rankings. Paterno was in his first year as head coach of the Nittany

Lions and a loss to Pitt would mark the first time Penn State had a losing season since 1939.

No worries. The Nittany Lions cruised 48–24, as Paterno piled it on with a score late in the game. This, of course, sparked accusations he was trying to run up the score and only added to the bitterness of the rivalry.

It was no less bitter than Penn State's rivalry with Syracuse, which also affected the bowl picture once upon a time.

"Where bowl bids were concerned, it always came down to Penn State and Syracuse," Syracuse's All-American defensive back Tony Kyasky said. "The Southern bowls liked to get the best teams in the East, and those teams usually were the best."

While Oklahoma and Texas A&M have been Texas's biggest rivals through the years, Arkansas could be added to that list for at least part of the twentieth century.

Started in 1894, the rivalry really took hold in the 1960s when Frank Boyles's Arkansas teams went head-to-head with close friend Darrell Royal at Texas in their annual battles for the Southwest Conference title.

That all changed when the SWC broke up in the 1990s as the result of recruiting scandals and NCAA violations by a number of conference teams that hurt TV revenue.

Arkansas left for the Southeastern Conference in 1992 and Texas, Texas A&M, Baylor, and Texas Tech joined the Big 8 in 1993, expanding it to the Big 12.

The SWC eventually dissolved in 1996.

But before Texas and Arkansas went their separate ways, the rivalry produced the kind of games, as the colorful Royal pointed out, "where you screw your belly to the ground."

In 1964, Royal gambled everything on a two-point conversion that would have given the Longhorns a 15–14 victory. But the play failed and Texas lost the game 14–13, and along with it the conference championship and a chance at the national title. It was also the first time Texas had lost in sixteen games.

The 1969 game produced the Big Shootout and the Big Controversy. It was also one of the greatest games ever produced by a No. 1 versus No. 2 team.

Texas was ranked No. 1 in the country and Arkansas was No. 2. But after the first three quarters, it looked like the pollsters had it wrong. The Razorbacks were dominating the Longhorns in all facets and led 14–0.

Then it was James Street time. The Texas quarterback, nicknamed "Slick" because of his flashy clothes, ran for one score and a two-point conversion. Then he led Texas on another touchdown drive for a dramatic 15–14 victory before a crowd that included President Richard Nixon.

After the game, Nixon visited the Texas locker room and personally handed a No. 1 plaque to the Longhorns in full view of a national television audience—and the controversy was on.

Paterno was outraged, to say the least. His Lions were also undefeated, and he thought his team deserved consideration for the national title.

As it turned out, Texas finished No. 1 and Penn State No. 2 after winning their respective bowl games to complete perfect seasons. The incident was not easily forgotten by Paterno, who later referenced Nixon in a graduation speech. Noted the Penn State coach:

"How could President Nixon know so much about college football and so little about Watergate?"

Paterno eventually had national championship rings made up for his team, which was in the midst of a school-record thirty-one-game unbeaten streak.

The Texas-Arkansas battles were indicative of the kind of fierce rivalries in the SWC for many years.

SMU's series with Texas Christian inspired deep and dark passions. During one game in Fort Worth, Texas, a man in the crowd stood up with a gun and screamed to SMU's Don Meredith: "Meredith, I'm going to kill you." Before anyone bothered to check whether the gun was loaded or not, the crazed fan was picked up by police and hauled off to the station house.

The featured game of that series came in 1935, when the two undefeated teams fought for the national championship. SMU won on a 50-yard touchdown pass from Bob Finley to Bobby Wilson on fourth-and-13 from punt formation. The victory earned the 12–0 Mustangs a berth in the Rose Bowl. TCU went to the Cotton in an era when only four bowls were available.

Another Texas shootout from the old SWC: Baylor-TCU, a highly competitive series for the better part of a century. After 102 meetings, the Texas rivals were separated by only one game.

That rivalry went to the sidelines when the schools headed to different conferences. Now they play only on a sometime basis.

Another long-standing rivalry that ended after a legendary association: North Dakota State-North Dakota.

For many years, the teams had played for the Nickel Trophy, a seventy-five-pound replica of the once-minted U.S. coin with the Indian head on it. The trophy was inaugurated in 1938 in a bitter, hard-hitting series.

Noted George Ellis, one-time sports information director at North Dakota State: "I remember the 1975 game where on one play five athletes were on the ground and had to be assisted off the field. One was admitted to a hospital."

Some significant moments in the series: In 1965, North Dakota State won its first national Division II title with a 6–3 victory over North Dakota. In 1971, North Dakota State had been unbeaten in thirty-six games, but was knocked out of the No. 1 spot by a 23–7 loss to North Dakota.

The teams last played in 2003, a 28–21 overtime victory for North Dakota. The series was discontinued when North Dakota State made the transition from the NCAA'S Division II to Division I-AA in football. North Dakota led the series at that point, 62-45-3.

Also in the dustbin are Norwich's rivalries with two other ancient foes, Middlebury and the Coast Guard Academy.

Once a rip-roaring rivalry, Norwich and Middlebury haven't played since 1991. Their relationship changed when Middlebury joined the New England Small College Athletic Conference (NESCAC).

One of the most exciting contests in the series was in 1967, when Middlebury's Charlie Brush fired a last-minute touchdown pass for a wild 40–38 victory in a great passing duel with Norwich's Ray Potter.

In the thirties and forties, when rail travel was the way to go, Norwich chartered a train for its entire cadet corps for the games at Middlebury. The cadets' march through town to the stadium added to the color and tradition of the rivalry. The cadets were not always on their good behavior.

After one loss at Middlebury, they tore down the goal posts on the main field as well as those on adjacent fields. Duke Nelson, who was athletic director as well as coach at Middlebury, sent Norwich a bill the next day.

"There are a lot of people that would love to put that (Middlebury-Norwich) game back on the schedule," said Brad Nadeua, the Middlebury sports information director. "Especially in Vermont, where the University of Vermont does not have football. So these are the only two college football teams in the state."

Norwich's game with the Coast Guard Academy was once known as the "Little Army-Navy Game." The series was halted after the 2005 game when the CGA joined the New England Football Conference.

Here was another rivalry where high jinks were always in high gear, much like the Army-Navy big boys.

Imagine trying to kidnap a live bear? Well, a group of Norwich students actually tried to pull that off one year when they made off with the Coast Guard Academy's mascot. These brave lads were ten miles out of town when the bear started rattling its cage. At that point, the students thought it was a better idea to get the angry animal back to the Coast Guard. They did so by nearly setting a land-speed record in the process.

No less competitive for many years were the Boston College-Holy Cross and Rutgers-Princeton rivalries before the schools went their separate ways athletically.

Rutgers and Princeton, of course, have the distinction of playing the first official intercollegiate football game in America in 1869.

Now the once-great rivalry, like many other memorable ones, is buried in history's end zone.

Index

About the Authors

Ken Rappoport is the author of dozens of sports books for young readers and adults, including *Profiles in Sports Courage* and *Ladies First: Women Athletes Who Made a Difference*. He has worked as an Associated Press writer for thirty-six years, covering every major professional and college sport. He lives in New Jersey with his wife, Bernice.

Barry Wilner has been a sportswriter for The Associated Press for thirty-two years. In that time, he has covered the Super Bowl, Olympics, World Cup, Stanley Cup finals, and many other major sporting events. He has written books on hockey, soccer, swimming, and Olympic sports. He lives in Garnerville, New York, with his wife Helene, daughters Nicole, Jamie, and Tricia, and son Evan.

FOOTBALL FEUDS

The
Greatest
College
Football
Rivalries